STRUCTURE OF ACCOUNTS

A practical guide to financial reporting and accounting standards

Second edition

Karl Harper

institute of financial services

Apart from any fair dealing for the purpose of research or private study, or criticism or review, as permitted under the Copyright, Designs and Patents Act 1988, this publication may be reproduced, stored or transmitted, in any form or by any means, only with the prior permission in writing of the publisher, or in the case of reprographic reproduction in accordance with the terms and licences issued by the Copyright Licensing Agency. Enquiries concerning reproduction outside those terms should be addressed to the publisher's agents at the undermentioned address:

Financial World Publishing
4-9 Burgate Lane
Canterbury
Kent
CT1 2XJ

T 01227 818602
F 01227 479641
E editorial@ifslearning.com

Financial World Publishing publications are published by The Chartered Institute of Bankers, a non-profit making registered educational charity.

The Chartered Institute of Bankers believes that the sources of information upon which the book is based are reliable and has made every effort to ensure the complete accuracy of the text. However, neither CIB, the author nor any contributor can accept any legal responsibility whatsoever for consequences that may arise from errors or omissions or any opinion or advice given.

Typeset by Kevin O'Connor
Printed by IBT Global, London

© Chartered Institute of Bankers 2002

Revised and reprinted 2002

ISBN 0-85297-703-4

FINANCIAL WORLD Publishing
THE CHARTERED INSTITUTE OF BANKERS

The Structure of Accounts

This textbook has been written for both students and practitioners of the subject. It has been written to a syllabus drawn up by subject experts, including current senior practitioners, which forms part of the Diploma in Financial Services Management (DFSM). This qualification is administered by the Institute of Financial Services, a wholly owned subsidiary of The Chartered Institute of Bankers and is awarded jointly by The CIB and the University of Manchester Institute of Science and Technology (UMIST). The role of UMIST in this partnership is to benchmark all aspects of the delivery of the DFSM, including this text, to first year undergraduate standard.

Though written to a syllabus specific to the DFSM it is intended that this text will serve a useful purpose for anybody studying for a business or finance-related qualification. Furthermore, this book will serve as an excellent reference tool for practitioners already working in this or related fields. All books in the DFSM series reflect the very latest regulations, legislation and reporting requirements.

Students of the DFSM will also receive a separate Study Guide to be used in conjunction with this text. This Study Guide refers the reader to further reading on the topic and helps to enhance learning through exercises based upon the contents of this book.

To Joseph Igstoligrips

Contents

Section A – Introduction			1
1	**An Introduction to Accounting**		3
		Introduction	3
	1.1	What is accountancy?	4
	1.2	What financial information do we need to record?	4
	1.3	Why do we need to record financial information?	5
	1.5	How do businesses record their financial information?	6
		Summary	7
2	**An Introduction to the Balance Sheet**		9
		Introduction	9
	2.1	The balance sheet format	10
	2.2	Buying and selling on credit	12
	2.3	Drawings	16
		Summary	17
Section B Preparation of Accounts			19
3	**From Double Entry to Trial Balance**		21
		Introduction	21
	3.1	Double-entry bookkeeping	22
	3.2	Expenses	25
	3.3	Stock	25
	3.4	Day books or journals	26
	3.5	Returns in and returns out	28
	3.6	Discounts	28

	3.7	Balancing off the accounts	31
	3.8	Trial balance	32
	3.9	Conclusion	33
		Summary	38
4		**Making Adjustments to the Trial Balance – Why and How**	**40**
		Introduction	41
	4.1	What adjustments we need to make	41
	4.2	Why we need to make these adjustments	42
	4.3	How we make the adjustments	42
	4.4	Conclusion	58
		Summary	61
5		**From Trial Balance to Final Accounts**	**63**
		Introduction	64
	5.1	The trading profit and loss account	64
	5.2	Preparing a trading profit and loss account and balance sheet from a trial balance	72
	5.3	Presenting the final accounts in a vertical format	76
		Summary	80
6		**Depreciation**	**82**
		Introduction	82
	6.1	What is depreciation?	83
	6.2	Causes of depreciation	83
	6.3	Calculating the depreciation charge for the year	83
	6.4	The effects of depreciation on the trading profit and loss account and balance sheet	86
	6.5	Examination questions	89
	6.6	The disposal or scrapping of a fixed asset	95
		Summary	102
7		**Partnership Accounts**	**103**
		Introduction	104

		Contents	
	7.1	The partnership agreement	105
	7.2	Producing the final accounts of a partnership	106
	7.3	Specimen layout of partnership accounts	112
		Summary	114
8	**Limited Company Accounts**		**115**
		Introduction	116
	8.1	Preparation of accounts – Limited company accounts	118
		Summary	129
9	**Manufacturing Company Accounts**		**131**
		Introduction	131
	9.1	Calculating the cost of manufacture	132
	9.2	Producing a trading profit and loss account for manufacturing businesses	137
	9.3	Producing a balance sheet for manufacturing businesses	139
		Summary	145
10	**Decision Making: Cost Behaviour and Break-even Analysis**		**146**
		Introduction	146
	10.1	Cost behaviour – How do costs behave in relation to manufacturing output and trading activity?	147
	10.2	What is break-even analysis?	148
	10.3	Break-even charts	151
	10.4	The implications of increasing or reducing output	153
	10.5	The use of break-even analysis as a decision-making tool and planning aid	155
		Summary	162
Section C – Cash and Liquidity			**165**
11	**Cash and Working Capital**		**167**
	11.1	Introduction – What is working capital?	167
	11.2	Assessing a company's working capital position	168
	11.3	Cash cycle/flow of funds	172

	11.4	The cost of maintaining working capital	175
	11.5	Conclusion – The importance of working capital	176
		Summary	177
12	**Bank Reconciliation Statements**	**178**
	12.1	Introduction – What are reconciliation statements?	178
	12.2	Bank reconciliation statements	179
	12.3	Dealing with different opening balances	185
		Summary	188
13	**Cashflow Statements (FRS 1)**	**189**
		Introduction	189
	13.1	Cashflow statements	190
	13.2	Preparing a cashflow statement	193
	13.3	The purchase and sale of fixed assets during the year	198
	13.4	Analysis of the cashflow statement	201
		Summary	202
14	**Cash Forecasts**	**204**
	14.1	Introduction – What is a cashflow forecast?	204
	14.2	How are cashflow forecasts constructed?	204
	14.3	Producing a forecast trading profit and loss account and balance sheet from a cashflow forecast	213
	14.4	The benefits of cashflow forecasts	215
		Summary	217
Section D – The Regulatory Regime and the Interpretation of Accounts			**219**
15	**The Regulatory Regime and Accounting Concepts**	**221**
	15.1	Introduction – The regulatory regime	222
	15.2	Standards or statements of best practice – Statement of Standard Accounting Practice (SSAPs) and Financial Reporting Standards (FRSs)	224
	15.3	International Accounting Standards (IASs)	233
	15.4	Stock Exchange rules	234

Contents

	15.5	Non-mandatory recommendations	234
	15.6	Conclusion	237
		Summary	240
16	**Asset Valuation and Profit Measurement**		**245**
		Introduction	246
	16.1	SSAP 9 – Stock and work in progress	251
	16.2	Accounting for depreciation	258
	16.3	Goodwill	259
	16.4	Asset revaluation and revaluation reserve	262
	16.5	Non-recurrent transactions, FRS 3 – Reporting Financial Performance	262
		Summary	270
17	**Interpretation of Accounts and Ratio Analysis**		**275**
		Introduction	276
	17.1	What is ratio analysis?	276
	17.2	Calculating accounting ratios	276
	17.3	Interpretation of account ratios	281
	17.4	Limitation of ratio analysis	287
		Summary	288
	Index		**292**

Structure of Accounts

PREFACE

This book is divided into four sections:

- Section A   Introduction
- Section B   Preparation of Accounts
    - Sole traders
    - Partnerships
    - Limited companies
    - Manufacturing companies
- Section C   Cash and Liquidity
- Section D   The Regulatory Regime and the Interpretation of Accounts

Section A provides you with an introduction to accounting:

- Nature and purpose of accounting;
- Financial information recorded;
- Importance of recording financial information;
- Major users of accounting information; and
- *Balance sheet*, which is a statement of a businesses financial position.

Section B examines how to prepare the *final accounts, (trading profit and loss account* and *balance sheet)* of various types of businesses:

- Sole traders;
- Partnerships;
- Limited companies;
- Manufacturing companies.

Section C focuses on the importance of *cash and liquidity*, making a distinction between liquidity and profitability and focusing on the following issues:

- *Cash and working capital* needs;
- *Bank reconciliation statements* (reconciling/checking the bank statement);
- Preparing and interpreting *cash flow statements* (*past* cash movements in and out of the business);

Structure of Accounts

- *Cash Forecasts* (forecasting *future* cash requirements).

Section D focuses on two issues:

- *The regulatory regime*, i.e. the regulations governing the way in which accounts are prepared and presented, and
- the *interpretation of accounts*, i.e. the assessment of a company's performance over time or in comparison with another company.

In summary therefore, this book aims to take you from a base of little or no accounting knowledge, to an ability to both *prepare* and *interpret* various accounting statements for various types of businesses:

- *trading profit and loss accounts*
- *balance sheets*
- *break-even statements*
- *bank reconciliation statements*
- *cashflow statements*
- *cash forecasts*

while also understanding and appreciating the implications of the *regulatory regime* governing the way in which accounts are prepared and presented.

Section A

INTRODUCTION

This section consists of two chapters:

Chapter 1: An Introduction to Accounting

After studying this chapter you should be able to:

1 Understand the nature and purpose of accounting;

2 List the financial information recorded by businesses;

3 Explain the importance of recording financial information;

4 Appreciate that while trading profitability is important, so too is a company's cashflow position.

Chapter 2: An Introduction to the Balance Sheet

After studying this chapter you should be able to:

1 Explain in simple terms the nature and purpose of a balance sheet;

2 Define various accounting terms such as assets, liabilities, capital, etc;

3 Distinguish between fixed and current assets, current and long-term liabilities;

4 Understand what happens when a business buys or sells goods on credit;

5 Produce a balance sheet in a horizontal format.

Structure of Accounts

1
AN INTRODUCTION TO ACCOUNTING

Syllabus Objectives
1.1   Accounting information

Learning Objectives
After studying this chapter you should be able to:
1   Understand the nature and purpose of accounting;
2   List the financial information recorded by businesses;
3   Explain the importance of recording financial information;
4   Appreciate that while trading profitability is important, so too is a company's cashflow position.

Introduction

You may well be wondering why you need to study accountancy; after all you are bankers not accountants.

The aim of this course, however, is not to turn you into accountants – preparing accounts for customers and helping them with their tax problems – but to help you to become better bankers, more capable of understanding a customer's financial position through an examination of his or her *accounts* (i.e. the financial information).

As banks have a variety of customers, we will examine the accounts of individuals trading as shopkeepers, taxi-drivers, etc., and also of partnerships and limited companies, first through the recording of their financial information, and then through the interpretation and use of this information in order to make decisions, assess loan applications and assist your customers.

1.1 What is accountancy?

Accountancy is concerned with *the recording of financial information.*

But what financial information do we need to record and why?

1.2 What financial information do we need to record?

Imagine that you have started your own business, let us say a clothes shop; what financial information would you record? Before reading any further, see if you can make a list of the information you would record.

Now let us see how our lists compare.

1 Details of any *items you purchased* in order to commence business such as:

- premises;
- fixtures and fittings (carpets, etc);
- equipment (cash till);
- van (to collect your stock);
- stock of clothes (for resale).

2 *Your source of finance* (where you obtained the money to purchase such items).

Most new businesses need to borrow money either to start their operation or to see them through the first years until the company is generating sufficient cash of its own. A loan may therefore be one of the company's sources of finance. Before agreeing to provide such finance the manager of your bank would wish to see that the owners of the company have also invested some of their own money in the business, i.e. capital.

Your sources of finance may therefore be a combination:

of your own money – capital, and

money from other sources, e.g. loans.

3 *Cash received*

In respect of sales.

4 *Cash paid out*

In respect of further purchases of stock and overheads such as gas, electricity and wages.

5 *Cheque and credit card transactions*

As a banker I am sure you will realize that not everybody pays for goods in cash, and

1 – An Introduction to Accounting

you will therefore need to record details of *all cheque and credit card transactions* which you both receive and pay.

6 *Purchases made on credit*

Hopefully, after a period of trading you will be able to purchase your stock on credit, and therefore *purchases made on credit* are another item that needs to be recorded.

7 *Sales made on credit*

After a while you may decide to allow your regular customers to buy on credit and only a fool would fail to record details of *sales made on credit*.

1.3 Why do we need to record financial information?

Now that we have outlined the financial information we need to record, see if you can make a list of the reasons for recording such information. Look back at the list of information in order to assist you, then compare your list with mine. While some of the points are obvious, others are more obscure, so do not worry if you do not manage to get all the points.

1 *To determine whether your clothes shop has achieved a profit or suffered a loss.*

More sophisticated bookkeeping could be used to indicate the strong and weak areas of your business, e.g. to determine whether the ladies' section of your shop is profitable.

2 *To determine whether or not the business will be able to meet its financial commitments as they fall due.*

This can be determined from an examination of the company's *cashflow position* (i.e. the flow of cash in and out of the business).

3 *To determine the financial strength and health of the business.*

4 *To assist cash management.*

Credit given to customers must be recorded to ensure that payment is received on the due date, and credit received must be recorded to ensure that we have the necessary funds available when payment is required.

5 *In order to assess your past performance.*

6 *To enable you to exercise control over your future progress.*

7 *To assist your decision-making.*

For example while you may *feel* that the ladies' section of your shop is running at a loss, the financial information will provide the answer and therefore assist, or even make, your decision to discontinue this side of your business.

8 *In order to comply with the law.*

As you will later discover, limited companies are required by law to publish an audited set of accounts.

9 *The financial information provides a valuable source of information and is of interest to a number of people.*

- *Investors (shareholders) existing and potential* who need to decide whether to buy or sell the company's shares or to subscribe for new shares when a rights issue is made
- *Employees* to assess the stability and profitability of the company and its ability to provide pay, retirement benefits and employment opportunities
- *Lenders* to determine whether their loans and interest will be repaid on time
- *Suppliers* to determine whether they will be paid on time
- *Customers* need information concerning the continuance of the company
- *Government and government agencies*, e.g. the Inland Revenue for tax purposes
- *The general public* (taxpayers, ratepayers, environmentalists) to determine the effect on the local economy
- *Analysts and advisers*, for example financial advisers, financial journalists, economists etc, who need to refer to the accounts
- *Auditors* who are responsible for checking the accounts to ensure that they reflect a *true and fair view* of the company's financial position

1.5 How do businesses record their financial information?

As you have discovered, a considerable amount of information needs to be recorded. It is the accountant's task to collate all the information and to present it in a meaningful manner and in accordance with regulatory requirements.

Just how this is done is the subject of *Section B – The preparation of accounts* and *Section D – The regulatory regime*. (*Section* C focuses on the cash and liquidity position of businesses.)

But before that, let us turn our attention to Chapter 2 for an introduction to the *balance sheet*, which is a financial statement of a business's financial position at a particular date.

1 – An Introduction to Accounting

Summary

1 Accountancy is concerned with the recording, collating and presenting of financial information in a meaningful manner.

2 The following financial information needs to be recorded:

   a) items purchased to commence business, such as premises, equipment, stock, etc.;

   b) your sources of finance (where you obtained the money to purchase such items);

   c) the amount of capital (money contributed by the owners of the business);

   d) cash received;

   e) cash paid out;

   f) cheques and credit card transactions;

   g) purchases on credit;

   h) sales on credit.

3 You need to record financial information in order to:

   a) determine your profit or loss;

   b) assess whether or not the business will be able to meet its financial commitments as they fall due through an examination of the company's cashflow position;

   c) determine the financial strength and health of the business;

   d) ensure payment is received from customers buying on credit on the due date;

   e) ensure you have adequate funds available to meet demands from suppliers who have allowed you to buy on credit;

   f) assess past performance;

   g) exercise control over future progress;

   h) assist management in decision-making;

   i) comply with the law;

   j) provide information to interested parties.

4 *Cashflow* refers to the flow of cash in and out of the business.

5 The financial position of a company is of interest to *the following people*:

   - *Investors (shareholders) existing and potential* who need to decide whether to buy or sell the company's shares or to subscribe for new shares when a rights issue is made

   - *Employees* to assess the stability and profitability of the company and its ability to provide pay, retirement benefits and employment opportunities

Structure of Accounts

- *Lenders* to determine whether their loans and interest will be repaid on time
- *Suppliers* to determine whether they will be paid on time
- *Customers* need information concerning the continuance of the company
- *Government and government agencies*, e.g. the Inland Revenue for tax purposes
- *The general public* (taxpayers, ratepayers, environmentalists) to determine the effect on the local economy
- *Analysts and advisers*, for example financial advisers, financial journalists, economists etc., who need to refer to the accounts
- *Auditors* who are responsible for checking the accounts to ensure that they reflect a true and fair view of the company's financial position

6 A *sole trader* is someone who is the sole owner of a business.

7 A *balance sheet* is a financial statement of a business's financial position at a particular date.

2

AN INTRODUCTION TO THE BALANCE SHEET

Syllabus Objectives
1.2   The accounting equation: assets = capital + liabilities

Learning Objectives
After studying this chapter you should be able to:

1   Explain in simple terms the nature and purpose of a balance sheet;

2   Define various accounting terms such as assets, liabilities, capital, etc.;

3   Distinguish between fixed and current assets, current and long-term liabilities;

4   Understand what happens when a business buys or sells goods on credit;

5   Produce a balance sheet in a horizontal format.

Introduction

You will recall from Chapter 1 that two important pieces of information recorded by businesses are:

1   *Items purchased* in order to commence or continue in business, such as premises, equipment and stock.

   These items **OWNED** by the business are known as **ASSETS**; and

2   *The source of finance* (where it obtained the money to purchase the assets). So far we have considered two sources:

   a)   *Capital*: Money contributed by the owners/shareholders to the business. This is therefore money **OWED** to the owners/shareholders by the business (we make a distinction between the owners and the business).

   b)   *Bank loans:* This also represents money owed by the business, but this time it is owed to people/institutions other than the owners/shareholders. These items are known as **LIABILITIES**.

Structure of Accounts

Clearly the items you have purchased (**ASSETS**) and where you got the money from, i.e. your source of funds (**CAPITAL + LIABILITIES**), must be equal.

What if you have not spent all the money you received I hear you cry?

The answer is that you will have some money left, which is an **ASSET** owned by the business. So **ASSETS** do equal **CAPITAL + LIABILITIES**.

This is the basic *accounting equation*.

$$\text{ASSETS} = \text{CAPITAL} + \text{LIABILITIES}$$

It also forms the basic structure of the balance sheet with assets on one side and the capital and liabilities on the other, reflecting the company's financial position at a particular date.

2.1 The balance sheet format

Balance sheet of example as at 1.9.X0

Items the business owns	Source of finance/money owed
ASSETS	**CAPITAL** (*owner's*)
	LIABILITIES (*outside providers*)

Let us look at an example.

Mr Davenport has just won £50,000 on the National Lottery and wishes to use the money to start his own business, designing and constructing conservatories (i.e. the £50,000 is a *source of finance*, and as it is contributed by him it is known as *capital*).

Having done some research he realizes that he needs a further £10,000 and therefore approaches the bank for a loan. As his plans for the business appear sound and in view of his creditworthiness the bank agrees to the loan but asks for a mortgage on his house as security (i.e. if Mr Davenport fails to repay the loan, the bank will be able to look towards the sale of the house for repayment). The loan is therefore another *source of finance*, but as it is contributed by someone other than the owner it is known as a *liability*.

Mr Davenport then purchases the following *assets* for his business:

Premises	£30,000
Fixtures	£5,000
Equipment	£2,000
Stock of material	£2,000

The balance sheet being a record of these details would appear as follows:

2 – An Introduction to the Balance Sheet

Table 2.1: Balance sheet of Davenport Conservatories as at 30.9.X0

a)
b)

		£	£		£
c)	*Fixed assets*			Capital	50,000
	Premises	30,000			
	Fixtures	5,000			
	Equipment	2,000	37,000		
				Liabilities	
c)	*Current assets*				
	Stock	3,000			
	Cash	20,000	23,000	Loan	10,000
d)			60,000		60,000

The important points to note are:

a) Title

The title should always indicate whose balance sheet it is, in our case Davenport Conservatories, which is not the same as Mr Davenport. As a result Mr Davenport's house, an asset owned by him, does not appear on the balance sheet, despite its importance to the bank. The only items in the balance sheet of a business are those owned or owed by the business. This is known as the *business entity concept*. (We shall look at more accounting concepts in Chapter 15.)

b) Date

*The balance sheet is like a photograph of the business's financial position **as at** a particular date only.*

c) There are two types of asset:

i) Fixed assets

Items of a permanent or semi-permanent nature, necessary for carrying out the business activities and therefore not normally changed in day-to-day trading. Fixed assets are listed in order of permanence and appear above current assets.

Structure of Accounts

ii) Current assets

Items acquired or produced for resale and conversion into cash – the least liquid being listed first.

d) A balance sheet must always balance

This is because one side represents the source of finance and the other what you have done with that money *plus*, in our case, the remaining cash of £20,000. After all, the cash remaining is something owned by the business and therefore an asset.

Remember the *accounting equation*:

$$\text{ASSET} = \text{CAPITAL} + \text{LIABILITIES}$$

(items owned)   =   (source of finance)

e) Layout

At this stage the balance sheet is presented in a horizontal format, but as you will see later there are other ways of presenting the information.

The important thing is to be neat:

i) underline titles such as 'fixed assets', etc. (printed in italics);

ii) do not simply list fixed and current assets in one column, use two, so the reader can see the sub-total for fixed and current assets at a glance;

iii) list the items in their correct order;

iv) put the total on the same line;

v) do not forget the heading.

Accountancy is concerned with conveying information and as a result some marks may be awarded in the examination for layout. These are easy marks to gain because they take little understanding, so do not lose these marks.

2.2 Buying and selling on credit

Buying on credit

Let us assume that Mr Davenport now decides to purchase another £2,000 of material (stock). On this occasion, however, he manages to secure credit terms of two months. How will this affect his balance sheet, shown above, and will any of the assets change?

Well, the first thing, which I am sure you have realized, is that stock will increase from £3,000 to £5,000 and with it the total of the assets.

2 – An Introduction to the Balance Sheet

Table 2.2: Balance sheet of Davenport Conservatories as at 31.10.X0

	£	£		£
Fixed assets			Capital	50,000
Premises	30,000			
Fixtures	5,000			
Equipment	2,000	37,000	*Liabilities*	
			Loan	10,000
Current assets				
Stock	5,000			
Cash	20,000	25,000		
		62,000		60,000

The problem now is that the assets equal £62,000 and the capital plus liabilities equal £60,000, i.e. the balance sheet does *not* balance, and as you know *a balance sheet must always balance*.

The reason for this is that, while we have recorded the increase in stock, we have not recorded the fact that Mr Davenport owes £2,000 to his supplier, (i.e. we have another *liability*).

In this case the liability is known as a *creditor* (someone to whom we owe money following the purchase of goods or services) and, as the debt is repayable within one year, it is a *current liability*.

Debts repayable after more than one year are known as *deferred* or *long-term liabilities*.

So if we record our creditor of £2,000 and the increase in stock of £2,000, the balance sheet will appear as follows:

Structure of Accounts

Table 2.3: Balance sheet of Davenport Conservatories as at 31.10.X0

	£	£		£
Fixed assets			Capital	50,000
Premises	30,000			
Fixtures	5,000		*Deferred liabilities*	
Equipment	2,000	37,000	**Loan**	10,000
Current assets			*Current liabilities*	
Stock	5,000		Creditors	2,000
Cash	20,000	25,000		
		62,000		62,000

Current and deferred liabilities

In the balance sheet above I have assumed that the loan is over a period of more than twelve months and is therefore a deferred or long-term liability.

What is the position, however, with an *overdraft*? Obviously, it is a liability (money owed by the business), but is it current or deferred? After all, many businesses have overdrafts outstanding for many years. While that is true, what determines the status of a liability is the earliest repayment date; an overdraft is normally repayable on demand and is therefore considered a *current liability*.

Selling on credit

Suppose Mr Davenport now designs and erects a conservatory for a customer at a price of £5,000. As the sale is to a friend he allows one month's credit. The materials and stock originally cost £2,000 and Mr Davenport will therefore earn a profit of £3,000 from this job.

Let us look at how this will affect the balance sheet. First of all, stock will obviously reduce by £2,000, as stock is recorded in the balance sheet at the cost price. But what else are we going to do to make the balance sheet balance?

Well, we need to record the profit of £3,000, earned by the business. As this belongs to the owners of the business, the amount is added to the capital, making the balance sheet appear as follows:

2 – An Introduction to the Balance Sheet

Table 2.4: Balance sheet of Davenport Conservatories as at 30.11.X0

	£		£		£
Fixed assets			Capital		50,000
Premises	30,000		**Profits**		**3,000**
Fixtures	5,000				53,000
Equipment	2,000	37,000	*Deferred liabilities*		
			Loan		10,000
Current assets			*Current liabilities*		
Stock	3,000		Creditors		2,000
Cash	20,000	23,000			
		60,000			65,000

Once again the balance sheet does not balance because we have failed to record something. We have failed to record the fact that £5,000 is owed to the business, i.e. there is a *debtor* (someone who owes the business money) of £5,000.

As *debtors* are, hopefully, converted into cash in the near future they are a *current asset*. The completed balance sheet appears as follows:

Table 2.5: Balance sheet of Davenport Conservatories as at 31.12.X0

	£		£		£
Fixed assets			Capital		50,000
Premises	30,000		**Profits**		**3,000**
Fixtures	5,000				53,000
Equipment	2,000	37,000	*Deferred liabilities*		
			Loan		10,000
Current assets			*Current liabilities*		
Stock	3,000		Creditors		2,000
Debtors	5,000				
Cash	20,000	28,000			
		65,000			65,000

Structure of Accounts

2.3 Drawings

When we calculated Mr Davenport's profit of £3,000 we simply stated that material (stock) originally cost £2000 and could be sold as a conservatory for £5,000. We have therefore ignored at this stage any money spent by Mr Davenport on overheads such as gas, electricity and wages paid to employees. Such expenses do not directly appear in the balance sheet but the trading profit and loss account, which we shall examine in Chapter 5.

Suppose, however, Mr Davenport wanted to withdraw £2,000 for his own living expenses. How would we deal with this item? It would be easy to think that it is dealt with in the same way as wages paid to employees in the trading profit and loss account but this is *not* the case, for a sole trader.

Money withdrawn by the owners of a business for their own personal use is known as *drawings* and is reflected in the balance sheet as a deduction from the money owed to them, i.e. as a deduction from capital and profits.

A withdrawal or *drawing* of £2000 would therefore be represented in the balance sheet as follows:

Table 2.6: Balance sheet of Davenport Conservatories as at 31.1.Y0

	£	£		£
Fixed assets			Capital	50,000
Premises	30,000		Profits	3,000
Fixtures	5,000			53,000
Equipment	2,000	37,000	**Drawings**	(2,000)
				51,000
Current assets			*Deferred liabilities*	
Stock	3,000		Loan	10,000
Debtors	5,000		*Current liabilities*	
Cash	**18,000**	26,000	Creditor	2,000
		63,000		63,000

Note how cash has reduced by £2,000 as a result of the drawing. A *double effect*, you might say, causing us to make a *double entry*.

In the next chapter we shall examine the double effect of transactions when we look at *double entry bookkeeping*, a subject you may be familiar with from your study of *business calculations*.

2 – An Introduction to the Balance Sheet

Summary

1. A balance sheet reflects the financial position of a business at a particular date only.
2. The title to the balance sheet should indicate whose accounts it represents.
3. The only items to appear in the balance sheet of a company are the items owned or owed by the business *not* the personal assets of the owners. This is the *business entity concept.*
4. A balance sheet in the horizontal format shows assets on one side and capital plus liabilities (source of finance) on the other.
5. *The accounting equation:* Assets = Capital + Liabilities.
6. A balance sheet must always balance.
7. *Assets* are items *owned* by the business, e.g. premises.
8. *Fixed assets* are of a permanent or semi-permanent nature, necessary for the continuation of the business and therefore not normally changed in the day-to-day trading.
9. *Current assets* are items acquired or produced for resale and conversion into cash.
10. *Capital* is the amount contributed by the owners of the business.
11. *Profits* are owed by the business to the owners and are therefore added to capital.
12. *Drawings* represent the money withdrawn by the owners and are deducted from capital plus profits.
13. *Liabilities* are amounts owed by the business.
14. *Long-term liabilities* are debts that are repayable after more than one year.
15. *Current liabilities* are debts that are repayable within one year.
16. *Overdrafts* are normally repayable on demand and are therefore considered to be a *current liability.*
17. *Creditors* are people to whom the business owes money and are hence a liability, and if repayable within one year, a current liability.
18. *Debtors* are people who owe the business money and are hence a *current asset.*

Structure of Accounts

Section B
PREPARATION OF ACCOUNTS

In this section we are concerned with the preparation of accounts for various types of businesses:

- Sole traders
- Partnerships
- Limited companies
- Manufacturing companies

We start with a *sole trader*, for example a shopkeeper, first by recording his or her day-to-day transactions (e.g. sales, purchases of stock and the payment of expenses), using *double-entry bookkeeping*. The effect of these transactions is then summarized in a *trial balance* before producing the *final accounts*, a trading profit and loss account and a balance sheet.

Using the knowledge gained from our examination of sole traders we then move on to examine *partnerships* and *limited companies*.

Finally, we turn our attention to *manufacturing companies*. Initially we will examine how to prepare the final accounts of a manufacturing company and in particular how to calculate the *cost of manufacture*. We then look at the costs of manufacture from a different angle, examining *the behavior of the costs* in relation to manufacturing output, the output required to break even (cover total costs) and the use of *break-even analysis* as a decision-making tool.

In summary, this section consists of the following chapters:

- Chapter 3: From Double Entry to Trial Balance
- Chapter 4: Making Adjustments to the Trial Balance – Why and How
- Chapter 5: From Trial Balance to Final Accounts
- Chapter 6: Depreciation
- Chapter 7: Partnership Accounts
- Chapter 8: Limited Company Accounts
- Chapter 9: Manufacturing Company Accounts
- Chapter 10: Decision-making: Cost Behaviour and Break-even Analysis

Structure of Accounts

3

FROM DOUBLE ENTRY TO TRIAL BALANCE

Syllabus Objectives

1.3 The double entry system, leading to the trial balance including:
- Debit and credit
- Ledger accounts – chart of accounts

Learning Objectives

After studying this chapter you should be able to:

1 Understand the nature of double-entry bookkeeping;

2 Produce a trial balance from a number of bookkeeping entries;

3 Explain the meaning of the following terms:
- Returns in
- Returns out
- Discount allowed
- Discount received
- Cash discount
- Trade discount

Introduction

In the last chapter we followed the activities of Mr Davenport and witnessed his balance sheet changing with every business transaction.

Imagine the situation if Mr Davenport and other businesses such as Marks and Spencer drew up a new balance sheet after every transaction, 'Sir, we've just sold another Chicken Kiev, I mean another two, sorry three...'. Obviously it would be impossible to do so.

Fortunately, it is also unnecessary because companies need to draw up a balance sheet only once a year at the end of their accounting period. While they need to produce a balance sheet only once a year they will still need to record certain accounting information on a regular basis in order to keep control of their business. For example, you would not simply wait until the balance-sheet date to calculate your debtors; you need to see how much is owed and by whom on any one day.

How does a company maintain records?

The recording of such information will differ from company to company. A newsagent may simply have a book with each customer's name on a separate page listing the amounts owed. Other companies may have their debtors listed on computer, with each debtor having a separate file or page. Then at the end of the accounting period, when the company wishes to produce its balance sheet, it can either manually total up the amounts owed from each debtor or ask the computer to produce a figure which could be transferred to the balance sheet.

As you can imagine, in practice it is a lot more difficult than I have outlined. When the accounts of a company such as Marks and Spencer are published, they may well be a few months old.

3.1 Double-entry bookkeeping

So far I have mentioned only the need to monitor debtors on a day-to-day basis, but the same could be said for creditors, cash and indeed most items. You will therefore need a separate account for each item so that the up-to-date position of each item can be seen at any time. These accounts are often known as *'T' accounts* and may be drawn as follows:

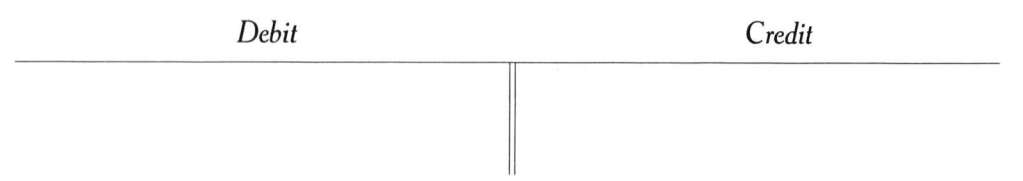

Debit	*Credit*

The terms *debit* and *credit* simply mean left and right and should *not* be confused with their meaning in banking.

But what information is recorded on the *debit (left)* and *credit (right)* side of the "T" accounts?

Here is the "T" account recording the banking transactions of a business.

3 – From Double Entry to Trial Balance

Table 3.1: T acount of bank account

Debit			Credit		
Date	Transaction	Amount	Date	Transaction	Amount
1 Jan 02	Sales	£5,000	5 Jan 02	Purchases	£2,000

This tells us that:

- On 1 January 02, the business *received* £5,000 in respect of sales, and
- On 5 January 02, the business *paid* £2,000 for purchases.

This is not a misprint. Remember, in accounts debit and credit simply mean left and right – a point that often confuses bankers.

The debit and credit sides record:

Debit (Left side)	**Credit side (Right side)**
Money/goods **IN**, i.e. we received £5,000	Money/Goods **OUT**, i.e. we paid £2,000
and/or	and/or
Items you **OWN**, i.e. we own the £5,000 it is an **ASSET**	Items you **OWE**

Example

Let us follow the transactions of Mr O'Neil of Wonder Records to see how the recording of information on the *debit and credit* side works.

Oct 1 *commenced business with £30,000 in the bank.*

Mr O'Neil will need to record:

- the amount of capital he has contributed and is therefore *owed* by the business *and*
- the cash the business has received.

He will therefore need two separate records.

The *double entries* are therefore:

1. Bank   money going *into* the business   on the left-hand side (Debit)
2. Capital   money *owed* by the business   on the right-hand side (Credit).

Bank account

Oct	1	Capital	£30,000	

Structure of Accounts

Capital account

	Oct	1 Bank		£30,000

The narrative is simply a cross-reference to the other account involved, describing the transaction.

Oct 1 *transferred £1,000 from the bank to the petty cash.*

The *double entries* are:

1. Bank — money going *out* — Credit
2. Petty cash — money going *in* — Debit

Bank account

Oct	1 Capital	£30,000	Oct	1 Petty cash	£1,000

Petty cash account

Oct	1 Bank	£1,000	

Oct 2 *purchased equipment for £5000 by cheque.*

The *double entries* are:

1. Bank — money going *out* — Credit
2. Equipment — something you *own* — Debit

Bank account

Oct	1 Capital	£30,000	Oct	1 Petty cash	£1,000
			Oct	2 Equipment	£5,000

Equipment account

Oct	2 Cash	£5,000	

So as you can see

- Each transaction has a *double effect*, with one entry being made on the debit side (left-hand side) of one "T" account and another entry being made on the credit side (right-hand side) of another "T" account.
- For every debit there is a credit. Hence the name *double-entry bookkeeping*.
- Money coming in or items purchased are on the debit side, whereas money going out and money owed are on the credit side.

3 – From Double Entry to Trial Balance

3.2 Expenses

So far we have ignored expenses such as gas, electricity, etc. Let us examine how we would deal with these in the case of Mr O'Neil.

Oct 3 *paid rent of £150 by cheque.*

Oct 4 *paid wages £200 by cheque.*

Bank account

							£
Oct	1	Capital	£30,000	Oct	1	Petty cash	1,000
					2	Equipment	5,000
					3	Rent	150
					4	Wages	200

Rent account

Oct	3	Cash	£150	

Wages account

Oct	4	Cash	£200	

As always, there are two entries for each transaction:

1. *Bank* recording the money going *out* — Credit
2. *Rent and wages* recording the expenses paid — Debit

We can therefore extend our rules relating to the recording of information on the *debit* and *credit* sides:

Debit (Left side)	Credit side (Right side)
Money/goods **IN**, i.e. we received £5,000	Money/Goods **OUT**, i.e. we paid £2,000
and/or	and/or
Items you **OWN**, i.e. we own the £5,000, it is an **ASSET**	Items you **OWE**
Expenses **PAID**	Income **RECEIVED** *(see later)*

3.3 Stock

Oct 5 *purchased a stock of 5000 records for £5,000 (i.e. £1 each) on two months' credit from A Black.*

Oct 6 *sold 2 500 records for £5,000 (i.e. £2 each), payment by cheque.*

We do not have a "T" account for stock, instead we have:

- a purchases account
- a sales account

This is because goods are purchased at cost price while hopefully sold at a profit.

The *double entries* for these transactions are:

Oct 5:	1	Purchases	goods coming *in*	Debit
	2	A Black	money we *owe*	Credit
Oct 6:	1	Sales	goods going *out*	Credit
	2	Bank	money coming *in*	Debit

Purchases account

Oct 5 A Black £5,000	

A Black (Creditor) account

	Oct 5 Purchases £5,000

Sales account

	Oct 6 Bank £5,000

Bank account

£		£	
Oct 1 Capital 30,000		Oct 1 Petty cash 1,000	
6 Sales 5,000		2 Equipment 5,000	
		3 Rent 150	
		4 Wages 200	

3.4 Day books or journals

Where companies buy and sell a large number of items on credit the purchases and sales accounts may well become cluttered. To avoid this such companies may use day books or journals to record all credit transactions.

Here is a look at the sales day book for another company – Forrester Ltd.

3 – From Double Entry to Trial Balance

Sales day book

Credit sales are entered in the sales day book at the point of sale. Then at the end of the accounting period the sales day book is totalled up and the balance transferred to the sales account.

Forrester Ltd Sales Day Book

Date		Debtor	Invoice no.	£
Jan	1	**Mather**	**1810**	**1,000**
	5	**Jennings**	**1911**	**5,100**
	8	Knowles	1812	2,610
	11	Peters	1813	4,200
	15	Gilzean	1814	650
	26	Hunt	1815	810
	31	**Transfer to sales ledger**		**14,370**

Sales account

	Jan 31 Credit sales for the month £14,370

NB: the double entries at the time of sale will therefore be:

1 Enter the sale in the sales day book.
2 Debit each individual debtors' account at the time of sale.

For example:

Mather (Debtor) account

Jan 1 Sales £1,000	

Jennings (Debtor) account

Jan 5 Sales £5,100	

Other day books

a) *Purchase day book* – credit purchases are listed in the purchases day book and at the end of the accounting period the balance is transferred to the purchase account;

Structure of Accounts

b) *Returns inwards day book;*

c) *Returns outwards day book.*

As the questions and examples that follow do not involve many transactions you will not be required to enter items in the day books.

Let us now return to Mr O'Neil and Wonder Records.

3.5 Returns in and returns out

a) *Returns in*   goods that have been returned to us possibly because they are faulty.

b) *Returns out*   goods that we have returned to our suppliers.

Let us see how we would deal with these.

October 7 *returned goods of £1000 to A Black, which were faulty.*

1. Open a new "T" account for returns out (remember every item has its own "T" account) and credit the returns out account – goods going *out*.

2. Debit A Black – his "T" account will therefore show that we originally owed him £5,000 but we have since returned goods of £1,000, indicating that we now owe him only £4,000.

Returns out account

	Oct 7 A Black	£1,000

A Black (creditor) account

| Oct 7 Ret out | £1,000 | Oct 5 Purchases | £5,000 |

Oct 8 *a customer returns faulty goods to Mr O'Neil in return for a cash refund of £100.*

Petty cash account

| Oct 1 Bank | £1,000 | Oct 5 Returns in | £100 |

Returns in account

| Oct 8 Petty cash | £100 | | |

3.6 Discounts

There are various types of discounts:

a) Discounts allowed:

   i) *Trade discount:* given to customers who buy in bulk.

   ii) *Prompt payment discount:* given to customers for prompt payment.

3 – From Double Entry to Trial Balance

b) Discounts received

  i) *Trade discount:* received from suppliers when buying in bulk.

  ii) *Prompt payment discount:* received from suppliers for prompt payment.

Discounts allowed

i) *Trade discount* given to customers who buy in bulk, e.g.

Oct 10 *sales of goods £500 to V Ahmed on credit terms of one month, with a trade discount of 5%.*

	£
Sales of goods	500
Less discount 5%	25
Net amount due	475

V Ahmed (Debtor) account

Oct 10 Sales	£475		

Sales account

		Oct 6	Bank	£5,000
		Oct 10	V Ahmed	£475

In this case the discount is deducted at the time of sale and therefore only the net amount appears in the "T" account.

ii) *Prompt payment discount:* given to customers for prompt payment.

Here the customer will have originally been invoiced for the total amount, e.g.

Oct 11 *sale of goods £100 to S Broady on credit terms of three months, with a 5% cash discount for prompt payment.*

Original entries:

S Broady (Debtor) account

Oct 11 Sales	£100		

Sales account

		Oct 6 Bank	£5,000
		Oct 10 V Ahmed	£475
		Oct 11 S Broady	£100

Structure of Accounts

Oct 20 *S Broady has unexpectedly received some money and calls to pay his bill early by cheque.*

This will qualify him for the 5% cash discount, i.e. 5% of £100 = £5. He therefore needs to pay only £95 (£100 – 5).

S Broady (Debtor) account

Oct	11	Sales	£100	Oct	20	Petty cash	£95

Petty cash account

Oct	20	Broady	£95		

As you can see, S Broady's "T" account still indicates that he owes £5. We therefore need to record details of the discount we have *allowed* him.

The transaction is therefore completed in the following manner:

Discounts allowed account

Oct	20	S Broady	£5		

S Broady (Debtor) account

Oct	11	Sales	£100	Oct	20	Petty cash	£95
					20	Dis. All.	£5

Discounts received

As we said, Mr O'Neil may also *receive discounts*, i.e. from suppliers, either for bulk orders (trade discount) or for prompt payment.

For example, on 5 October Mr O'Neil purchased £5000 worth of goods from Mr A Black and on 7 October returned £1,000 worth of goods as they were faulty.

Oct 30 *decides to pay Mr A Black in full by cheque after deducting £100 for prompt payment.*

A Black (Creditor) account

Oct	7	Ret. Out	£1,000	Oct	5	Purchases	£5,000
	30	Dis. recvd.	£100				

Discount received account

				Oct	30	A Black	£100

The balance to pay is £3,900 (£5,000 – (1,000 + 100)) and the transaction is therefore completed as follows:

3 – From Double Entry to Trial Balance

A Black (Creditor) account

Oct	7	Returns out	1,000	Oct	5	Purchases	5,000
	30	Discount received	100				
	30	**Bank**	**3,900**				

Bank account

Oct	1	Capital	30,000	Oct	1	Petty cash	1,000
	6	Sales	5,000		2	Equipment	5,000
	20	S Broady	95		3	Rent	150
					4	Wages	200
					30	A Black	3,900

So:

Discounts allowed – represents cash discounts we have allowed our customers.

Discounts received – represents cash discounts we have received from our customers.

3.7 Balancing off the accounts

Earlier in the chapter I mentioned that companies need to produce a balance sheet only at the end of their accounting period and that in the meantime they will record details of their transactions in "T" accounts.

Suppose Mr O'Neil has now come to the end of his accounting period and wishes to produce his final accounts.

First of all he must balance off the "T" accounts by adding up the greater side, which then forms the total of the account, i.e. £35,095 (30,000 + 5,000 + 95).

Bank account

Oct	1	Capital	30,000	Oct	1	Petty cash	1,000
	6	Sales	5,000		2	Equipment	5,000
	20	S Broady	95		3	Rent	150
					4	Wages	200
					30	A Black	3,900
			35,095				**35,095**

But the right hand side (credits) does *not* really add up to £35,095 because Mr O'Neil has spent only £10,250 (1,000 + 5,000 + 150 + 200 + 3,900). In other words Mr O'Neil has paid £35,095 into his bank account and written cheques for £10,250, which means that according *to him* his bank balance should be:

$$£35\,095$$
$$\text{less } \underline{£10\,250}$$
$$\underline{£24\,845}$$

The balancing figure of £24,845 is recorded as follows in order to balance off the account:

Bank Account

Oct	1	Capital	30,000	Oct	1	Petty cash	1,000
	6	Sales	5,000		2	Equipment	5,000
	20	S Broady	95		3	Rent	150
					4	Wages	200
					30	A Black	3,900
					30	**Balance**	**24,845**
			35,095				35,095
Nov	1	Balance c/o £24,845					

The balance is *carried over* as the starting balance of the next accounting period and is the amount entered in the trial balance.

Clearly, if some cheques have not yet been presented to Mr O'Neil's bank or if Mr O'Neil has not yet paid the £95 received from S Broady into his bank account, the bank will record a different balance than £24,945. We will return to this in Chapter 12, Bank Reconciliation Statements, when we examine how customers check (reconcile) their accounts with their bank statement.

3.8 Trial balance

The trial balance is a summary of the balances remaining in the various accounts, with debits on one side and credits on the other. You may not be surprised to notice that the trial balance, (shown below), balances. This, you will recall, is because an entry has been made on one side of one account and the other side of another account, i.e. for every debit there is a credit.

Obviously, if it does not balance, then we have made a mistake, and the trial balance therefore provides a check on the accuracy of the accounts. Unfortunately, that does not necessarily mean that our accounts are accurate if the trial balance does balance. We may have:

1 omitted details of a transaction on either side;

2 entered details twice;

3 entered the wrong amount in both accounts;

4 entered the correct amount but in the wrong accounts.

3.9   Conclusion

A full recap of Mr O'Neil's transactions, together with a record of his accounts, is given below, illustrating:

a) the recording of entries;

b) the balancing of accounts;

c) the construction of a trial balance.

Mr O'Neil of Wonder Records

Oct 1 Commenced business with £30,000 in the bank.

   1 Transferred £1,000 from the bank to the petty cash.

   2 Purchased equipment for £5,000 by cheque.

   3 Paid rent of £150 by cheque.

   4 Paid wages £200 by cheque.

   5 Purchased a stock of 5,000 records for £5,000 on two months' credit from A Black.

   6 Sold 2 500 records for £5,000, payment by cheque.

   7 Returned goods of £1,000 to A Black which were faulty.

   8 Customers returned faulty goods to us of £100 in exchange for a cash refund.

  10 Sale of goods £500 to V Ahmed on credit terms of one month with a trade discount of 5%.

  11 Sale of goods £100 to S Broady on credit terms of three months, with a 5% cash discount for prompt payment.

  20 S Broady unexpectedly received some money and calls to pay his bill early by cheque.

  30 Paid A Black in full by cheque, after deducting £100 for prompt payment.

Structure of Accounts

Table 3. 2: Full recapitulation of Mr O'Neil's transactions

Bank Account

Oct	1	Capital	30,000	Oct	1	Petty cash	1,000
	6	Sales	5,000		2	Equipment	5,000
	20	S Broady	95		3	Rent	150
						Wages	200
					30	Bank	3,900
					31	Balance	24,845
				35 095			35,095
Nov	1	Balance c/o	24 845				

Capital account

Oct	31	Balance c/o	30,000	Oct	1	Bank	30,000
				Nov	1	Balance c/o	30,000

Petty cash account

Oct	1		1,000	Oct	8	Return in	100
					31	Balance	900
			1,000				1,000
Nov	1	Balance c/o	900				

Equipment account

Oct	2	Bank	5,000	Oct	31	Balance	5,000
Nov	1	Balance c/o	5,000				

Rent account

Oct	31	Bank	150	Oct	31	Balance	150
Nov	1	Balance c/o	150				

Wages account

Oct	3	Bank	200	Oct	31	Balance	200
Nov	1	Balance c/o	200				

3 – From Double Entry to Trial Balance

Purchases account

Oct	5	A Black	5,000	Oct	31	Balance	5,000
Nov	1	Balance c/o	5,000				

A Black (Creditor)

Oct	7	Returns out	1,000	Oct	5	Purchases	5,000
	30	A Black	100				
	30	Bank	3,900				
			5,000				5,000

Sales account

				Oct	6	Bank	5,000
					10	Ahmed	475
Oct	31	Balance	5,575		11	S Broady	100
			5,575				5,575
				Nov	1	Balance c/o	5,575

Returns out account

Oct	31	Balance	1,000	Oct	7	A Black	1,000
				Nov	1	Balance c/o	1,000

Returns in account

Oct	8	Petty cash	100	Oct	31	Balance	100
Nov	1	Balance c/o	100				

V Ahmed (Debtor) account

Oct	10	Sales	475	Oct	31	Balance	475
Nov	1	Balance c/o	475				

S Broady (Debtor) account

Oct	11	Sales	100	Oct	20	Discount allowed	5
					20	Bank	95
			100				100

Structure of Accounts

Discount allowed account

Oct	20	S Broady	5	Oct	31	Balance	5
Nov	1	Balance c/o	5				

Discount received account

Oct	31	Balance	100	Oct	30	A Black	100
				Nov	1	Balance c/o	100

Table 3.3: Trial balance of Wonder Records as at 31.10.Y0

	£	£
Bank	24 845	
Capital		30,000
Petty cash	900	
Equipment	5,000	
Rent	150	
Wages	200	
Purchases	5,000	
A Black		
Sales		5,575
Returns out		1,000
Returns in	100	
V Ahmed (Debtor)	475	
S Broady		
Discounts allowed	5	
Discounts received		100
	36 675	**36 675**

Please note: you will *not* be asked to record entries in "T" accounts and produce a trial balance in the examination. The questions in the examination that ask you to prepare accounts will give you the trial balance from which you will be asked to produce final accounts – the trading profit and loss account and a balance sheet.

3 – From Double Entry to Trial Balance

So why have we spent a chapter learning how to record entries in "T" accounts, I hear you say?

Well, in the first place, I hope this chapter has taught you more than how to record entries and construct a trial balance. You should by now be able to explain the meaning of the following:

- Returns in
- Returns out
- Discount allowed
- Discount received
- Cash discount
- Trade discount

In addition, the chapter should also have given you an appreciation of the double-entry system which will be useful to you in the next chapter when we examine the trial balance in more detail and look at the possible adjustments that you **may be asked** to make to the trial balance in the examination.

Structure of Accounts

Summary

1. A company will draw up its balance sheet only at the end of its accounting period, usually once a year.

2. Double-entry bookkeeping is a system of record keeping that enables a business to record its daily transactions.

3. A separate account is kept for each item.

4. The left-hand side of the account is known as the debit side.

5. The right-hand side of the account is known as the credit side.

6. Debit and credit simply mean left and right and should not be confused with their meaning in banking.

7. The rules relating to the recording of information on the *debit* and *credit* sides are:

Debit (Left side)	*Credit side (Right side)*
Money/goods **IN**, i.e. we received £5,000	Money/Goods **OUT**, i.e. we paid £2,000
Items you **OWN**, i.e. we own the £5,000, it is an **ASSET**	Items you **OWE**
Expenses **PAID**	Income **RECEIVED** (see later)

8. Each transaction has a *double effect*, with one entry being made on the debit side (left-hand side) of one "T" account and another entry being made on the credit side (right-hand side) of another "T" account.

9. For every debit there is a credit. Hence the name *double-entry bookkeeping*.

10. The purchase of stock is recorded in a purchases account at the cost price and not in a stock account.

11. The sale of stock is recorded in a sales account at the sale price.

12. Returns in refers to goods that have been returned to us possibly because they are faulty.

13. Returns out refers to goods we have returned to our suppliers.

14. Where companies buy and sell a large number of items on credit they may enter details of purchases and sales in a purchases day book and sales day book.

15. The balance in the day books is then transferred to the purchases and sales accounts at the end of the accounting period.

16. Companies may also have day books for returns inwards and return outwards.

17. Trade discounts are often given to customers who buy in bulk. Such a discount will be deducted at the time of sale and will therefore not appear in the ledger.

3 – From Double Entry to Trial Balance

18 Prompt payment discounts may be given for prompt payment and will be recorded in the account of the company as either a discount allowed or a discount received.

19 Discount allowed is the discount we allow to customers.

20 Discount received is the discount we receive from our creditors.

21 At the end of the accounting period the accounts are balanced off and the balance transferred to a trial balance.

22 The trial balance is a summary of the balances of the accounts.

23 A trial balance should always balance.

24 If the trial balance does not balance it indicates that an error has been made in the bookkeeping.

25 Even if the trial balance does balance, mistakes may still have been made, e.g. because we

- omitted details of a transaction on either side;
- entered details twice;
- entered the wrong amount in both accounts;
- entered the correct amount but in the wrong accounts.

4

MAKING ADJUSTMENTS TO THE TRIAL BALANCE – WHY AND HOW

Syllabus Objectives

1.4   The trial balance

Adjust for:

- Prepayments
- Accruals
- Bad and doubtful debts
- Stock
- Depreciation   (See Chapter 6)

Learning Objectives

After studying this chapter you should be able to:

1   Explain *why* you need to make adjustments to the trial balance.

2   Illustrate *how* to make the following adjustments to the trial balance:

- Stock
- Prepayments
- Accruals
- Bad and doubtful debts

Depreciation is covered in detail in Chapter 6.

3   Explain the importance of matching revenue and related expenditure;

4   Appreciate the time at which revenue is recognized;

5   Recognize and explain the need for prudence.

4 – Making Adjustments to the Trial Balance

Introduction

In the previous chapter we followed the activities of Mr O'Neil by entering details of his transactions in his "T" accounts, with debits on one side and credits on the other. We then produced a trial balance – a summary of the balances remaining in each account with, once again, debits on one side and credits on the other. As you know, you will *not* be asked to do this in the examination.

But you *may well* be asked to make adjustments to the trial balance, profit and loss account and balance sheet in order to produce a set of final accounts which reflect a "true and fair view" of a company's financial position, in line with regulatory requirements.

In this chapter we will make the adjustments to the trial balance and in the next chapter we will go on to produce the final accounts (trading profit and loss account and balance sheet). Later in the book we will also examine the regulatory requirements relating to the preparation of final accounts.

Throughout this chapter you will be introduced to items that will appear in the trading profit and loss account and reminded of those which appear in the balance sheet. Do not worry too much about them at this stage, simply concentrate on *why* and *how* we adjust the trial balance.

It may be worth knowing at this stage, however, that the *basic calculation of profit* is:

Sales (income)

less

Expenses (outgoings)

As you will see, a number of the adjustments we make affect the *expenses* of the business.

So, let us move on and look at:

- What adjustments we need to make
- Why we need to make them and
- How we make them.

4.1 What adjustments we need to make

According to the syllabus you may need to make adjustments for:

- Stock
- Prepayments
- Accruals
- Bad and doubtful debts
- Depreciation (See Chapter 6)

Structure of Accounts

4.2 Why we need to make these adjustments

Because, when preparing accounts, we, along with everyone else, must observe certain regulations, in particular:

- Legislation – UK and EU
- Standards or statements of best practice, in particular Statements of Standard Accounting Practice (SSAPs) and Financial Reporting Standards (FRSs)
- International Accounting Standards (IASs)
- Stock Exchange rules
- Non-mandatory recommendations

These regulations have been established over time in order to narrow (minimize) and regularize the range of permissible accounting treatments applicable to transactions or situations and thereby aid the comparability of accounts across time (from year to year), and between companies.

We will examine the regulatory regime in great detail in Chapter 16. In this chapter we will also touch on **FRS 18** and a number of the **Accounting Concepts and Conventions** upon which accounts are based, when we examine the necessary adjustments and explain in more detail *why* we need to make each adjustments.

4.3 How we make the adjustments

Here is the trial balance of Mario's Restaurant, together with a number of notes at the foot of the trial balance.

4 – Making Adjustments to the Trial Balance

Table 4.1: Trial balance of Mario's Restaurant as at 31.12.01

	Dr £	Cr £
Capital		50,000
Sales		150,000
Stock	**5,000**	
Purchases	90,000	
Rent	1,100	
Rates	3,000	
Electricity	200	
Gas	100	
Telephone	50	
Insurance	150	
Debtors	12,170	
Creditors		10,980
Premises	60,000	
Fixtures	20,000	
Vehicles	19,210	
	210,980	210,980

Notes:

1. Stock as at 31.12.01   £20,000
2. Prepayment – Insurance   £100
3. Accrual – Electricity owing   £50

The *notes* at the foot of the trial balance inform you of any adjustments that you will need to make to the trial balance.

Therefore when presented with a trial balance and asked to produce the final accounts (trading profit and loss account and balance sheet) you must always deal with the *notes* first by making the necessary adjustments.

Let us look at each *note* in turn.

Structure of Accounts

1. Adjusting the trial balance for stock

In the trial balance (the third item down on the debit or left hand side) you will see stock £5,000. This refers to the *opening stock* at the beginning of the accounting period, let us say 01.01.01.

Note 1 at the foot of the trial balance indicates the value of the *closing stock* as at 31.12.01. We will look at how companies value their closing stock later in the book.

For now we do not need to consider stock valuation or make any adjustments to our trial balance; simply remember:

- *Opening stock* appears in the body of the trial balance   £5,000
- *Closing stock* is given as a note at the foot of the trial balance   £20,000

2. Adjusting the trial balance for prepayments and accruals

What are prepayments and accruals?

Let us consider the position of Mario's Restaurant in greater detail for a moment. Mario needs to calculate his net profit for the year ending, i.e. from 01.01.01 to 31.12.01.

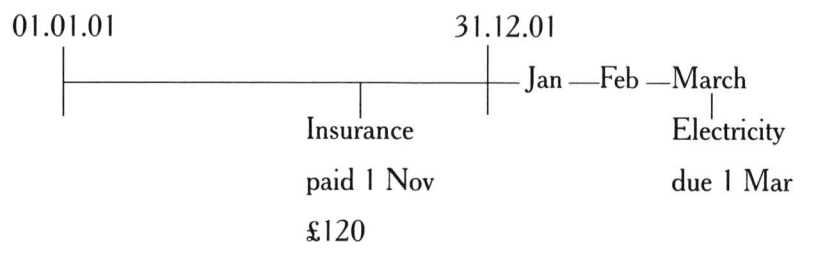

```
01.01.01                          31.12.01
|─────────────────────┬──────────────|── Jan ── Feb ── March
                      |                              |
                   Insurance                    Electricity
                   paid 1 Nov                   due 1 Mar
                      £120
```

Insurance

Mario's annual insurance premium was paid on 1 November but this related to November and December of this accounting year and ten months of the next accounting period, i.e. at the end of this accounting year Mario will have paid 10 months of his insurance bill in advance. He has made a *prepayment*.

Prepayment: Money paid this accounting period in respect of an expense due in the next accounting period.

Annual insurance premium paid on 1 November (this related to November and December of this accounting year and ten months of the next year)	£120
Prepayment = (if 12 months = £120, we can say 10 months = £100)	£100

4 – Making Adjustments to the Trial Balance

Electricity

Mario is not due to receive his next electricity bill until 1 March next year. This bill will cover his electricity for December of this accounting period and January and February of next accounting period, i.e. at the end of this accounting period Mario will still owe for his electricity consumption during December. He needs to make an *accrual*.

Accruals: Money owing at the end of the accounting period in respect of benefits enjoyed during the accounting period.

At the end of this accounting year we need to estimate what the bill will be and then take 1/3 (1 month out of 3) as the amount owing for December

Estimated bill	£150
Amount owing (*accrual*) = £150 x 1/3 =	£50

So how do we deal with the prepayment and accrual? Do we simply include the full amount paid for insurance and forget the electricity bill because it is not payable until next year?

You may feel this would be fair because each year's accounts would suffer in the same way and therefore even things up. Unfortunately, however, we are not allowed to simply ignore such matters, otherwise we would over- or underestimate the profit figure for the year. A trading profit and loss account should reflect a company's performance for a particular account period, e.g. for the year ending 31.12.01.

```
1.1.01                                                    31.12.01
├──────────────────────────────────────────────────────────┤
```

We are required to match all income relating to a particular period with the expenditure incurred that relates to that period and not to the cash receipts and payments (accruals or matching concept).

So, we cannot simply ignore the insurance prepayment and the electricity accrual, and we need to adjust the amounts paid during the year in order to calculate the amount of expense incurred during the accounting year.

Let us return to our trial balance to see how the adjustments are made.

Prepayments

1 – *Reduce* the insurance paid during the year so that it represents the cost for this accounting period. This should be done on the trial balance, as follows:

Structure of Accounts

Table 4.2: Trial balance of Mario's Restaurant as at 31.12.01

	Dr	Cr
	£	£
Capital		50,000
Sales		150,000
Stock	5,000	
Purchases	90,000	
Rent	1,100	
Rates	3,000	
Electricity	200	
Gas	100	
Telephone	50	
Insurance	(-100) 150	
Debtors	12,170	
Creditors		10,980
Premises	60,000	
Fixtures	20,000	
Vehicles	19,210	
	210,980	210,980

But if we reduce insurance by £100, the left hand column reduces by £100 and the trial balance does not balance. We therefore have to make another entry, or should I say the *double entry*, by recording details of the amount prepaid and therefore owing to Mario's Restaurant.

2 – Record details of the prepayment at the foot of the trial balance as follows:

4 – Making Adjustments to the Trial Balance

Table 4.3: Trial balance of Mario's Restaurant as at 31.12.01

	Dr	Cr
	£	£
Capital		50,000
Sales		150,000
Stock	5,000	
Purchases	90,000	
Rent	1,100	
Rates	3,000	
Electricity	200	
Gas	100	
Telephone	50	
Insurance	(-100) 150	
Debtors	12,170	
Creditors		10,980
Premises	60,000	
Fixtures	20,000	
Vehicles	19,210	
	210,980	210,980
Prepayments – insurance	100	

As you will see in the next chapter, in order to produce the final accounts (a trading profit and loss account and balance sheet) all we need to do is to rearrange the items in the trial balance (including the prepayment of £100), into an accepted order and format.

It is a bit like doing a jigsaw!

However if we do not make the adjustments correctly or if we do not insert all the pieces then we will not balance. I therefore include the prepayment of £100 at the foot of the trial balance as another item, so that when it comes to produce the final accounts I shall remember to put in all the pieces.

We will consider where the pieces go in the jigsaw in the next chapter.

But why record the prepayment of £100 in the debit (left-hand) column?

Basically Mario has paid £100 to his insurance company in advance. Therefore at the end

Structure of Accounts

of the accounting period the insurance company *owes* Mario's Restaurant £100. Prepayments are therefore like debtors (people who owe you money) and as you can see from the trial balance, debtors are listed in the left-hand column.

The trial balance now balances and therefore so too will our final accounts.

Accruals

As with every adjustment there are two entries. In the case of accruals these are:

1) Add the amount owing £50, to the amount paid £200

2) Create an accrual of £50 at the foot of the trial balance.

This should be done on the trial balance, as follows:

Table 4.4: Trial balance of Mario's Restaurant as at 31.12.01

		Dr	Cr
		£	£
Capital			50,000
Sales			150,000
Stock		5,000	
Purchases		90,000	
Rent		1,100	
Rates		3,000	
Electricity	(+50)	200	
Gas		100	
Telephone		50	
Insurance	(-100)	150	
Debtors		12,170	
Creditors			10,980
Premises		60,000	
Fixtures		20,000	
Vehicles		19,210	
		210,980	210,980
Prepayments – insurance prepaid		100	
Accruals – electricity owing			50

4 – Making Adjustments to the Trial Balance

Remember amounts *we owe* are listed on the right-hand side (credit column).

The guide to help you in this case is creditors (people who you owe money). As you can see from the trial balance creditors are listed on the right-hand side and, as accruals also represent money owed, then they too are listed on the right-hand side.

So:

Prepayment: Money paid this accounting period in respect of an expense due in the next accounting period.

1. Reduce the expense in the trial balance by the amount of prepayment.
2. Create a prepayment on the debit (left) side at the foot of the trial balance (money owed *to you* similar to *debtors*).

Accruals: Money owing at the end of the accounting period in respect of benefits enjoyed during the accounting period.

1. Increase the expense in the trial balance by the amount of accrual.
2. Create an accrual on the credit (right) side at the foot of the trial balance (money *you owe*, similar to *creditors*).

Please do not worry too much about which side you record the adjustments at the foot of the trial balance. You will see later that as long as you record them at the foot of the trial balance and put them into the final accounts *in their correct place* you will balance anyway. The important thing is to be able to calculate the correct adjustment and to remember to make *two* entries.

3. Adjusting the trial balance for bad and doubtful debts

Bad debts

When you sell goods on credit you run the risk of not getting paid. For example your customer may go bankrupt and be unable to pay or simply disappear! When a debt actually *goes* bad this is known as a *bad debt*. Where a sale actually goes bad, we simply write it off immediately.

e.g.

| Jan 1 | Sale of goods to V Iqbal | £2,000 |

V Iqbal account

| Jan 1 | Sales | £2,000 | | | |

Sales account

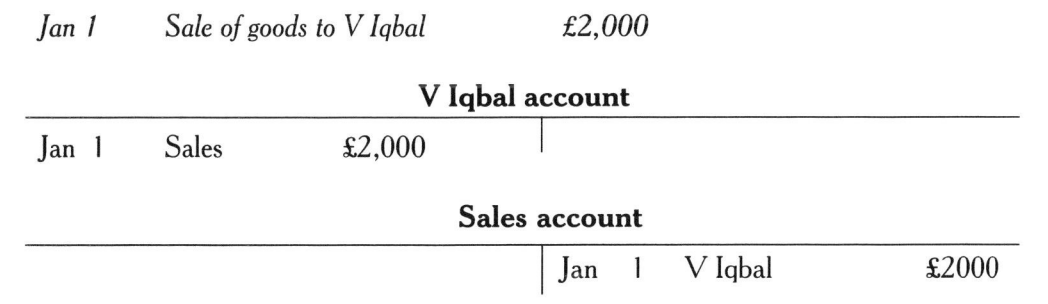

| | | | Jan 1 | V Iqbal | £2000 |

March 1: We are advised that V Iqbal has been declared bankrupt and that as an unsecured creditor we will not receive a dividend.

Therefore, we write off the debt of £2,000 in V Iqbal's account and create a bad debt which is included with all other accounts in the trial balance and as an expense in the trading profit and loss account.

V Iqbal account

Jan 1	Sales	£2,000	Mar 1	Bad debts	£2,000

Bad debts account

Mar 1	V Iqbal	£2,000			

In effect you do not need to adjust the trial balance for bad debts, the bad debts will have been accounted for in the above manner. At the end of the accounting period the bad debts "T" account will be balanced off and the balance, in our case £2,000, will be transferred to the trial balance along with all other items.

In the next chapter we will see exactly what we do with this and all other items in the trial balance.

Doubtful debts

Bad debts are entirely different from doubtful debts.

Doubtful debts are debts which you *feel may go bad in the future.*

But *why* are we concerned with what might happen in the future? Why do we not simply wait until the debts go bad and deal with them as bad debts?

If we go back to double-entry bookkeeping for a moment, you will recall that a sale on credit is entered in the accounts as follows:

Dec 1: Sale of £5,000 to A White on credit of three months.

Sales account

			Dec 1	A White	£5,000

A White (Debtor) Account

Dec 1	Sales	£5,000			

At the end of the accounting period the accounts are balanced off and the balances transferred to the trial balance, therefore:

Sales	The sales account will include the £5,000 of goods sold to A White despite the fact that we have not yet been paid.
A White	The balance of A White's account will form part of the debtors' figure (money owed), appearing in the balance sheet, despite the fact that we may not get paid.

4 – Making Adjustments to the Trial Balance

As a result:

Profit   The profit figure calculated in the trading profit and loss account may be overoptimistic. As we will see in the next chapter, profit is basically calculated as Sales – Expenses = Profit.

Debtors   (and hence assets) may be overstated, therefore:

SSAP 2 and the accounting concept of prudence and conservatism requires us to take account of all foreseeable losses, while only recognizing profits when they are realized or when realization is reasonably certain.

The normal time for recognizing profits is *when the goods are sold with a provision being made for bad and doubtful debts and future interest payments.*

By making such a provision we are:

- *Acting prudently.*
- Attempting to match the bad debts that result from the sales of the same period (i.e. *matching concept*).
- Taking steps to ensure that the accounts reflect a "true and fair view" of a company's financial position.

How do we make a provision for doubtful debts?

The provision for bad and doubtful debts should take account of all *foreseeable losses*.

Where it seems probable that the loss will be incurred, an *estimate* of the loss must be included in the final accounts.

If, however, the loss is doubtful, there is no need to include it in the trading profit and loss account or balance sheet, but, in order to remain prudent, a detail of the possible loss should be revealed as a note accompanying the final accounts. For example, if Company A is acting as a guarantor for Company B (which can happen if both companies are members of the same group), Company A must provide details of the guarantee, as there is a possibility that they may be called upon to pay the debts of Company B. This is known as a *contingent liability*.

The problem with creating a provision for bad and doubtful debts is that while we realize some debts will go bad we do not know which debts, and therefore how much will go bad.

An estimate must therefore be made, based on past experience. But an estimate of what?

Well, an estimate of the people who owe the business money, i.e. of the debtors.

One company may estimate bad and doubtful debts as follows, taking into consideration how long the debts have been outstanding:

Structure of Accounts

Length outstanding	Amount	Estimate of bad and doubtful debts	Amount
	£	%	£
0–3 months	15,000	1	1,500
3–6 months	10,000	5	500
6–9 months	7,000	10	700
9–12 months	1,000	15	150
Over 12 months	500	20	100
	33,500		**2,950**

Another company may simply make a provision based on the outstanding debtors. If for example they have found from past experience that 5 per cent of their debts turn bad and at the end of the year their debtors equal £100,000 then:

Debtors £100,000

Provision for bad and doubtful debts = 5% = £5,000

Adjusting the trial balance for provision for bad and doubtful debts

Here is the trial balance of a trader at the end of Year 1. As you can see from the note at the foot of the trial balance he has decided to create a provision for bad and doubtful debts of 5% of debtors.

4 – Making Adjustments to the Trial Balance

Table 4.5: Trial balance as at 31.12.01

	£	£
Purchases and sales	100,000	200,000
Stock at 1.1.X9	20,000	
Rent	3,000	
Bad debts	**1,000**	
Other expenses	20,000	
Premises	77,000	
Bank	2,000	
Cash	1,000	
Van	15,000	
Debtors	**42,000**	
Creditors		6,000
Capital		75,000
	281,000	281,000

Notes:

1. Stock as at 31.12.01 £15,000
2. Create a provision for bad and doubtful debts of 5% of debtors

Please note:

- The trial balance includes bad debts of £1,000. This has been accounted for.
- The closing stock is £15,000. (No adjustments are required for this).

How much should the provision for Year 1 be?

It should be 5% of debtors, i.e. 5% of £42,000 = £2,100

How is the adjustment recorded on the trial balance?

Let us return to double-entry bookkeeping for a moment, though you will NOT need to record the entries in "T" accounts in the examination.

We need to open two "T" accounts for the provision for bad debts:

1. **The expense for the year**

    You will recall that the reason we are providing for bad debts is so that we do not overestimate our profit when we know from experience that some of our income from sales will not materialize. The provision for the year is therefore an *expense*.

    As this is an expense it is recorded on the debit (left) side, and

Structure of Accounts

2. **The provision for bad and doubtful debts account,** which as you will see in the next chapter is deducted from debtors in the balance sheet so that our assets are not overvalued. We are basically saying that we think £2,100 of the debtors will not pay.

This is recorded on the Credit (Right) hand side.

Do not worry too much about which side of the "T" accounts the entries are recorded or on which side they are recorded at the foot of the trial balance.

The main thing is to remember to make two entries:

- the expense, and
- the provision that will be deducted from Debtors (remember we are providing for debtors going bad).

Provision for bad and doubtful debts (Expense) account

31.12.01	Prov. for year 2001 £2,100	

Provision for bad and doubtful debts account

	31.12.01	Prov. for year 2001 £2,100

I would suggest that you record the adjustment on the trial balance as follows:

Table 4.6: Trial balance as at 31.12.01

	£	£
Purchases and sales	100,000	200,000
Stock at 1.1.X9	20,000	
Rent	3,000	
Rates	1,000	
Other expenses	20,000	
Premises	77,000	
Bank	2,000	
Cash	1,000	
Van	15,000	
Debtors	42,000	
Creditors		6,000
Capital		75,000
	281,000	281,000
Bad and doubtful debts expense	2,100	
Provision for bad and doubtful debts		2,100

4 – Making Adjustments to the Trial Balance

Let us look at the situation at the end of Year 2.

Table 4.7: Trial balance as at 31.12.02

	£	£
Purchases and sales	150,000	257,000
Fixtures	15,000	
Rent	6,500	
Bad debts	500	
Provision for bad and doubtful debts		**2,100**
Other expenses	22,000	
Premises	80,000	
Motor vehicles	45,000	
Stock as at 01.01.02	**15,000**	
Van	15,000	
Bank	8,900	
Debtors	50,000	
Creditors		4,900
Capital		75,000
Profit		**68,900**
	407,900	407,900

Notes:
1. Stock as at 31.12.02 £30,000.
2. Create a provision for bad and doubtful debts of 5% of debtors.

Please note the following in the body of the trial balance for Year 2:
- The balance of provision for bad and doubtful debts account which we created in Year 1.
- The closing stock at the end of Year 1, £15,000, is the opening stock at the beginning of Year 2. (The closing stock for Year 2 is £30,000, as detailed in the *notes* at the foot of the trial balance above.)
- In Year 1 a profit of £68,900 was achieved and is carried forward to Year 2. This appears on the credit side as it is money *owed* by the business to the owners/shareholders.

What about the other "T" account for the provision for bad and doubtful debts which we created in Year 1, i.e. the bad and doubtful debts (expense) account?

Structure of Accounts

At the end of Year 1 this account was closed, following the calculation of profit. The balance of the account was treated as an *expense for that year.*

So what do we do with the note for Year 2 asking us to create a provision for bad and doubtful debts of 5% of debtors?

We follow the same procedure as we did in Year 1:

- calculate the provision

    The provision should be 5% of debtors, i.e. 5% of £50,000 = £2,500

- enter details of the provision in the *two* "T" accounts

    As the balance of the provision account is already £2,100, we simply need to increase the provision this year by £400, making it the required £2,500.

Provision for bad and doubtful debts

	31.12.01 Prov. for year 2001 £2,100
	31.12.02 Prov. for year 2002 £400
	£2,500

The *double entry* is an entry of £400 in the bad and doubtful debts (expense) account.

Bad and doubtful debts (expense) account

31.12.02 Prov. for year 2002 £400	

We therefore need to adjust the trial balance as follows:

4 – Making Adjustments to the Trial Balance

Table 4.8: Trial balance as at 31.12.02

	£	£
Purchases and sales	150,000	257,000
Stock at 1.1.X0	15,000	
Rent	6,000	
Rates	1,000	
Provision for bad and doubtful debts		2 100 (+ 400)
Other expenses	22,000	
Premises	80,000	
Van	15,000	
Debtors	50,000	
Creditors		4,900
Capital		75,000
	339,000	339,000
Bad and doubtful debts (expense)	**400**	

We therefore have *two* amounts for bad and doubtful debts:

1. In the body of the trial balance (2100 + 400 = 2,500), which represents the balance of the provision account, which will be deducted from debtors in the balance sheet.
2. £400, at the foot of the trial balance which represents *this year's* provision, which is included as an expense in the trading profit and loss account (see Chapter 5).

Let us suppose the debtors at the end of Year 3 are only £10,000 and we are asked once again to make a provision for bad and doubtful debts of 5%, i.e. £500.

The balance of the provision for bad and doubtful debts appearing in the trial balance will be £2,500.

The *double entries* are therefore:

1. *Reduce* the provision by £2,000, to leave £500 in the provision account.
2. Enter £2,000 in the bad and doubtful debts (expense) account.

Structure of Accounts

Provision for bad and doubtful debts

	£		£
31.12.03 Provision for year 2003	2,000	31.12.01 Provision for year 2001	2,000
		31.12.2 Provision for year 2002	400
• 31.12.03 balance	500		
	2,500		2,500
		1.1.Y1 Balance c/o	500

Bad and doubtful debts (Expense) account

	£
31.12.03 Provision for year 2003	2,100

The balance of £500 remaining in the provision account, as a credit balance, will then be deducted from debtors in the balance sheet. What, however, do we do with the balance in the so-called expense account, which we can see is a credit balance of £2,000?

In the past the balance of this account, like all expense accounts, has been a debit balance. But as we have reduced the provision this year, rather than increased it, the £2,000 is not an expense, it is in fact a reduction in expenses.

4.4 Conclusion

Throughout this chapter I have, I hope, explained *why* and *how* we need to make adjustments for:

- Stock
- Prepayments
- Accruals
- Provision for bad and doubtful debts

In the examination you may well be asked *why* you need to make adjustments. In which case you should:

- outline the accounting concepts and conventions requested, and/or
- discuss, with examples, the relevance/need for accounting concepts and conventions

We will discuss these further in Chapter 15. You are also likely to be presented with a trial balance such as the one below, which requires a number of adjustments to be made, and asked to prepare final accounts (a trading profit and loss account and balance sheet) for a sole trader or limited company.

4 – Making Adjustments to the Trial Balance

Given its importance I have, therefore, illustrated the way in which these adjustments should be made.

Table 4.9: Trial balance of Mrs A Bowden at 31.3.02

	Dr £	Cr £
Purchases and sales	60,297	100,000
Stock at 31.3.02	31,301	
Premises	70,000	
Equipment	21,000	
Debtors and creditors	20,109	17,109
Bank		2,700
Provision for bad and doubtful debts		1,500
Cash	170	
Wages	20,105	
Rent and rates	4,000	
Insurance	1,500	
Electricity	715	
Office expenses	951	
Bad debts	700	
Capital		140,115
Drawings	21,768	
	261,424	261,424

Notes:

1 Stock at 31.3.02 £61,206.
2 Rent and rates prepaid £700.
3 Insurance owing £500.
4 Increase provision for bad and doubtful debts to £2,000.

Structure of Accounts

Illustration of how to make the adjustments

Table 4.10: Trial balance of Mrs A Bowden at 31.3.02

	Dr £	Cr £
Purchases and sales	60297	100,000
Stock at 31.3.01	40,109	
Premises	70,000	
Equipment	21,000	
Debtors and creditors	20,109	17,109
Bank		2,700
Provision for bad and doubtful debts		(+500) 1,500
Cash	170	
Wages	20,105	
Rent and rates	(-700) 4,000	
Insurance	(+500) 1,500	
Electricity	715	
Office expenses	951	
Bad debts	700	
Capital		140,115
Drawings	21,768	
	261,424	261,424
Closing stock	61,206	
Provision for bad and doubtful debts	500	
Prepayments – rent and rates	700	
Accrual – insurance		500

4 – Making Adjustments to the Trial Balance

Summary

1 The basic calculation of profit is:

   Sales (Income)

   less

   Expenses

2 According to the syllabus you may need to make adjustments for:
   - Stock
   - Prepayments
   - Accruals
   - Bad debts
   - *Depreciation*   (See Chapter 6)

3 Adjustments are required *in order to observe regulatory requirements*:
   - Legislation – UK and EU
   - Standards or statements of best practice, in particular Statements of Standard Accounting Practice (SSAPs) and Financial Reporting Standards (FRSs)
   - International Accounting Standards (IASs)
   - Stock Exchange rules
   - Non-mandatory recommendations

4 *Opening stock:* appears in the body of the trial balance

   Closing stock is given as a note at the foot of the trial balance

5 *The accruals or matching concept* is concerned with matching all income relating to a particular period with the expenditure incurred which relates to that period, not the cash receipts and payments.

6 *Prepayment*: Money paid in this accounting period in respect of an expense due in the next accounting period.

   Adjustment 1: Reduce the expense in the trial balance by the amount of prepayment

   2 Create a prepayment on the debit (left) side at the foot of the trial balance (money owed *to you* similar to *debtors*)

7 Accruals: Money owing at the end of the accounting period in respect of benefits enjoyed during the accounting period.

   Adjustment 1 Increase the expense in the trial balance by the amount of accrual

Structure of Accounts

      2 Create an accrual on the credit (Right) side at the foot of the trial balance (money *you owe* similar to *creditors*)

8 *Bad debts* are debts that have actually turned bad.

9 Doubtful debts are debts that you *feel may go bad in the future.*

10 The accounting concept of prudence and conservatism requires us to take account of all foreseeable losses, while only recognizing profits when they are realized or when realization is reasonably certain.

11 *Foreseeable losses* are included in the final accounts if their payment is probable or simply as a note to the accounts if their payment is doubtful.

12 *Recognition of sales/turnover* is normally made when the goods are sold with a provision being made for bad and doubtful debts where appropriate.

13 *Provision for bad and doubtful debts* is an estimate of the amount of debts (debtors) that will turn bad, based on past experience and the length of time debts have been outstanding.

14 *In dealing with provision for bad and doubtful debts* we need to open two "T" accounts for the provision for bad debts:

    1. **The expense for the year**

    We are providing for bad and doubtful debts so that we do not overestimate our profit when we know from experience that some of our income from sales will not materialize. The provision for the year is therefore an *expense*.

    As this is an expense it is recorded on the debit (left) side, and

    2. **The provision for bad and doubtful debts account,** which is then deducted from debtors in the balance sheet so that our assets are not overvalued. In the example of Mrs Bowden, we feel £2000 of the debtors will not pay.

15 Any reduction in the provision is a reduction in expenses.

5
FROM TRIAL BALANCE TO FINAL ACCOUNTS

Syllabus Objectives

1.5 Individual transactions and adjustments

The effects of individual transactions and adjustments on the trading and profit and loss account and balance sheet

1.6 Final accounts

- Prepared from trial balance or cash records

    These should be presented in vertical format; it is not necessary to memorize the exact format of published accounts, but candidates should be able to present them in "good format"

- The appropriation of profits

2.1 Sole trader

- Capital injection and withdrawal
- Risk

Learning Objectives

After studying this chapter you should be able to:

1 Distinguish between items appearing in a trading profit and loss account and items appearing in a balance sheet;

2 Define capital and revenue expenditure;

3 Explain what is meant by gross and net profit;

4 Calculate gross and net profit;

5 Produce both a trading profit and loss account and a balance sheet from a trial balance in vertical format;

6 Define working capital and explain its importance.

Structure of Accounts

Introduction

In Chapter 3 we recorded details of transactions in ledgers before producing a trial balance. In Chapter 4 we made various adjustments to the trial balance.

In this chapter we will use the trial balance as the starting point in the construction of the final accounts, namely:

- The *trading profit and loss account*, which is drawn up to determine the profit or loss of a company by deducting a company's expenses from its income, and

- The *balance sheet* which reflects the assets (items you own) and liabilities (money you owe/source of funds) of the business.

Assuming the company uses day books, the account procedure from invoice to balance sheet may therefore take the pattern seen in Figure 5.1 on the next page:

Preparing the final accounts from the trial balance

As I mentioned in the last chapter, preparing the final accounts from a trial balance is like doing a jigsaw. If we rearrange the items in the adjusted trial balance in the correct order and format then our accounts will look correct, show the correct profit for the year and balance!

So, we are simply re-arranging the items in the adjusted trial balance to produce a trading profit and loss account and balance sheet.

One of the problems is separating those items which appear in the trading profit and loss account from those which appear in the balance sheet.

You may well recall from Chapter 2 which items go in the balance sheet and in which order but what about the trading profit and loss account?

5.1 The trading profit and loss account

The trading profit and loss account is concerned with a company's *income* and *expenses*, but let us look closer at these two items.

Income

As we are trying to establish whether our business is profitable we are concerned with income generated from business, i.e. sales, and not with money received in the form of loans or capital. You will no doubt recall that loans and capital represent a company's source of finance which enables it to commence or continue in business and hence they appear in the balance sheet.

5 – From Trial Balance to Final Accounts

Figure 5.1

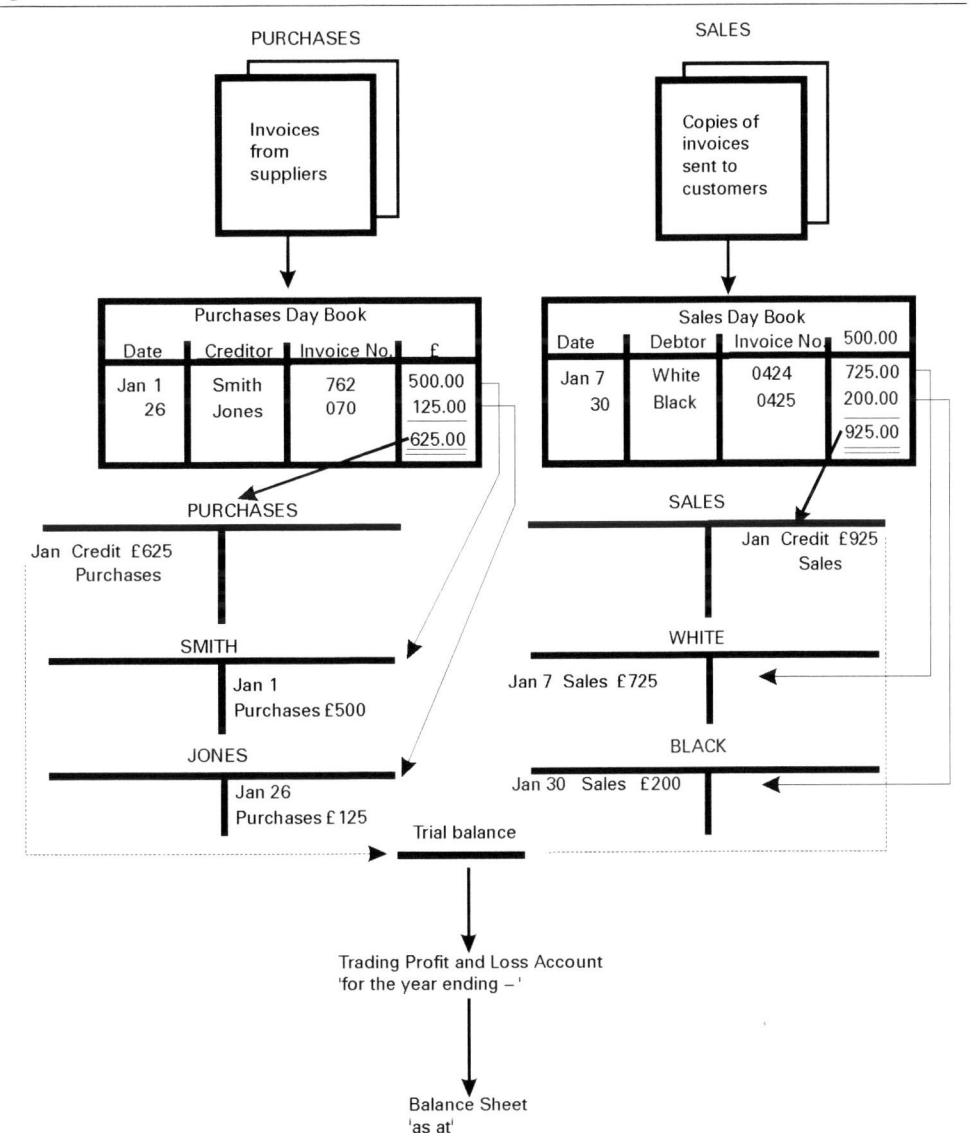

Expenses

While both the purchase of machinery and the payment of rent can be considered as expenditure, the trading profit and loss account is concerned only with expenditure incurred in the day-to-day running of the company, e.g. rent, rates, gas, etc., i.e. *revenue expenditure*.

The purchase of machinery or equipment, etc. represent the purchase of *assets* which will be reflected in the balance sheet, i.e. *capital expenditure*.

The trading profit and loss account can be broken up into two parts:

Trading account – In which we calculate the *gross profit*, i.e. the profit achieved on *trading*

Structure of Accounts

(buying and selling the goods of your business which could be second-hand cars, groceries, toys, etc.)

Profit and loss account – in which we calculate the *net profit*, i.e. the profit achieved after deducting expenses from gross profit.

Example

Let us imagine that you buy and sell second-hand cars. During your first month of trading you purchase a car for £1,000 and sell it for £2,000 following an advertisement which cost £50.

Your trading profit and loss account for the month would therefore be as follows:

Table 5.1: Trading profit and loss account of Car Dealer for the month ending 31.10.X8

			£
Trading account		Sales	2,000
	less	Purchases	(1,000)
		Gross profit	1,000
Profit and loss account	less	*Expenses*	
		Advertising	(50)
		Net Profit	950

So:

    Gross profit = Sales less the cost of the goods you sold

If the goods you sold actually cost more than you received for them, then this is known as a *gross loss* and is obviously a bad sign for any company.

    Net profit = Gross profit less expenses

Closing stock

In the next example let us imagine you purchased ten cars for £1,000 each and then sold one at £2,000. What is your profit?

You may think that the company has made purchases of £10,000 (10 x £1,000) while it achieved a sale of only £2,000 and therefore incurred a loss of £8,000. But this is *not* the case.

True expenditure exceeds income by £8,000 but the trading account is concerned with calculating the profit on the goods *which we have traded (i.e. bought and sold)*. As spelt out above, gross profit is the difference between sales and the cost of the goods sold, i.e.

5 – From Trial Balance to Final Accounts

Sales	=	£2,000
The cost of the car we sold	=	£1,000
Gross profit on that car	=	£1,000

We are then left with nine cars in stock which cost a total of £9,000 and represent an *asset* owned by the company.

The trading account shows the complete story as follows:

	£	£
Sales		2,000
less cost of goods sold		
Purchases	10,000	
less Closing Stock	(9,000)	1,000
Gross profit		1,000

Yes, more money has been spent on the purchase of goods than actually received from sales but we have a closing stock of £9,000 of goods which can, hopefully, be sold in the future. The cost of the goods we sold was £1,000 (£10,000 – £9,000). The company is able to trade profitably, having sold goods for £2,000 which cost it only £1,000.

Before we go on to look at opening stock, can you think where else the closing stock might be reflected? Remember the stock left at the end of the accounting period is something of value, owned by the business.

Well, the answer I am looking for is the *balance sheet* as a *current asset*.

Opening stock

The closing stock at the end of Year 1 is the opening stock at the begining of Year 2. Our company had a closing stock of nine cars at a cost of £9,000 and therefore the opening stock for Year 2 is £9,000.

Suppose that over their second year the company purchased a further 20 cars for £20,000 and sold 25 cars for £50,000. (Not a giant company in the industry but it serves as an example.)

What is the company's gross profit if it has a closing stock of four cars at a cost of £4,000?

Let us recap for a moment.

Gross profit =	Sales	less	the cost of the goods you sold
	25 cars worth £50,000	less	?

What is the cost of the goods you sold?

Structure of Accounts

Well we:

started with opening stock of	9 cars at a cost of	£9,000
Purchased a further	20 cars at a cost of	£20,000
	29 cars at a cost of	£29,000
have a closing stock of	4 cars at a cost of	£4,000
Cost of goods sold =	**25 cars at a cost of**	**£25,000**

The formula for the cost of goods sold is therefore:

	£
Opening stock	9,000
+ Purchases	20,000
	29,000
– Closing Stock	4,000
Cost of the goods sold	25,000

and the trading account appears as follows:

Table 5.2: Trading account of AB Co. For the year ending 31.12.X8 (a)

	£	£ (b)
Sales		50,000
less cost of goods sold		
Opening stock	9,000	
+ Purchases	20,000	
	29,000	
– Closing Stock **(c)**	(4,000)	25,000
Gross profit		25,000

Note:

a) As we are calculating the profit achieved over a certain period, the title should always reflect this.

b) Use two columns to improve the presentation.

c) Closing stock is valued at cost and not the amount you feel you will be able to sell it for.

Returns in and returns out

Can you remember what we mean by returns in and returns out?

5 – From Trial Balance to Final Accounts

Just in case you cannot, let us recap and consider how they are dealt with in the trading profit and loss account.

Returns in – Goods you have previously sold but which have since been returned to you, possibly because they are faulty. They are therefore shown *as a deduction from sales*.

Returns out – Goods you previously purchased but which you have since returned to your supplier and are shown *as a deduction from purchases*.

	£	£	£
Sales			50,000
Less Returns In			(2,000)
			48,000
Less cost of goods sold			
Opening stock		10,000	
+ Purchases	35,000		
Less Returns Out	(1,000)	34,000	
		44,000	
– Closing Stock		(20,000)	24,000
Gross profit			24,000

Note:

The third column is used to calculate the net figure for purchases which is then carried over and added to opening stock. Do *not* add opening stock to purchases and then deduct returns out. Returns out are deducted from purchases to find the purchase figure.

Carriage in and carriage out

Carriage out is the cost of transporting goods out and is treated as any other expense such as rent, rates, etc. and is therefore *listed as an expense* deducted from gross profit to determine the net profit.

Carriage in is the cost of transporting goods in and, as it is incurred as a direct result of purchasing and not selling, it is dealt with differently from other expenses and is therefore one to watch out for. As an expense incurred as a result of purchase *it is added to purchases*.

The trading profit and loss account may now appear as follows:

Table 5.3: Trading Profit and Loss Account of AB Co. for the year ending 31.12.X8

	£	£	£
Sales			50,000
less returns in			(2,000)
			48,000
less cost of goods sold			
Opening stock		10,000	
+ Purchases	35,000		
less Returns Out	(1,000)		
	34,000		
Plus carriage in	500	34,500	
		44,500	
– Closing Stock		(20,000)	24,500
Gross profit			23,500
less expenses			
Rent		1,000	
Carriage out		250	
Wages		5,000	(6,250)
Net profit			17,250

Discount allowed and discount received

Discount allowed: An expense incurred by a company, being the amount of discount they allow their customers. They are therefore listed with all other expenses.

Discount received: A form of income received and is therefore *added to gross profit* before deducting the expenses.

Other forms of income

Please note there are other forms of income which should also be added to gross profit, such as:

- interest received (from your investments), and
- rent received (income from renting out premises).

5 – From Trial Balance to Final Accounts

Example layout

Here then is an example layout of a trading profit and loss account including all the items you may come across, though not – you will be pleased to learn – all in the same question.

Table 5.4: Trading profit and loss account for example company for the year ending 31.10.X8

	£	£	£
Sales			50,000
less returns in			(2,000)
			48,000
less cost of goods sold			
Opening stock		10,000	
+ purchases	35,000		
– returns out	(1,000)		
	34,000		
+ carriage in	500	34,500	
		44,500	
– closing stock		(20,000)	(24,500)
Gross profit			23,500
add income			
Discount received		1,000	
Rents received		500	
Interest received		250	1,750
			25,250
less expenses			
Rent		1,000	
Carriage out		250	
Wages		5,000	
Discount allowed		300	(6,550)
Net profit			18,700

5.2 Preparing a trading profit and loss account and balance sheet from a trial balance

So, as you can see, there are a number of items which appear in a trading profit and loss account. The real problem comes when you are asked to produce both a trading profit and loss account and a balance sheet from a trial balance similar to that below.

Table 5.5: Trial balance of E Loughlan as at 31.10.X8

Code		Dr	Cr
CAP	Capital		60,000
TRADE	Sales		55,950
TRADE	Stock at 1.1.X7	17,105	
CAP	Drawings	5,000	
FA	Premises	50,000	
TRADE	Returns in	210	
CA	Debtors	3,105	
CL	Creditors		8,410
TRADE	Carriage in	309	
DL	Loan		20,000
TRADE	Returns out		108
TRADE	Purchases	41,807	
EXP	Rates	1,000	
EXP	Discounts allowed	410	
EXP	Electricity	300	
INC	Interest received		250
FA	Fixtures and fittings	15,000	
FA	Van	5,000	
CL	Bank		2,923
EXP	Wages	6,000	
EXP	Insurance	500	
CA	Cash	1,895	
		147,641	147,641

5 – From Trial Balance to Final Accounts

Notes:

1. Closing stock: £15,000
2. Electricity prepaid £150
3. Insurance owing £200
4. Create a provision for bad debts of £150

Procedure

It would be very easy to forget to use one of the items or remember that you should have added Carriage In to Purchases when you come to list the expenses. I would therefore suggest the following procedure:

Step 1

Make all the necessary adjustments to the trial balance, as detailed in the previous chapter.

Step 2

Go down the trial balance and code each item (*as shown above*), e.g.

INC	(Income)
EXP	(Expenses)
TRADE	(Items which appear in the trading account, i.e. the calculation of gross profit)
CAP	(Relating to capital in the balance sheet)
LTL	(Long-term liabilities)
CL	(Current liabilities)
FA	(Fixed assets)
CA	(Current assets)

You do not need to use my codes. You can use your own. The important thing is to identify things correctly.

Step 3

Rearrange the items in their correct order to produce:

a) *Trading profit and loss account*

b) *Balance sheet*. Do not forget that the net profit you have calculated in the trading profit and loss account is added to capital.

Place a tick against each item as you use it. Then if you forget to use an item, it will clearly stand out.

Structure of Accounts

Step 4

If you do not balance, find the difference and check whether there is an item for this amount which you have forgotten.

You will be pleased to learn that not many questions will include all the items we have considered above, so if you can prepare the final accounts of E Loughlan you will have no problems.

Why not have a go at preparing the final accounts yourself before reading further.

Note

In the trial balance, 'Bank' is listed on the right hand side (credit side). This means that it is a bank overdraft and therefore a current liability.

The Answer is as follows (see over the page):

Table 5.6: Trading profit and loss account of E Loughlan for the year ending 31.10.X8

	£	£	£
Sales			55,950
less returns in			(210)
			55,740
less cost of goods sold			
Opening stock		17,105	
+ purchases	41,807		
less returns out	(108)		
	41,699		
+ carriage in	309	42,008	
		59,113	
– closing stock		(15,000)	44,113
Gross profit			11,627
add income			
Interest received			250
			11,877
less expenses			
Rates		1,000	
Discount allowed		410	
Electricity	300		
– prepaid	(150)	150	
Wages		6,000	
Insurance	500		
+ accrued	200	700	
Provision for bad and doubtful debts		150	(8,410)
Net profit			3,467

Structure of Accounts

Table 5.7: Balance sheet of E Loughlan as at 31.10.X8

	£	£		£	£
Fixed assets			Capital		60,000
Premises	50,000		+ Net profit		<u>3,467</u>
Fixtures	15,000				63,467
Van	<u>5,000</u>	70,000	– Drawings		(5,000)
					58,467
Current assets					
Stock		15,000	Long-term liabilities		
Debtors	3,105				
less Provision	(150)	2,955			
Prepayment		150	Loan		20,000
Cash		<u>1,895</u> 20,000			
			Current liabilities		
			Creditors	8,410	
			Accruals	200	
			Bank overdraft	<u>2,923</u>	<u>11,533</u>
		<u>90,000</u>			<u>90,000</u>

Note:

A trading profit and loss account is always 'for the year ending ...' or 'for the month ending ...' etc, as you are calculating the profit achieved over that period.

A balance sheet, being a photograph of a company's assets and liabilities, is always 'as at' a particular date and will change the following day.

The question will normally reveal this by asking for a trading profit and loss account for the year ending and a balance sheet as at a particular date, but try to remember this, it is important and often worth a mark in the examination.

5.3 Presenting the final accounts in a vertical format

In the answer above, you will see that the trading profit and loss account is written in a vertical format with the details running down the page.

<blockquote>
Sales
<u>less cost of goods sold</u>
Gross profit
<u>less expenses</u>
Net profit
</blockquote>

5 – From Trial Balance to Final Accounts

while the balance sheet is written in a horizontal format with assets on one side and capital and liabilities on the other.

It is now more common to present both the trading profit and loss account and balance sheet in a vertical format. In fact your syllabus states that the final accounts should be presented in vertical format. We therefore need to change the presentation of the balance sheet.

This can be done quite simply as follows, by moving the assets above the capital and liabilities.

Table 5.8: Balance sheet of E Laughlan as at 31.10.X8

	£	£	£
Fixed assets			
Premises		50,000	
Fixtures		15,000	
Van		5,000	70,000
Current assets			
Stock		15,000	
Debtors	3,105		
less Provisions	150	2,955	
Prepayments		150	
Cash		1,895	20,000
			90,000
Capital			60,000
+ net profit			3,467
			63,467
– drawings			5,000
			58,467
Long-term liabilities			
Loan			20,000
Current liabilities			
Creditors		8,410	
Accruals		200	
Bank overdraft		2,923	11,533
			90,000

But if we rearrange the order of the components further, we are able to gain a better picture of the company's position.

Rather than present the balance sheet as shown above we should therefore present the information in the format shown below:

Table 5.9: Balance sheet of E Loughlan as at 31.10.X8

	£	£	£	
Fixed assets				
Premises		50,000		
Fixtures		15,000		
Van		5,000	70,000	Fixed assets
Current assets				
Stock		15,000		
Debtors	3,105			
less Provisions	(150)	2,955		
Prepayments		150		
Cash		1,895		
		20,000		plus
Current liabilities				
Creditors	8,410			
Accrual	200			
Bank overdraft	2,923	(11,533)	8,467	Working capital
			78,467	Total assets less Current liabilities
less				
Long-term liabilities				less
Loan			(20,000)	Long-term liabilities
			58,467	**Balance**
Financed by:				
Capital			60,000	Financed by
+ Net Profit			3,467	
			63,467	
– Drawings			(5,000)	
			58,467	**Balance**

5 – From Trial Balance to Final Accounts

While the balance sheet now balances to a different figure – this does not matter, after all:

ASSETS = CAPITAL + LIABILITIES

e.g. 10 = 6 + 4

and

ASSETS - LIABILITIES = CAPITAL

10 - 4 = 6

This form of presentation is preferred for a number of reasons:

1. It clearly shows the company's *working capital*, i.e. the difference between current assets and current liabilities.

    Working Capital = Current Assets – Current Liabilities

    Working capital examines the company's liquidity and trading position by deducting current liabilities (money the company owes and must repay within twelve months) from current assets (cash, or items the company can convert into cash in the near future).

    We shall examine the importance of working capital later (Chapter 11), but for now let us just concentrate on using the new form of presentation which reveals the working capital.

2. It clearly shows the *shareholders' capital employed*, i.e. the money invested in the business by the owners/shareholders

e.g. Fixed assets		70,000
plus		
Current assets	20,150	
less		
Current liabilities	(11,533)	
Working capital		8,617
		78,617
less		
Long term liabilities		(20,000)
Total net assets		**58,617**
Financed by:		
Total shareholders' capital employed		**58,617**

Structure of Accounts

Summary

1 *The trading profit and loss account* is drawn up to determine the profit or loss of a company for a particular period.

2 *The balance sheet* reflects the assets and liabilities of a company as at a particular date.

3 *Revenue expenditure* is the expenditure incurred in the day-to-day running of the company, e.g. rent, electricity.

4 *Capital expenditure* relates to the purchase or improvement of a company's assets and is reflected in the balance sheet.

5 The trading account *shows the calculation of gross profit.*

6 *Gross profit* is the profit achieved on trading (i.e. on buying and selling the goods of your business).

7 *Sales – cost of goods sold = gross profit*

8 The profit and loss account *shows the calculation of net profit.*

9 *Net profit* is the profit achieved after deducting expenses from gross profit plus any other revenue received, such as discounts received.

10 *Returns in*, being goods previously sold but since returned, are shown as a deduction from sales.

11 *Returns out*, being goods previously purchased but since returned to suppliers, are shown as a deduction from purchases.

12 *Carriage in* is the cost of transporting goods in and, as an expense incurred as a direct result of purchasing, it is added to purchases and not listed with other expenses.

13 *Carriage out* is treated in the same way as other expenses and deducted from gross profit.

14 *Discount allowed* is the amount of discount allowed to customers and treated in the same way as other expenses.

15 *Discount received*, like rent received and interest received, is a form of income which is added to gross profit before deducting expenses.

16 A trading profit and loss account is 'for the year ending ...' or 'for the month ending ...' etc., as it reflects the profit or loss for that period.

17 A balance sheet, being like a photograph of a company's assets and liabilities, is always, '*as at*' a particular date.

18 *Questions* will normally reveal the way the final accounts are to be headed up by asking for a trading profit and loss account for the year ending ... and a balance sheet as at a particular date, but try to remember this, it is important and often worth a mark in the examination.

5 – From Trial Balance to Final Accounts

19 *Working capital = Current Assets – Current Liabilities*

20 *Working capital* examines the company's liquidity and trading position by deducting current liabilities (amounts the company owes and must repay within twelve months) from current assets (cash, or items the company can convert into cash in the near future).

6
DEPRECIATION

Syllabus Objectives

1.7   Depreciation

- Straight line and reducing balance methods (FRS 15)

Learning Objectives

After studying this chapter you should be able to:

1   Outline the nature and purpose of depreciation;

2   Calculate rates of depreciation using the following methods;

   a)   straight line,

   b)   reducing balance;

3   Explain the nature of the various methods of calculating depreciation;

4   Construct trading profit and loss accounts and balance sheets which require the provision for depreciation;

5   Take the appropriate action required on the disposal or scrapping of fixed assets;

6   Identify the profit or loss arising upon the disposal or scrapping of fixed assets.

Introduction

In Chapter 4 we made adjustments for *prepayments and accruals* as well as providing for the possibility of *bad and doubtful debts* in order to match all the income relating to a particular period with the expenditure incurred which relates to that period and not simply the cash receipts and payments.

In other words we adopted the *matching concept* in order to calculate the true profit figure for the accounting period.

Depreciation is yet another item we must consider if we are to calculate the true profit figure.

6 – Depreciation

6.1 What is depreciation?

The easiest way for most people to think of depreciation is to think of a car. How often do you hear people talk about how much the value of their car has depreciated? Strictly, in accounting terms, depreciation is concerned with the way an asset is used up. According to FRS 15 depreciation is:

The measure of the cost or revalued amount of the economic benefits of the tangible fixed asset that have been consumed during the period.

which, put more simply, means:

Depreciation is the amount of the value of the asset which has been used up by the firm in the period.

For example:

Motor van cost 19X1	£5,000
Motor van sold 19X5	£1,000
Depreciation	£4,000

6.2 Causes of depreciation

1. *Wear and tear* – signifies loss of value arising from use.
2. *Obsolescence* – machinery made obsolete by later inventions and better models, e.g. computers, robots in the car industry.
3. *Inadequacy* – when the asset becomes useless because the firm has grown or changed its requirements.
4. *Depletion* – if an asset is of a wasting nature.
5. *Time factor* – when assets depreciate through passage of time or if the asset is for a fixed period of time, e.g. a lease on premises.

6.3 Calculating the depreciation charge for the year

The amount of depreciation can obviously be determined when we sell a fixed asset, but we cannot simply wait until the date of sale to account for depreciation; otherwise we would not be obeying the matching concept, and as a result we would be overstating the profit achieved over the life of the asset. The year in which the sale takes place would also bear the full reduction in value.

The matching concept requires the depreciation cost to be charged to the accounting periods which benefit from the use of the asset, i.e. if the motor van is expected to last for three years then the depreciation should be spread over the three years and not just be charged in Year 3 when the van is scrapped or sold.

The calculation can be done in a number of ways, i.e. there are a number of methods which are acceptable under FRS 15, which outlines recommendations for Accounting for Depreciation.

The most common methods and the two methods covered in your syllabus are:

a) Straight line;

b) Reducing balance.

Each method is based on the historical cost of the asset and requires an estimate of:

- The expected life of the asset, e.g. if a motor van is expected to last for three years, then the depreciation is spread over the three years, as each year benefits from use of the asset and should therefore show a part of the cost as an expense.

- The residual value of the asset (the estimated value at the end of the asset's expected life with the owner, i.e. what the owner feels he will be able to sell the van for, if it lasts three years, as expected).

The asset may in fact last longer than three years and be worth more than the estimated residual value upon sale. As a result adjustments will need to be made, but we will consider this later. For now let us look at the various methods of calculating depreciation.

Straight line method

The straight line method charges an equal amount of depreciation in each year of the asset's life.

For example:

Van cost	£12,000
Expected life	3 years
Estimated residual value	£1,500

Calculation

Total depreciation over 3 years = £12,000 − £1,500 = £10,500

Annual depreciation = $\dfrac{£10,500}{3}$ = £3,500

6 – Depreciation

or expressed as a formula:

$$\frac{\text{Cost} - \text{Estimated value}}{\text{Number of years of expected life}} = \text{Annual depreciation}$$

This is known as the straight line method, as the depreciation charge, when plotted graphically, forms a straight line

Figure 6.1

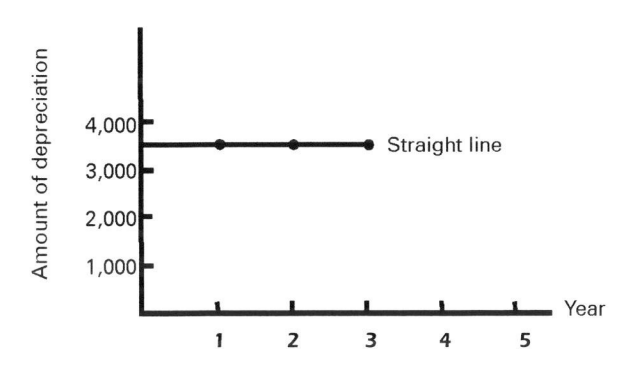

Reducing balance method

This method applies a fixed percentage each year.

Example

Rather than depreciate £3,500 each year, as in the straight line method, the company may choose to depreciate (reduce) the balance of the asset remaining in the accounts *(i.e. the book value)* by say 50% each year.

	£
Cost day 1	12,000
Depreciation charge for Year 1 50%	6,000
Net book value/balance sheet value at end of Year 1	6,000
Depreciation charge for Year 2 50%	3,000
Net book value/balance sheet value at end of Year 2	3,000
Depreciation charge for Year 3 50%	1,500
Net book value/balance sheet value at end of Year 3	1,500

As illustrated above the reducing balance method charges more depreciation in the earlier years which, for certain assets such as motor vans, may be considered more realistic.

The rate used in the reducing balance method is found by the following complicated formula.

$$r = 1 - \sqrt[n]{\frac{s}{c}}$$

where r = rate of depreciation to be used

n = number of years (estimated life)

s = net residual value

c = cost of asset

Example

$$r = 1 - \sqrt[3]{\frac{1,500}{12,000}}$$

$$r = 1 - \sqrt[3]{0.125}$$

$$r = 1 - 0.5$$

$$r = 0.5 \text{ or } 50\%$$

Do not worry, you will not be asked to determine the percentage rate for the reducing balance method in the examination. The rate to use will always be given to you

6.4 The effects of depreciation on the trading profit and loss account and balance sheet

The depreciation charge for the year is an *expense* and as such is deducted from sales when calculating the *net profit for the year*. The choice of method will therefore affect the amount of depreciation charged to each year's accounts, and as a result the profit calculation for the year. It will also affect the reported value of the fixed asset in the balance sheet because the *accumulated (total) depreciation charged over the life of the asset* is deducted from the cost of the asset in the balance sheet.

Here is an illustration of the effects of adopting both straight line and reducing balance on the trading profit and loss account and balance sheet. Using our example:

Cost of van	£12,000
Expected life	3 years
Estimated residual value	£1,500

You will recall from our calculations above that the annual depreciation charges are as follows:

Straight line	£3,500
Reducing balance	50%

The accounts would therefore appear as follows:

6 – Depreciation

Table 6.1: YEAR 1

	Straight line		Reducing balance	
Trading profit and loss extract end of Year 1				
	£	£	£	£
Gross profit		20,000		20,000
less expenses				
Rent	5,000		5,000	
Rates	2,000		2,000	
Depreciation expenses	**3,500**	(10,500)	**6,000**	(13,000)
Net profit		9,500		7,000
Balance sheet extract as at end of Year 1				
	£	£	£	£
Fixed assets				
Land and buildings		120,000		120,000
Motor van (at cost)	12,000		12,000	
less accumulated provision for depreciation	(3,500)	8,500	(6,000)	6,000
		128,500		126,000

Table 6.2: YEAR 2

Trading profit and loss extract end of Year 2				
	£	£	£	£
Gross profit		30,000		30,000
less expenses				
Rent	6,000		6,000	
Rates	3,000		3,000	
Depreciation expense	**3,500**	(12,500)	**3,000**	(12,000)
Net profit		17,500		18,000

Structure of Accounts

Balance sheet extract as at end of Year 2

	£	£	£	£
Fixed assets				
Land and buildings		120,000		120,000
Motor van (at cost)	12,000		12,000	
less accumulated provision for depreciation	**(7,000)**	5,000	**(9,000)**	3,000
		125,000		123,000

Table 6.3: YEAR 3

Trading profit and loss extract end of Year 3

	£	£	£	£
Gross profit		40,000		40,000
less expenses				
Rent	6,000		6,000	
Rates	3,000		3,000	
Depreciation expense	**3,500**	12,500)	1,500	(10,500)
Net profit		27,500		29,500

Balance sheet extract as at end of Year 3

	£	£	£	£
Fixed assets				
Land and buildings		120,000		120,000
Motor van (at cost)	12,000		12,000	
less accumulated provision for depreciation	**(10,500)**	1,500	(10,500)	1,500
		121,500		121,500

The important points to note are:

a) The trading profit and loss account *includes only the charge for the year.*

6 – Depreciation

b) The *net profit for the year* will be different if the depreciation charge for the year is different. However the total depreciation charged over the life of the asset against profits is be the same under either method (in our case £10,500).

c) *Reducing balance* charges a higher amount in the earlier years and a lower amount in the later years.

d) the *balance sheet* shows:

- i) the asset at *cost*

less ii) *the total amount of depreciation (i.e. the accumulated depreciation) which has been charged against the asset over its life, e.g. in YEAR 3 it is the charges for YEAR 1 +YEAR 2 + YEAR 3*

- iii) the net book value (cost less accumulated depreciation).

e) The n*et book value* at the end of the three years is the same no matter which method is adopted.

6.5 Examination questions

The need to provide for depreciation is often part of a question asking you to produce a trading profit and loss account and balance sheet from a trial balance, with the instruction given by way of a note.

Example:

Structure of Accounts

Table 6.4: Trial balance of L Peat as at 31.12.X9

	Dr £	Cr £
Purchases and sales	179,841	200,000
Stock as at 1.1.X9	21,679	
Capital		75,000
Creditors		36,000
Machinery	**30,000**	
Premises	60,000	
Debtors	20,000	
Carriage inwards	510	
Telephone	216	
Loan		2,328
Electricity	313	
Rates		1,000
Rent	518	
Office expenses		821
Discount	1,000	2,500
Returns	105	175
	316,003	316,003

Notes:

Depreciate machinery on the straight line basis. The owners estimate that the machinery will last ten years and have a residual value of nil. (In some questions it may simply say "Depreciate machinery 10% on cost.)

Adjusting the trial balance for depreciation – straight line method

The procedure, including the *double-entry bookkeeping*, would be as follows. However in the examination you will NOT be required to show the "T" accounts.

1. Calculate the amount of depreciation for the year, i.e. 10% of 30,000 = £3,000 pa

   30,000/10 years = £3,000 pa

2. Open two "T" accounts for depreciation

6 – Depreciation

1 Represents the *expense* for that year and is therefore a *debit* entry (i.e. on the left-hand side).

2 Represents the *depreciation over the life of the asset*, which is a *credit* entry (i.e. on the right-hand side).

Depreciation (expense) account

31.12.X9 Dep for year X9 3,000	

Provision for depreciation account

	31.12.X9 Dep for year X9 3,000

3 At the end of the accounting period the "T" accounts would be balanced off and the balances transferred to the trial balance as follows:

Table 6.5: Trial balance of L Peat as at 31.12.X9

	Dr £	Cr £
Purchases and sales	179,841	200,000
Stock as at 1.1.X9	21,679	
Capital		75,000
Creditors		36,000
Machinery	30,000	
Premises	60,000	
Debtors	20,000	
Carriage inwards	510	
Telephone	216	
Loan		2,328
Electricity	313	
Rates	1,000	
Rent	518	
Office expenses	821	
Discount	1,000	2,500
Returns	105	175
	316,003	316,003
Provision for depreciation (expense)	3,000	
Accumulated provision for depreciation		3,000

91

Structure of Accounts

We have therefore made two adjustments:

a) Including the amount of depreciation as an *expense* at the foot of the trial balance on the *debit* (left) side;

b) Indicating the amount to be deducted from the cost of the asset in the balance sheet, i.e. the *accumulated depreciation*, on the *credit* (right) side.

Adjusting the trial balance for depreciation – reducing balance method

In the above question the asset was being depreciated for the first time, but in some questions the asset may already have been depreciated in previous years.

The trial balance under such circumstances would appear as follows:

Table 6.6: Trial balance of V Sunderland as at 31.12.X9

	Dr £	Cr £
Purchases and sales	71,059	92,100
Capital		60,000
Loan		30,000
Stock as at 1.1.X9	10,000	
Debtors and creditors	16,100	10,000
Premises	75,000	
Motor van (at cost) (*See 1 below*)	**10,000**	
Provision for depreciation motor van (2)		**1,000** (*See 2 below*)
Bank	3,000	
Cash	1,562	
Wages	5,000	
Electricity	369	
Gas	510	
Insurance	1,000	
Provision for bad debts		500
	193,600	193,600

6 – Depreciation

Notes:

Depreciate motor vans on a reducing balance basis at the rate of 10% per annum. (*See 3 below.*)

The important points to note are:

1. The cost price of the motor van (£10,000) is given in the trial balance and should be shown in the balance sheet.

2. The provision for depreciation in the trial balance (£1,000) refers to depreciation that has been charged in previous years. It is the balance of the provision for depreciation "T" account.

3. The *note* indicates *this year's depreciation charge which should be included as an expense in the trading profit and loss account*.

Procedure

1. Calculate the amount of depreciation for the year, *in this case we are told to depreciate on a reducing balance basis*.

	£.
Cost	10,000
– previous provision for depreciation	1,000
Net Book Value	9,000

10% on a reducing balance basis means 10% of the net book value:

= 10% of £9,000 = 900

2. The *double-entry bookkeeping entries* (though not required for the examination) would be:

Depreciation (expense) account

31.12.X9 Dep for year X9 900	

Provision for depreciation account

	31.12.X8 Dep for year X9	1,000
	31.12.X9 Dep for year X9	900

Note: The previous year's provision for depreciation (expense) account of £1,000 will have been closed, when calculating the profit for that year.

3. Adjust the trial balance as follows:

Structure of Accounts

Table 6.7: Trial balance of V Sunderland as at 31.12.X9

	Dr	Cr
	£	£
Purchases and sales	71,059	92,100
Capital		60,000
Loan		30,000
Stock as at 1.1.X9	10,000	
Debtors and creditors	16,100	10,000
Premises	75,000	
Motor van (at cost)	10,000	
Provision for depreciation		
motor van		1,000 (+900)
Bank	3,000	
Cash	1,562	
Wages	5,000	
Electricity	369	
Gas	510	
Insurance	1,000	
Provision for bad debts		500
	193,600	193,600
Depreciation of motor van (expense)	900	

Once again we have therefore made two adjustments:

a) Including the amount of depreciation as an *expense* at the foot of the trial balance on the *debit* (left) side;

b) Indicating the amount to be deducted from the cost of the asset in the balance sheet, i.e. the *accumulated depreciation* on the *credit* (right) side. In this case I have not added at the foot of the trial balance as we already have an account opened for depreciation. I have therefore added this years provision of £900 to the £1,000 in the body of the trial balance.

6 – Depreciation

6.6 The disposal or scrapping of a fixed asset

The calculation of depreciation is based on the cost of the asset, but you will recall that this requires an estimate to be made of the expected life of the asset and of the residual value.

Our first example was as follows:

Van cost	£12,000
Expected life	3 years
Estimated residual value	£1,500

As a result, using the *straight line method*, our "T" accounts would appear as follows:

Provision for depreciation account

	31.12.01 prov for year 01	3,500
	31.12.02 prov for year 02	3,500
	31.12.03 prov for year 03	3,500
		10,500

Motor van

01.01.01 Bank (Cost) 12,000	

i.e. according to *our books* the van is worth £1,500 at the end of Year 3.

The asset would appear in the balance sheet as follows:

Balance sheet extract

Fixed assets

Motor van (at cost)	12,000
less accumulated provision for depreciation	10 500
	1 500

But suppose we sold it for £2,000 at the end of Year 3; how would we deal with this?

First we need to deal with the sale of the van. As we no longer own that particular van we need to remove its value from our accounts, together with all the depreciation relating to the van.

Secondly we need to record the receipt of £2,000.

This will either increase the cash or bank by the sales proceeds £2,000.

Here then are the entries we would make in our "T" accounts, in order to:

Structure of Accounts

- remove the asset (van) and its depreciation from our accounts, and
- record the receipt of £2,000

As you can see the disposal of the van is recorded in a disposal of motor van "T" account.

Provision for depreciation account

31.12.03 Disposal	10 500	31.12.01 Prov for year 01	3,500
		31.12.02 Prov for year 02	3,500
		31.12.03 Prov for year 03	3,500
	10 500		10 500

Motor van account

01.01.01 Bank (Cost)	12,000	31.12.03 Disposal	12000

Bank account

31.12.03 Disposal of van 2,000	

Disposal of motor van account

31.12.03 Motor van	12,000	31.12.03 Prov for depreciation	10,500
		31.12.03 Bank	2,000
	12,000		12 500

Can you see anything wrong with the disposal account?

Hopefully you have spotted that it does not balance. That is because we have not yet recorded the profit or loss on the sale of the van. By that I mean the *book profit or loss*, which in our case is:

Cash received	2,000
Book value	1,500
Book profit	500

The important thing to realize is that the profit or loss is only a *book* profit or loss, which simply arises because the estimated residual value is different from the actual sale price and cash received. This is recorded as follows,

Disposal of motor van account

31.12.03 Motor van	12,000	31.12.03 Prov for depreciation	10,500
31.12.03 **Profit on disposal**	500	31.12.03 Bank	2,000
	12,500		12 500

6 – Depreciation

Profit on disposal of motor van

	31.12.03 Disposal	500

The "T" account for the profit on disposal of motor van will be closed off and the £500 deducted from the expenses for the year, thereby increasing the profit.

A *book loss* however is treated as an expense.

Dealing with disposals in the trial balance

In the trial balance below we can see that motor vans at cost were £30,000, while the depreciation charged against these vans so far is £16,000.

Table 6.8: Trial balance as at 31.12.X9

	Dr	Cr
	£	£
Purchases and sales	50,000	100,000
Stock at 1.1.X9	10,000	
Premises	80,000	
Motor vans	**30,000**	
Provision for depreciation: motor vans		**16,000**
Fixtures and fittings	11,500	
Provision for depreciation: Fixtures		3,500
Debtors	21,000	
Bank	1,000	
Cash	500	
Creditors		17,000
Loan		15,000
Capital		70,000
Wages	12,000	
Office expenses	3,903	
Electricity	397	
Rates	1,000	
Insurance	200	
	221,500	221,500

Structure of Accounts

Notes:

1. Depreciation has been and is to be charged on motor vans, at an annual rate of 20% on cost.

2. On 1.1.X9 a motor van which originally cost £5,000 on 1.1.X6 was sold for £1,000 cash. No entries have been made for this sale.

Before we can calculate the depreciation charge for the year (Note 1) we must deal with the sale of the van which took place on the 1.1.X9 (Note 2). Otherwise we would charge depreciation for the year on an asset which did not belong to the company that year.

Note 2: The disposal of a van on 1.1.X9.

As explained above you will need to make the following adjustments:

- remove the asset (van) and its depreciation from our accounts, and
- record the receipt of £1,000 cash, and
- calculate and record the book profit or loss on sale.

1. Removing the asset (van) and its depreciation from our accounts

We can see that the van cost £5,000 on 1.1.X6, and therefore motor vehicles need to be reduced by £5,000, but how much depreciation has been charged against this van since purchase?

We can calculate this as follows:

1.1.X6	Purchased at cost		5,000
	Depreciation for X6	20% on cost	1,000
1.1.X7	Net book value		4,000
	Depreciation for X7	20% on cost	1,000
1.1.X8	Net book value		3,000
	Depreciation for X8	20% on cost	1,000
1.1.X9	Net book value		2,000

Note: The question stated depreciate at the rate of *20% on cost*, i.e. cost £5000 x 20% = £1,000 p.a. It does *not* say depreciate by 20% on a reducing balance basis. Do not simply assume it to be reducing balance when use see a % rate. Read the question.

From the above table we can see that since purchase the van has been depreciated by a total of £3,000. Therefore in order to remove the asset (van) and its depreciation from our accounts, we need to:

Reduce the motor vans (at cost) by £5,000

Reduce the provision for depreciation: motor vans by £3,000

6 – Depreciation

As you know the *double entries* would be entries in the disposal account. I am not showing that in this example, I am simply going to mark the adjustment on the trial balance, so that it is ready to prepare the final accounts.

2. Record the receipt of £1,000 cash

Increase the cash by	£1,000

3. Calculate and record the book profit or loss on sale

Net book value on 1.1.X9	£2,000
Sale proceeds	£1,000
Book loss	**£1,000**

A book loss is recorded on the trial balance as an expense at the foot of the trial balance. Here is the trial balance with a record of the adjustments. Both the debit and the credit side have been reduced by the same amount £3,000. Our trial balance therefore balances and so too can our final accounts.

Structure of Accounts

Table 6.9: Trial balance as at 31.12.X9

	Dr £	Cr £
Purchases and sales	50,000	100,000
Stock at 1.1.X9	10,000	
Premises	80,000	
(1) Motor vans	(- 5,000) 30,000	
(1) Provision for depreciation: motor vans		16,000 (- 3,000)
Fixtures and fittings	11,500	
Provision for depreciation: Fixtures	3,500	
Debtors	21,000	
(2) Bank	(+1000) 1,000	
Cash	500	
Creditors		17,000
Loan		15,000
Capital		70,000
Wages	12,000	
Office expenses	3,903	
Electricity	397	
Rates	1,000	
Insurance	200	
	221,500	221,500
3) Loss on sale of van	1,000	

Now that we have dealt with Note 2, and removed the vans we have sold from our accounts we can deal with Note 1 and depreciate the vans which we did own during the year at the appropriate rate for the year.

Note 1: Depreciate motor vans 20% on cost

The motor vans we owned during the year are therefore:

Motor vans at cost	30,000
less disposal	5,000
	25,000

6 – Depreciation

Depreciation for the year is therefore:

    25,000 x 20% =   5,000

The completely adjusted trial balance appears as follows:

Table 6.10: Trial balance as at 31.12.X9

	Dr £	Cr £
Purchases and sales	50,000	100,000
Stock at 1.1.X9	10,000	
Premises	80,000	
Motor vans	(- 5000) 30,000	
Provision for depreciation: motor vans		16,000 (- 3000) (+ 5000)
Fixtures and fittings	11,500	
Provision for depreciation: Fixtures		3,500
Debtors	21,000	
Bank	(+1000) 1,000	
Cash	500	
Creditors		17,000
Loan		15,000
Capital		70,000
Wages	12,000	
Office expenses	3,903	
Electricity	397	
Rates	1,000	
Insurance	200	
	221,500	221,500
Loss on sale of van *(expense)*	1,000	
Provision for depreciation *(expense)*	5,000	

As a result the motor vans will appear in the balance sheet as:

Balance sheet extract

Fixed assets

Motor vans at cost	25,000
Provision for depreciation: motor vans	18,000
	7,000

Structure of Accounts

Summary

1 *FRS 15 accounting for depreciation* defines depreciation as:

   'The measure of the cost or revalued amount of the economic benefits of the tangible fixed asset that have been consumed during the period', i.e. it is the amount by which the value of an asset is estimated to have reduced because the business has been using it.

2 The *matching concept* requires the depreciation cost to be charged to the accounting periods which benefit from the use of the asset.

3 The most popular methods of calculating depreciation are:

   a) straight line;

   b) reducing balance.

4 The *calculation is* based on the historical cost of an asset and requires an estimate of the expected life and residual value of the asset.

5 *Estimated residual value* is the owner's estimate of the value of the asset at the end of its life with him.

6 *Straight line* charges an equal amount of depreciation in each year of the asset's life.

7 *Straight line rate*

$$= \frac{\text{cost} - \text{estimated value}}{\text{number of years of expected life}}$$

8 *Reducing balance* applies a fixed percentage each year to the reducing value of the asset.

9 Trading profit and loss account *includes only the charge for the year, as an expense.*

10 Balance sheet shows

   a) The asset at *cost*

         less

   b) The *total amount of depreciation charged over the life of the asset*, i.e. net book value.

11 Procedure upon disposal:

   a) Deal with the sale of the asset – deduct the cost price and all previous depreciation;

   b) Deal with the cash receipt;

   c) Calculate the book profit or loss

   - book profits are added to gross profit
   - book losses are treated as an expense and deducted from gross profit.

12 The profit or loss on sale are *book profits or losses* which simply arise because the estimated residual value is different from the actual sale price and cash received.

7
PARTNERSHIP ACCOUNTS

Syllabus Objectives

1.5 Individual transactions and adjustments

The effects of individual transactions and adjustments on the trading and profit and loss account and balance sheet

1.6 Final accounts

- Prepared from trial balance

These should be presented in vertical format; it is not necessary to memorize the exact format of published accounts, but candidates should be able to present them in "good format".

- The appropriation of profits

2.1 Sole trader

- Capital injection and withdrawals
- Risk

2.2 Partnerships

- Risk
- Division of profit – the partnership act 1890
- Capital and current accounts

Learning Objectives

After studying this chapter you should be able to:

1 Define a partnership;

2 Outline some of the agreements which may be made upon forming a partnership;

3 Appreciate how these agreements affect partnership accounts;

4 Produce final accounts for a partnership.

Introduction

So far we have been concerned with the accounts of *sole traders* but in the next three chapters we will consider the accounts of:

- Partnerships (Chapter 7, i.e. this chapter)
- Limited companies (Chapter 8)
- Manufacturing companies (Chapter 9)

Let us start by comparing sole traders with partnerships in terms of their general advantages and disadvantages (risks):

	Sole traders	**Partnerships**
Definition	Someone who is the sole owner of a business, say a shopkeeper	'A partnership is the relation which subsists between persons carrying on a business in common with a view of profit': **Partnership Act 1890, s.1.**
Advantages	All the profits are your own	Share the risk
	You make all the decisions	Share the workload and possible to bring new expertise into the business
	Few formalities (i.e. accounts do not have to be published or audited as with many limited companies)	A partner will usually inject new capital into the business
Disadvantages (Risks)	All the losses are yours alone	Joint and several liability – you are liable for your partners business debts and it is not unknown for one partner to leave another partner to pay the bills
	Unlimited liability – you are liable not only to the extent of money involved in the business but also to the extent of your personal assets	Unlimited liability – you are liable not only to the extent of money involved in the business but also to the extent of your personal assets
	While you make all the decisions, you may lack expertise in certain areas, e.g. marketing	Disputes between partners

7 – Partnerships

Sole traders	Partnerships
Difficult to take holidays unless you have competent and trusted staff	A partner may decide to leave the partnership at an inappropriate time
Finance is limited to what you can contribute in terms of capital and if you can borrow, which in itself costs money in terms of interest	

Now we know a little bit about partnerships, let us take a look at one and how we prepare its accounts.

7.1 The partnership agreement

Luke and Joshua decide to go into business together, selling computer games, trading under the name of 'CompuGames'.

Upon forming the partnership they make the following *financial agreements*:

1. Luke is to contribute £50,000 capital, while Joshua will contribute £30,000.
2. In order to reward Luke for the extra capital he is contributing they decide that interest should be paid on capital at the rate of 10 per cent per annum.
3. As they realize that the first year of trading will be difficult they feel that drawings should be kept to a minimum. They therefore agree to pay interest on any drawings at the rate of 5%.
4. Each partner will be paid a salary of £10,000 per annum.
5. Profits or losses will be shared equally.

Partners can make any agreements they wish regarding the operation of their partnership. For example, although Luke and Joshua have decided to share profits equally, they may have decided to share profits:

a) In proportion to their contribution of capital, e.g.

Luke:	Capital	£50,000
Joshua:	Capital	£30,000
	Total	£80,000

therefore Luke receives 5/8 of the profits because he contributes 5/8 of the capital, and Joshua receives 3/8 of the profits.

Structure of Accounts

Distribution of profits, assuming profits of £25,000

Luke: 5/8 of £25,000   =   £15,625
Joshua: 3/8 of £25,000   =   £9,375
                              £25,000

b) In accordance to a pre-agreed ratio, e.g. 3:1

therefore Luke receives 3 of 4 parts or 3/4

Joshua receives 1 of 4 parts or 1/4

Distribution of profits

Luke: = 3/4 of £25,000 =   £18,750
Joshua: = 1/4 of £25,000 = £6,250
                              £25,000

Where no agreements have been made either express or implied, section 24 of the Partnership Act 1890 will decide the outcome:

- in the case of profits and losses *Section 24*, states that they should be shared equally

In respect to the other financial agreements, *Section 24* states:

- no interest is allowed on capital;
- no interest is charged on drawings;
- no salaries are allowed;
- any capital contributed in excess of the sum agreed will earn interest of 5 per cent per annum.

7.2   Producing the final accounts of a partnership

So, how do we prepare the accounts of CompuGames, whose financial agreements are outlined above?

Their trial balance at the end of their first year of trading appears as follows.

7 – Partnerships

Table 7.1: Trial balance of CompuGames as at 31.12.X9

	£	£
Sales		100,000
Purchases	50,000	
Expenses	10,000	
Fixed assets	80,000	
Current assets	30,000	
Current liabilities		10,000
Long-term liabilities		10,000
Capital:		
Luke		50,000
Joshua		30,000
Drawings:		
Luke	20,000	
Joshua	10,000	
	200,000	200,000

Notes:

1. Stock as at 31.12.X9 = nil
2. Interest on capital: 10%
3. Interest on drawings: 5%
4. Salaries:
   Luke   £10,000
   Joshua   £10,000
5. Profits or losses are to be shared equally.

As you can see many of the details of their partnership agreement are given in the notes at the foot of the trial balance and we must therefore take these into consideration when constructing the final accounts:

1. *Interest on capital* must be calculated and given to each partner

   Luke   50,000 x 10%   =   5000
   Joshua   30,000 x 10%   =   3000

2. *Interest on drawings* must be calculated and deducted from each partner

   Luke 20,000 x 5% = 1,000

   Joshua 10,000 x 5% = 500

3. *Salaries* must be given to each partner

   Luke   10,000

   Joshua   10,000

4. *Profits or losses* must be shared

   Luke   50%

   Joshua   50%

Producing the trading profit and loss account

The only difference between a trading profit and loss account of a sole trader and that of a partnership is the inclusion of an *appropriation account*.

The net profit or loss is calculated in *exactly* the same way as you did for sole traders.

The *appropriation account* is concerned with the partnership agreements and the distribution of profits, showing:

a) Amounts payable *by the partners to the partnership*, i.e. interest on drawing.

b) Amounts payable *to the partners from the partnership*, i.e. interest on capital, salaries.

c) The resulting profit or loss is then available for distribution.

Look at the example on the next page:

7 – Partnerships

Table 7.2: Trading profit and loss account of CompuGames for the year ending 31.12.X9

			£	£
Sales				100,000
less cost of goods sold				(50,000)
Gross profit				50,000
less expenses				(10,000)
Net profit				40,000
Appropriation account				
+ interest on drawings:	Luke		1,000	
	Joshua		500	1,500
				41,500
– interest on capital:	Luke		5,000	
	Joshua		3,000	(8,000)
				33,500
– salaries	Luke		10,000	
	Joshua		10,000	(20,000)
Balance of profits				13,500
shared as follows	Luke 50%		6,750	
	Joshua 50%		6,750	13,500

Producing the balance sheet

From the previous chapters you will be aware that the balance sheet of a sole trader is shown as follows:

	£	£
Fixed assets		200,000
Current assets	100,000	
less current liabilities	(20,000)	80,000
		280,000
less long-term liabilities		(80,000)
		200,000

Structure of Accounts

Financed by

Capital		180,000
+ net profit		50,000
		230,000
− drawings		(30,000)
		200,000

The balance sheet of a partnership is exactly the same, except for the capital section highlighted above. This section is represented in one of two ways:

a) Fixed capital plus current account;
b) Fluctuating capital account.

Fixed capital plus current account

This is where the capital is shown as the amount contributed by Luke and Joshua. Profits, interest on capital and salaries less drawings and interest on drawings are then shown in a separate account known as the *current account*.

Table 7.3: Balance sheet extract

			£	£
Capital:				
Luke			50,000	
Joshua			30,000	80,000
Current accounts	Luke	Joshua		
	£	£		
Opening balance	nil	nil		
Share of profit	6,750	6,750		
Interest on capital	5,000	3,000		
Salary	10,000	10,000		
	21,750	19,750		
less drawings	(20,000)	(10,000)		
	1,750	9,750		
less interest on drawings	(1,000)	(500)		
	750	9,250	10,000	
				90,000

110

7 – Partnerships

Fluctuating capital account

This is where the share of profits, interest on capital and salaries are added to the capital and the drawings and interest on drawings are deducted. The balance will therefore fluctuate/change each year.

Table 7.4: Balance sheet extract

	Luke £	Joshua £	
Capital	50,000	30,000	
Share of profit	6,750	6,750	
Interest on capital	5,000	3,000	
Salary	10,000	10,000	
	71,750	49,750	
less drawings	(20,000)	(10,000)	
	51,750	39,750	
less interest on drawings	(1,000)	(500)	
	50,750	39,250	90,000

The *fixed capital plus current account* (method a) is preferred to the fluctuating capital account, which would conceal a situation where a partner was taking out more than his share of profits, salaries, etc. With separate accounts this is revealed by a debit balance on the current account.

7.3 Specimen layout of partnership accounts

Table 7.5: Trading profit and loss account of CompuGames for the year ending 31.12.X9

			£	£
Sales				100,000
less cost of goods sold				(50,000)
Gross profit				50,000
less expenses				(10,000)
Net profit				40,000
+ interest on drawings:	Luke		1,000	
	Joshua		500	1,500
				41,500
− interest on capital:	Luke		5,000	
	Joshua		3,000	(8,000)
				33,500
− salaries:	Luke		10,000	
	Joshua		10,000	(20,000)
Balance of profits				13,500
shared as follows:	Luke 50%		6,750	
	Joshua 50%		6,750	13,500

7 – Partnerships

Table 7.6: Balance sheet of CompuGames as at 31.12.X9

	£	£	£
Fixed assets			80,000
Current assets		30,000	
less current liabilities		(10,000)	20,000
			100,000
less			
Long-term liabilities			
Loan			(10,000)
			90,000
Capital:			
Luke		50,000	
Joshua		30,000	80,000
Current accounts	*Luke*	*Joshua*	
Opening balance	nil	nil	
Share of profit	6,750	6,750	
Interest on capital	5,000	3,000	
Salary	10,000	10,000	
	21,750	19,750	
less drawings	(20,000)	(10,000)	
	1,750	9,750	
less interest on drawings	(1,000)	(500)	
	750	9,250	10,000
			90,000

Structure of Accounts

Summary

1. A *sole trader* is someone who is the sole owner of a business, e.g. a shopkeeper.

2. A *partnership is the relationship which subsists between persons carrying on a business in common with a view of profit (Partnership Act 1890, Section1).*

3. Final accounts of partnerships are often affected by the following *financial agreement:*

    a) amount of interest to be paid on capital;

    b) amount of interest to be charged on drawings;

    c) amount of salaries paid to each partner;

    d) the amount of capital to be contributed by each partner;

    e) the distribution of profits or losses.

4. *Details of the partnership agreement* are given in the notes to the trial balance.

5. *Net profit* is calculated in exactly the same way as for sole traders.

6. The *appropriation account* is concerned with the payment of interest by and to the partners and the payment of salaries to determine the amount of profit available for distribution.

7. The *balance sheet* is exactly the same as for a sole trader except for the *capital section*.

8. The preferred method for presenting the capital and profits, etc. is in the form of a *fixed capital plus current account*.

9. A *fixed capital plus current account* would clearly reveal a situation where a partner was withdrawing more than his or her balance of profits etc, with a debit balance on the current account.

10. Generally speaking, partners are left to make their own arrangements but where there are no agreements, *Partnership Act 1890, Section 24*, will decide the outcome.

8
LIMITED COMPANY ACCOUNTS

Syllabus Objectives

1.6 Final accounts

- Prepared from trial balance

  These should be presented in vertical format; it is not necessary to memorize the exact format of published accounts, but candidates should be able to present them in "good format".

- The appropriation of profits

2.3 Limited company

- Limited liability – separation of ownership and management
- Formation
- Risk
- Corporation tax as an accrual (calculation is not covered)
- Dividends
- Share capital
- Rights issues
- Bonus issues
- Share premium
- Debentures
- Provisions and reserves

2.4 Setting up a business

- Sources of funds (equity shares, preference shares, debentures) and their related obligations, consequences and application

2.5 Capital structure

2.6 Capital and revenue expenditure

Structure of Accounts

Fixed assets and current assets

2.7 Long-term and short-term liabilities

2.8 Profit

Its distribution or reinvestment

Learning Objectives

After studying this chapter you should be able to:

1   Outline the nature of a limited company;

2   Describe the essential differences between companies and partnerships;

3   Produce final accounts of a limited company.

Introduction

As promised we will now turn our attention to another type of business: *limited companies*. In the last chapter we started with a comparison of sole traders and partnerships in terms of their nature and advantages/disadvantages. Let us continue to develop our understanding of the various businesses we might meet with a comparison of partnerships and limited companies

8 – Limited Company Accounts

	Limited companies	**Partnerships**
Formation	Registered in accordance with the Companies Acts. As a result they are bound by these Acts, e.g. their accounts must be drawn in accordance with the Acts (See Chapter 15).	By agreement, express or implied, by deed, in writing or oral. This leaves partners to make any agreements they wish. The Partnership Act 1890 will only be referred to where agreements have not been made.
Members (Owners)	These are the shareholders. Minimum two, maximum unlimited. This provides an opportunity to raise capital by issuing more shares.	The partners. Minimum two, maximum 20 except in special cases, e.g. solicitors. The ability to raise further capital is therefore limited.
Separate legal entity	A company is a separate legal entity from its members, i.e. from its shareholders.	A partnership is not a separate legal entity from its members.
Liability	Each member's liability is limited to the amount of shares he/she owns, i.e. in the event of liquidation the shareholder may lose the money he or she has invested in the company but not personal assets.	Partners have unlimited liability. i.e. in the event of the partnership going bankrupt partners will be liable not only to the extent of money invested in the business but also to the extent of their personal assets. In addition, one partner is liable for the business debts of another partner.
Succession	A limited company continues independently unless it is wound up. i.e. the retirement of a director does not affect a company in the same way as the retirement of a partner affects a partnership.	Upon certain events the partnership will come to an end, e.g. if there are two partners and one retires.
Taxation	As a separate legal entity companies pay corporate tax on their profits, which therefore appears in the company accounts.	Partners pay income tax on the firm's profit.

Structure of Accounts

Limited Liability Partnership

It is worth mentioning in passing that since 2000 there has been a further structure possible, that of Limited Liability Partnership. As the name suggests these give such partnerships some of the protection of limited liability status in exchange for taking on some of the reporting and statutory obligations of limited companies.

8.1 Preparation of accounts – Limited company accounts

The accounts of a limited company are different from those of a partnership and sole trader. However, as you will see there are many common elements which makes your task of constructing the final accounts from a trial balance that much easier.

Let us look at a specimen trading profit and loss account of a limited company and in particular the differences between limited companies, partnerships and sole traders as indicated by the notes below.

8 – Limited Company Accounts

Specimen layout of trading profit and loss account

Table 8.1: Trading profit and loss account of Example Ltd for the year ending 31.12.X9

Notes		£	£
	Sales		500,000
	Less cost of good sold		
	Opening stock	50,000	
	+ purchases	<u>250,000</u>	
		300,000	
	– closing stock	<u>(60,000)</u>	240,000
	Gross profit		260,000
	Less expenses		
	Rent and rates	5,000	
	Provision for bad and doubtful debts	3,000	
	Light and heat	6,000	
	Wages	50,000	
	Motor expenses	20,000	
1:	Directors' remuneration	40,000	
2:	Auditors' remuneration	3,000	
3:	Debenture interest	2,000	
4:	Amortization of goodwill	2,000	
	Depreciation:		
	Equipment	5,000	
	Fixtures and fittings	<u>5,000</u>	(141,000)
	Net profit for the year before taxation		119,000

Structure of Accounts

Table 8.1 continued: Trading profit and loss account of Example Ltd for the year ending 31.12.X9

Notes		£	£	£
5:	Less corporation tax			(40,000)
	Net profit for the year after taxation			79,000
	Plus retained profits from previous year			72,000
				151,000
	Less appropriation			
6:	Transfer to general reserve		5,000	
	Transfer to other reserves		6,000	
			11,000	
7:	Preference dividends			
	Final proposed		3,000	
	Ordinary dividends:			
	Interim paid	2,000		
	Final proposed	5,000	7,000	21,000
8:	Retained profits			130,000

Notes re trading profit and loss account

The trading profit and loss account is exactly the same as for partnerships and sole traders except that you may find some new expenses in the trial balance, such as:

Note 1: Directors' remuneration, i.e. the directors' wages/salary

Note 2: Auditors' remuneration, i.e. fees paid to auditors. The accounts of a limited company must be drawn in accordance with the Companies Act and give a 'true and a fair view' of the company's affairs. The person/firm who checks the accounts are known as auditors.

Note 3: Debenture interest A debenture is a loan received by the company and as a result the company may need to make interest payments.

Note 4: Amortization of good will Amortization is the same as depreciation but the word amortization is used in the context of intangibles. Goodwill must be amortized over its useful life.

8 – Limited Company Accounts

Note 5: Taxation As stated earlier, companies are subject to corporation tax which must be deducted before any distribution of the profits can be made.

Questions may state 'ignore taxation', so do not simply include it without being directed to in the notes at the foot of the trial balance.

Appropriation account

This section deals with the distribution of profits, the effect of which will also be seen in the balance sheet.

After calculating the profit for the year, add the retained profits from previous years (given in the trial balance) and then make all the necessary distributions of profit.

As with partnerships accounts, the need for such distribution will be revealed in the notes at the foot of the trial balance.

There are three types of distributions you need to be aware of:

Note 6: Transfers to various reserves (see balance sheet notes)

Note 7: Dividends Dividends are payments made by the company to their shareholders, in return for the shareholders investing money in the company. In a sense it represents the shareholder's interest on his or her investment, except that unlike interest on, say, bank loans, companies are not required to pay dividends.

In our case we can see we have:
  a) dividends paid, i.e. shareholders have actually received their dividend payment in cash
  b) dividends proposed, i.e. the company propose to pay the dividend to the shareholders in the future.

Note 8: Retained profits The profit remaining after all distributions is simply carried forward to the balance sheet.

Specimen layout of balance sheet

Look at the specimen balance sheet of a limited company and in particular the differences between limited companies, partnerships and sole traders as indicated by the notes below.

Structure of Accounts

Table 8.2: Balance sheet of Example Ltd at 31.12.X8

Notes		£	£	£
	Fixed assets			
9	Intangible:			
	Goodwill		6,000	
	less goodwill written off		(2,000)	4,000
	Tangible:			
	Premises		160,000	
	Equipment	30,000		
	– depreciation	(10,000)	20,000	
	Fixtures and fittings	18,000		
	– depreciation	(5,000)	13,000	
	Motor vehicles		21,000	214,000
				218,000
	Current assets			
	Stock		60,000	
	Debtors	20,000		
	– provision for bad and doubtful debts	(5,000)	15,000	
	Bank		20,000	
	Cash		1,000	
	less		96,000	

Table 8.2 continued: Balance sheet of Example Ltd at 31.12.X8

Notes		£	£	£
10	*Creditors: amounts falling due within one year*			
	Creditors	10,000		
11	Proposed dividends:			
	Preference	3,000		
	Ordinary	5,000		
12	Taxation	40,000	58,000	
13	Net current assets			38,000
				256,000
	less			
14	*Creditors: amounts falling due after more than one year*			
15	10% debenture 2006			(20,000)
				236,000
	Capital and reserves		Authorized	Issued
16	*Capital*			
	Ordinary shares of £1 each fully paid		70,000	50,000
	10% preference shares of £1 each		30,000	30,000
			100,000	80,000
17	*Reserves*			
	General reserves		10,000	
	Other reserves		16,000	
	Retained profits		130,000	156,000
				236,000

Notes re balance sheet

Basically it is the same as sole traders and partnerships except for the following:

Structure of Accounts

Note 9: Intangible assets, **e.g. goodwill.** In the balance sheet above you will note that intangible assets are listed separately and above tangible assets.

Tangible assets are items of value owned by the company, which can be seen, touched or even kicked, such as premises, fixtures, motor vehicles, etc.

Intangible assets are items of value owned by the company which *are not* clearly visible, such as goodwill, patents, trade marks and research and development.

We will examine *goodwill* in detail in Chapter 16. For now, simply concentrate on where intangible and tangible assets appear in the balance sheet. As we have said intangible assets are listed separately and above tangible assets.

In addition you should also note that the balance sheet shows:

Goodwill	£6,000
less goodwill written off	£2,000
	£4,000

The £2,000 written off goodwill is an expense as outlined in Note 4 above.

Note 10: Creditors: amounts falling due within one year. This title simply replaces that of current liabilities.

Note 11: Proposed dividends These are the dividends you *propose* to pay in the future. As you have not yet actually paid them to the shareholders they appear under the heading 'Creditors: amounts falling due within one year'.

If you look back to Note 7 you will see that the dividends you have *paid* do *not* appear as part of *creditors: amounts falling due within one year* as they have actually been paid and are therefore *not due*.

Note 12: Taxation Companies are liable for corporation tax based on the net profit. Therefore at the time of drawing the accounts the payment of tax is still outstanding. As a result taxation appears as a deduction from net profit in the trading profit and loss account (Note 5) and as an amount falling due within one year in the balance sheet.

Note 13: Net current assets That is the difference between current assets and

8 – Limited Company Accounts

	accounts falling due within one year. This is the same therefore as *working capital*.
Note 14: Creditors: Amounts falling due after more than one year	Simply another change of title, this time the title replaced is long-term liabilities.
Note 15: Debentures	These are loans received by the company, which are usually for long periods. In our case the loan is for £20,000 and due to be repaid in 2006.
	The interest rate on the loan is 10 per cent (i.e. £2,000 pa), hence this amount appears in the *trading profit and loss account* as interest paid (Note 3).
Note 16: Capital	You must show:
	Authorized share capital, i.e. the amount of share capital the company is allowed to issue.
	Issued share capital, i.e. the amount they have actually issued, which may be less than the authorized capital and is found in the body of the trial balance.
	The issued shares may be in many forms, the most common being:
	Ordinary shares
	These allow the shareholders a share of the profits after all other classes of shareholders;
	Preference shares
	Such shareholders are entitled to a specified percentage rate of dividends, in our case 10 per cent;
	Cumulative preference shares
	The holders of these shares are entitled to a specified percentage rate of dividend, which is carried forward to future years if there are insufficient profits to pay the dividend in say Year 1.
Note 17: Reserves	These are shown as an addition to the share capital and can be either:
	Revenue reserves, i.e. retained profits which can be distributed to shareholders in the form of dividends, if you have the cash of course!
	Capital reserves, i.e. reserves that have been built up from the transfer of profits in the appropriation account. These reserves are not distributable.

Structure of Accounts

e.g. *General reserves* – £5,000 was transferred to the General Reserve from retained profits in the appropriation account.

e.g. *Share premium reserve*

Where shares are issued at more than their nominal value, for example £1 ordinary shares issued at £1.50, the amount in excess of the nominal value (i.e. 50p per share) is credited to a share premium account.

An issue of 10,000 £1 ordinary shares at £1.50 each will therefore have the following effects on the balance sheet:

£1 ordinary shares	increase the nominal value by	£10,000
Share premium reserve	increase the premium by	£5,000
Bank/Cash	increase cash injected by	£15,000

Hence the balance sheet balances!

e.g. *Revaluation reserve*

It is possible to revalue your assets regularly in order that the balance sheet reflects a true picture and more importantly so that your assets are not shown below their true value.

However if fixed assets valued in the balance at £100,000 were found to have a true value of £150,000, how would you account for this revaluation?

If you simply increase the fixed assets by £50,000, the balance sheet would not balance, therefore you:

create a	revaluation reserve of	£50,000
increase	fixed assets by	£50,000

Hey presto, the balance sheet balances again!

Two other terms relating to share capital and reserves that you need to be aware of are:

- Rights issues, and
- Bonus issues.

8 – Limited Company Accounts

Rights issue

This occurs where the existing shareholders have the right to *purchase* additional shares in the company, in proportion to their existing shareholding.

For example, suppose you currently own 10% of the 50,000 ordinary shares currently in issue, i.e. 5,000 shares, and that the company is about to issue another 10,000 shares at £1 each. You have the right to purchase 10% of new shares being issued. If you take up your right to 10% of the new issue, i.e. 1,000 shares, you will maintain your 10% stake in the business. After the issue you will still own 10% of the business: 6,000 of the 60,000 shares.

Clearly if you do not take up the right your stake in the business will reduce: 5,000 of 60,000 = 8.33%.

The rights issue will have two effects on the balance sheet:

Share capital will increase	£10,000
Cash will increase	£10,000

as a result, the balance sheet will balance.

Bonus issue

This occurs where new shares are *given* to existing shareholders in proportion to their existing shareholding as a *bonus*, e.g. one new share for every five currently held. Because these shares are given away no additional cash comes into the business.

So how does this work, after all if share capital increases but cash does not how does the balance sheet balance?

It is really very simple. Here is existing share capital taken from the balance sheet above:

Table 8.3: Capital and reserves

		Authorized	Issued
16	Capital		
	Ordinary shares of £1 each fully paid	70,000	50,000
	10% preference shares of £1 each	30,000	30,000
		100,000	80,000
17	Reserves		
	General reserves	10,000	
	Other reserves	16,000	
	Retained profits	130,000	156,000
			236,000

The retained profits, which belong to the owners of the business, i.e. the shareholders = £130,000. However, it is important to realize that the company does not have a drawer with

Structure of Accounts

£130,000 cash just sitting there. Profits like capital are simply a source of finance – they show where you got the money from and who you owe the money to.

What you have done with the money is shown on the asset side.

If you look back at the assets of the company you will see that the capital and reserves, including the retained profits, have mainly been used to purchase Fixed assets worth £218,000 and stock worth £60,000. The only cash available is £1,000 with an additional £20,000 available in the bank account; as indicated by the current assets.

In many ways it is silly to leave £130,000 as retained profit as it is unlikely that the company will be able to pay it back to the shareholders. The company could therefore *capitalize* it, (make it a permanent feature of the company – which after all is what it is), by making a *bonus issue* of say 1:5, i.e. one new share for every five currently held. This will have the following effect:

Ordinary shares will increase by	£10,000
Retained profits will reduce by	£10,000

Table 8.4: Capital and reserves

16 *Capital*	Authorized	Issued
Ordinary shares of £1 each fully paid	70,000	60,000
10% preference shares of £1 each	30,000	30,000
	100,000	90,000
17 *Reserves*		
General reserves	10,000	
Other reserves	16,000	
Retained profits	12,000	146,000
		236,000

Compare the balance sheets before and after the bonus issue to note the effects.

8 – Limited Company Accounts

Summary

1 A limited company is registered in accordance with the *Companies Acts* and as a result is bound by these acts. It is a separate legal entity from its members, with each member's liability being limited to the amount of shares he or she owns.

2 *Trading profit and loss account* is exactly the same as that for a partnership and sole trader except that it may include new expenses such as directors' remuneration, auditors' remuneration and debenture interest.

3 *Taxation*. Limited companies are subject to corporation tax which may therefore appear as a deduction from net profit.

4 *Appropriation account*. This outlines the distributions of profit which may be in the form of:

   a) transfers;

   b) write-offs;

   c) dividends.

5 *Balance sheet* is basically the same as for sole traders except for the inclusion of new items and changes of heading.

6 *Intangible assets* are items that cannot physically be seen, yet are considered of value to the company, e.g. goodwill, patents and trademarks, research and development.

7 *Proposed dividends* are dividends you propose to pay in the future. As such they are still outstanding and appear as a creditor, due within 12 months.

8 *Debentures* are loans received by the company, often for long periods.

9 *Authorized share capital* is the amount of shares the company is allowed to issue.

10 *Issued share capital* is the amount of shares the company has actually issued.

11 *Ordinary shares* allow the shareholders a share of the profits after all other classes of shareholders.

12 *Preference shares* allow shareholders a specified percentage rate of dividend.

13 *Cumulative preference shares*. This is where the entitlement to a specified percentage rate is carried forward to future years if there are insufficient profits to pay the dividend in any particular year.

14 *Rights issue*. This is where the existing shareholders have the right to *purchase* additional shares in the company, in proportion to their existing shareholding.

15 *Bonus issue*. This is where new shares are *given* to existing shareholders in proportion to their existing shareholding as a *bonus*, e.g. one new share for every five currently held. Because these shares are given away no additional cash comes into the business.

Structure of Accounts

16 *Reserves* represent retained profits whether held as profits or transferred to a specific reserve.

17 *Revenue reserves* are retained profits that can be distributed to shareholders as dividends.

18 *Capital reserves* are non-distributable and are built up from transfers from retained profits. Reserves are *not* cash held in a drawer.

19 *Share premium reserve*. Where shares are issued at more than their nominal value the amount in excess of the nominal value is credited to a share premium account.

20 *Revaluation reserves*. When assets are revalued, they are shown at their new valuation in the assets and the increase or decrease in value is recorded in a revaluation reserve

21 *Liabilities (Capital, reserves, creditors)* are sources of finances that the company has issued to purchase the assets.

9
Manufacturing Company Accounts

Syllabus Objectives

1.6 Final accounts

- Prepared from trial balance

  These should be presented in vertical format; it is not necessary to memorize the exact format of published accounts, but candidates should be able to present them in "good format".

- The appropriation of profits

2.9 Manufacturing company

- The cost of manufacture

Learning Objectives

After studying this chapter you will be able to:

1. See the need for manufacturing accounts;
2. Calculate the *prime* cost of manufacture;
3. Calculate the total cost of manufacture;
4. Produce trading profit and loss accounts and balance sheets for manufacturing businesses.

Introduction

So far we have looked at businesses that have simply bought and sold goods; as a result, their trading accounts have appeared as follows:

Structure of Accounts

Table 9.1: Trading account of Example Limited for the year ending 31.12.Y0

	£	£
Sales		100,000
less cost of goods sold		
Opening stock	30,000	
+ purchases	**80,000**	
	110,000	
− closing stock	<u>20,000</u>	<u>90,000</u>
Gross profit		<u>10,000</u>

But suppose a company manufactured the goods they sold rather than purchased them. They would therefore need to calculate the cost of manufacture which would then replace the purchases figure in the trading account.

We therefore need to produce a *manufacturing account* before we can move on to the trading profit and loss account and balance sheet.

9.1 Calculating the cost of manufacture

A manufacturing account includes only costs relating to the *manufacture of goods*.

All administrative, selling/distribution and financial expenses appear in the trading profit and loss account just as we have seen in previous chapters.

So what are the costs of manufacture?

The *prime costs* of manufacture (or the major cost of manufacture) are:

1. *Direct material:* This is the cost of material directly used in manufacturing the goods.

2. *Direct labour:* This is the cost of labour actually employed in manufacturing the goods and therefore may also be referred to as manufacturers' wages, etc.

3. *Direct expenses:* This does *not* mean expenses such as light and heat, etc., and I cannot stress that enough. It refers to expenses specifically relating to the product, such as royalties or patents.

So, the basic structure of a manufacturing account is therefore:

1	Direct material	138,000
2	Direct labour	30,000
3	Direct expenses	<u>—</u>
	Prime cost of manufacture	<u>168,000</u>

9 – Manufacturing Company Accounts

To this we then add:

4 *Manufacturing overheads*: The overheads such as light and heat, rent, rates, etc. incurred in the manufacture of the goods.

The manufacturing account now appears as follows:

1	Direct material	138,000
2	Direct labour	30,000
3	Direct expenses	—
	Prime cost of manufacture	168,000
4	Add manufacturing overheads	41,000
		209,000

Finally we include:

5 Work in progress (W.I.P.)   partly manufactured items.

The manufacturing account is therefore:

1	Direct material	138,000
2	Direct labour	30,000
3	Direct expenses	—
	Prime cost of manufacture	168,000
4	Add manufacturing overheads	41,000
		209,000
5	Add opening stock of W.I.P.	15,000
		224,000
	less closing stock of W.I.P.	(14,000)
	Total cost of manufacture	210,000

Let us take a closer look at the account, starting with the calculation of the prime cost of manufacture.

The prime cost of manufacture

As you know the prime costs of manufacture are:

- Direct material
- Direct labour
- Direct expenses

Structure of Accounts

Direct labour and direct expenses are normally given to you in the trial balance, although as stated earlier *direct labour* could be referred to as manufacturers' wages, or any other term to describe the labour costs relating to the manufacture of the goods.

Direct material (the cost of material directly used in manufacturing the goods) may require calculating from a number of items in the trial balance as shown below. However, as the calculation is similar to others we have seen before, this should not worry you.

Table 9.2: Manufacturing account of Wonder Toys Limited for the year ending 31.12.Y0

Notes		£	£
	Opening stock of raw materials		30,000
	add purchases of raw materials	125,000	
	add carriage in of raw materials	5,000	
		130,000	
	less returns out of raw materials	(2,000)	128,000
			158,000
	– closing stock of raw materials		(20,000)
1	**Direct material**		138,000
2	Direct labour		30,000
3	Direct expenses		—
	Prime cost of manufacture		168,000

So we have now got the prime cost of manufacture, but remember this is not the total cost of manufacture. We must now add to this the manufacturing overheads.

Manufacturing overheads

The important thing to remember is that the manufacturing account is concerned only with the *cost of manufacture*.

All administrative, selling/distribution and financial expenses appear in the trading profit and loss account as before.

9 – Manufacturing Company Accounts

So which of the following are manufacturing overheads?

> Factory heat and light
> Factory rent
> Office salaries
> Warehouse expenses
> Office expenses
> Office insurance
> Depreciation of office equipment
> Warehouse wages
> Selling expenses
> Factory supervisors' wages
> Salesmen's salaries
> Discounts allowed
> Factory insurance
> Depreciation of machinery

Hopefully you picked:

> Factory heat and light
> Factory rent
> Factory supervisors' wages
> Factory insurance
> Depreciation of machinery

What about the next one – rent of premises?

Part of the premises may be used for manufacturing and part for administrative, selling or financial matters and remember, in the manufacturing account we are concerned only with *the proportion of these costs that relate to the manufacture of the goods.*

Unless the trial balance indicates the cost of rent for each function (for the factory, sales department, etc.) you may need to apportion the cost to each function in accordance with information provided (usually in the notes at the foot of the trial balance).

For example:

> Rent of premises   £3,000 per annum

Note

The factory space occupies 2/3 of the premises and office space 1/3.

It would be fair to apportion the rent in accordance with the space each function occupies, i.e:

Structure of Accounts

Factory rent £2,000   manufacturing overhead (manufacturing account)

Office rent £1,000   admin expense (trading, profit and loss account)

The manufacturing account

The manufacturing account, therefore, appears as follows:

Table 9.3: Manufacturing account of Wonder Toys Limited for the year ending 31.12.Y0

Notes		£	£
	Opening stock of raw materials		30,000
	and purchases of raw materials	125,000	
	+ carriage in of raw materials	5,000	
		130,000	
	less Returns out of raw materials	(2,000)	128,000
			158,000
	less Closing stock of raw materials		(20,000)
	Direct material		138,000
	Direct labour		30,000
	Direct expenses		—
	Prime cost of manufacture		168,000
1	**add manufacturing overheads**		
	Factory heat and light	4,000	
	Factory rent	5,000	
	Factory supervisors' wages	15,000	
	Factory insurance	7,000	
	Depreciation of machinery	10,000	41,000
			209,000
2	**add opening stock of work in progress**		**15,000**
			224,000
2	**less closing stock of work in progress**		**14,000**
	Cost of manufacture		210,000

9 – Manufacturing Company Accounts

Notes

1. We are trying to calculate the total cost of manufacture, therefore *add* factory overheads to the prime cost of manufacture. Many students are so used to deducting expenses from gross profit that they deduct factory overheads. Do not make that mistake.

2. Having added the factory overheads we must then:

    a) add the opening stock of work in progress (i.e. half-finished items); and

    b) deduct the closing stock of work in progress, for as you will see, the stock of these partly finished items is an asset belonging to the company and therefore not a cost.

9.2 Producing a trading profit and loss account for manufacturing businesses

The format is exactly the same as we have seen for other limited companies except that:

1. The *cost of manufacture* is carried forward from the manufacturing account, replacing purchases;

2. The trading account, in which we calculate the gross profit on sales, includes the opening and closing stocks of *finished goods* because it is these items that have been traded and on which the gross profit is calculated;

3. The expenses are those expenses that relate to areas other than the manufacture of the goods, e.g

    - administration
    - selling and distribution
    - financial.

As you can see below, the profit and loss account may show a sub-total for each of these categories rather than simply listing all the expenses.

Structure of Accounts

Table 9.4: Trading profit and loss account for Wonder Toys Limited for the year ending 31.12.Y0

	£	£	£
Sales			500,000
less cost of goods sold			
Opening stock of *finished goods* (2)		50,000	
and cost of manufacture (1)		<u>210,000</u>	
		260,000	
– closing stock of *finished goods* (2)		<u>40,000</u>	<u>220,000</u>
Gross profit			280,000
***less expenses* (3)**			
Administration			
Office salaries	60,000		
Office heat and light	4,000		
Office expenses	5,000		
Office rent	5,000		
Office insurance	7,000		
Depreciation of office equipment	<u>5,000</u>	86,000	
Selling and distribution			
Warehouse wages	20,000		
Warehouse expenses	4,000		
Selling expenses	5,000		
Salesmen's salaries	<u>30,000</u>	59,000	
Financial			
Depreciation of premises	2,000		
Discounts allowed	<u>3,000</u>	<u>5,000</u>	<u>150,000</u>
Net profit for the year before tax			130,000
less taxation			<u>40,000</u>
Net profit for the year after tax			90,000
less appropriation			
Transfer to reserves			<u>5,000</u>
			85,000
Proposed dividends – ordinary shares			<u>5,000</u>
Retained profits			<u>80,000</u>

9.3 Producing a balance sheet for manufacturing businesses

Can you think of the *one* thing that will be different in the balance sheet of a manufacturing business when compared with other limited companies?

The answer is the *stock*. While some limited companies simply have a closing stock of goods (which they have purchased), a manufacturing business has:

- closing stock of raw material;
- closing stock of work in progress;
- closing stock of finished goods;

all of which are current assets because they represent items owned by the company.

Here then is the balance sheet of Wonder Toys, the manufacturing company we have followed throughout this chapter.

Table 9.5: Balance sheet of Wonder Toys Ltd as at 31.12.Y0

	£	£	£
Fixed assets			
Premises (cost)		186,000	
– provision for depreciation		23,306	162,694
Motor vehicles (cost)		31,000	
– provision for depreciation		9,100	21,900
Office equipment (cost)		26,000	
– provision for depreciation		13,000	13,000
			197,594
Current assets			
Closing stock of raw material		20,000	
Closing stock of work in progress		14,000	
Closing stock of finished goods		40,000	
		74,000	
Debtors		57,100	
Cash		2,467	
		133,567	
less current liabilities			
Creditors	36,161		
Proposed dividend: ordinary	5,000		
Taxation	40,000	81,161	52,406
			250,000
Authorized and issued share capital		Authorized	Issued
£1 ordinary shares fully paid		150,000	150,000
Reserves			
Balance of profits		80,000	
General reserve		20,000	100,000
			250,000

9 – Manufacturing Company Accounts

Conclusion

When asked to produce a manufacturing trading profit and loss account and balance sheet from a trial balance you need to:

1. Deal with the notes at the foot of the trial balance (e.g. prepaids; accruals; provision for bad debts; depreciation etc.), making any necessary adjustments to the items in the trial balance.

2. Identify which items belong in the manufacturing account, the trading profit and loss account and balance sheet.

3. Prepare the manufacturing account, which is basically:

    Direct material

    Direct labour

    Direct expenses

    Prime cost of manufacture

    + Manufacturing overheads

    + Opening stock of work-in-progress

    – Closing stock of work-in-progress

    Cost of manufacture

4. Prepare the trading profit and loss account, remembering that the trading account appears as follows:

Sales		500,000
less cost of goods sold		
Opening stock of *finished goods*	50,000	
+ cost of manufacture	210,000	
	260,000	
– closing stock of *finished goods*	40,000	220,000
Gross profit		280,000

5. Prepare the balance sheet remembering that current assets include:
   - closing stock of raw material;
   - closing stock of work in progress;
   - closing stock of finished goods.

Here is a look at the complete final accounts of Wonder Toys from manufacturing account, to trading profit and loss account, to balance sheet.

Table 9.6: Manufacturing account of Wonder Toys Limited for the year ending 31.12.Y0

	£	£
Opening stock of raw materials		30,000
and purchases of raw materials	125,000	
+ carriage in of raw materials	5,000	
	130,000	
less Returns out of raw materials	2,000	128,000
		158,000
less Closing stock of raw materials		20,000
Direct material		138,000
Direct labour		30,000
Direct expenses		—
Prime cost of manufacture		168,000
add manufacturing overheads		
Factory heat and light	4,000	
Factory rent	5,000	
Factory supervisors' wages	15,000	
Factory insurance	7,000	
Depreciation of machinery	10,000	41,000
		209,000
add opening stock of work in progress		15,000
		224,000
less closing stock of work in progress		14,000
Cost of manufacture		**210,000**

9 – Manufacturing Company Accounts

Table 9.7: Trading profit and loss account for Wonder Toys Limited for the year ending 31.12.Y0

	£	£	£
Sales			500,000
less cost of goods sold			
Opening stock of *finished goods*		50,000	
and cost of manufacture		210,000	
		260,000	
– closing stock of *finished goods*		40,000	220,000
Gross profit			280,000
less expenses			
<u>Administration</u>			
Office salaries	60,000		
Office heat and light	4,000		
Office expenses	5,000		
Office rent	5,000		
Office insurance	7,000		
Depreciation of office equipment	5,000	86,000	
<u>Selling and distribution</u>			
Warehouse wages	20,000		
Warehouse expenses	4,000		
Selling expenses	5,000		
Salesmen's salaries	30,000	59,000	
<u>Financial</u>			
Depreciation of premises	2,000		
Discounts allowed	3,000	5,000	150,000
Net profit for the year before tax			130,000
less taxation			40,000
Net profit for the year after tax			90,000
less appropriation			
Transfer to reserves			5,000
			85,000
Proposed dividends – ordinary shares			5,000
Retained profits			**80,000**

143

Structure of Accounts

Table 9.8: Balance sheet of Wonder Toys Ltd as at 31.12.Y0

	£	£	£
Fixed assets			
Premises (cost)		186,000	
– provision for depreciation		<u>23,306</u>	162,694
Motor vehicles (cost)		31,000	
– provision for depreciation		<u>9,100</u>	21,900
Office equipment (cost)		26,000	
– provision for depreciation		<u>13,000</u>	<u>13,000</u>
			197,594
Current assets			
Closing stock of raw material		20,000	
Closing stock of work in progress		14,000	
Closing stock of finished goods		<u>40,000</u>	
		74,000	
Debtors		57,100	
Cash		<u>2,467</u>	
		133,567	
less current liabilities			
Creditors	36,161		
Proposed dividend: ordinary	5,000		
Taxation	<u>40,000</u>	<u>81,161</u>	<u>52,406</u>
			250,000
Authorized and issued share capital		Authorized	Issued
£1 ordinary shares fully paid		<u>150,000</u>	150,000
Reserves			
Balance of profits		80,000	
General reserve		<u>20,000</u>	<u>100,000</u>
			<u>250,000</u>

9 – Manufacturing Company Accounts

Summary

1. Where businesses manufacture goods they will need to produce a *manufacturing account* in order to calculate the cost of manufacture.

2. *Prime cost* of manufacture examines the major costs of manufacture which are:
   - direct material;
   - direct labour;
   - direct expenses.

3. *Direct material* is the cost of material directly used in manufacturing the goods.

4. *Direct labour* refers to the wages of those actually manufacturing the goods.

5. *Direct expenses* are such things as patents or royalties relating to the particular goods.

6. *Factory overheads* are added to the prime cost of manufacture.

7. The cost of manufacture is *transferred* into the trading profit and loss account in order to calculate the cost of goods sold.

8. *Work in progress* – this refers to partly completed items.

9. The trading profit and loss account is exactly the same as for any other limited company *except*:

   a) cost of manufacture replaces purchases;

   b) the trading account features opening and closing stock of *finished* goods;

   c) expenses are often those which relate to areas other than the manufacture of goods, e.g. administration, selling, financial.

10. The only difference in the balance sheet of a manufacturing business is that it may include more than one *closing stock*, i.e.
    - raw materials;
    - work in progress;
    - finished goods.

10

DECISION MAKING: COST BEHAVIOUR AND BREAK-EVEN ANALYSIS

Syllabus Objectives

3.1 Information

   Preparation and use of accounting reports as a basis for decision making

3.2 Cost behaviour

   Fixed and variable costs; contribution costing

3.3 Break-even analysis;

   - Calculation of break-even point
   - Limitations

3.4 Capacity and output compared

   Revenue and cost implications of different levels of activity

Learning Objectives

After studying this chapter you should be able to:

1 Explain the meaning and purpose of break-even analysis;

2 Distinguish between fixed and variable costs;

3 Calculate the break-even point;

4 Use break-even analysis as a decision-making tool and planning aid;

5 Outline the assumptions on which break-even analysis is based.

Introduction

In the last chapter we prepared the final accounts of a manufacturing company. This entailed

10 – Decision Making

calculating the cost of manufacture before preparing the trading profit and loss account and balance sheet.

You will no doubt recall that the major or *prime costs* of manufacture are:

- Direct material – material directly used in manufacturing the goods
- Direct labour – labour costs of those actually manufacturing the goods
- Direct expenses – expenses specifically relating to the goods, e.g. royalties and patents

The other *costs* (expenses), such as electricity, depreciation, administration expenses, etc. were divided into:

- Manufacturing (or factory) overheads – as part of the manufacturing account
- Administration expenses – as part of the trading profit and loss account
- Selling and distribution expenses – as part of the trading profit and loss account
- Financial expenses – as part of the trading profit and loss account

In this chapter we shall look at these *costs* (the prime costs and the various expenses) from a different angle. We shall:

- examine the *behaviour* of these costs in relation to manufacturing output and trading activity
- calculate the output required in order to cover total costs, i.e. break even (the *break-even point*)
- consider the implications of increasing or reducing output
- use *break-even analysis* as a decision-making tool and planning aid when deciding/ calculating:
- decide whether or not to accept new orders at reduced rates
- calculate the maximum profit with limited resources (e.g. limited supply of material)
- calculate the sales necessary to achieve a target profit
- decide whether to manufacture or buy goods for resale

10.1 Cost behaviour – How do costs behave in relation to manufacturing output and trading activity?

Generally, the more units you manufacture or buy and sell the more costs you incur, i.e. generally as output/trading activity increases so too do costs.

Think about the *direct material and direct labour*, these may *vary in direct proportion to the level of output*, e.g.

Structure of Accounts

Direct material   A table manufacturer who needs one piece of wood costing £10 to manufacture one table, will need two pieces, costing £20, to manufacture two tables, etc (assuming no wastage or discounts for bulk buying). The cost will therefore vary in direct proportion to output.

Direct labour   If employees are paid £5 for every table they manufacture (i.e. piece rate) the *direct labour cost* of one table is £5; two tables are £10, etc. The cost will therefore vary in direct proportion to output.

But not all costs vary in direct proportion to output, some costs are *fixed (unaffected by changes in the output)*, e.g.

Rent   A company may pay £10,000 p.a. for the rent of its factory. It is £10,000 whether they manufacture one item or ten million items. *The cost is therefore unaffected by changes in the output.*

Insurance   The company may pay £2,000 p.a. Once again this *cost is unaffected by changes in output.*

This does not mean that *fixed costs* will not alter, e.g. next year the rent may increase to £1,200, but this increase (or change) is not as a direct result of an increase in output.

Are all costs either variable or fixed?

No.

Some costs, such as electricity, may be *partly fixed and partly variable*, e.g:

Electricity   The lights and heating will be running whether tables are being produced or whether the workers are sitting idle *(fixed cost element)*, but the electricity used to power the cutting machines will be used only when production takes place *(variable cost element)*.

So, when we are considering cost behaviour in relation to output we can divide costs into three types:

Variable costs   Those that vary in direct proportion to the level of output

Fixed costs   Those that are unaffected by changes in the output

                and

Semi-variable   Costs partly fixed and partly variable

Let us use this knowledge to calculate the break-even point

10.2 What is break-even analysis?

Break-even analysis is a method of identifying the volume of sales required at a given sales price in order to break even, i.e. in order to cover total costs (fixed; variable and semi-variable), neither making a profit nor a loss.

10 – Decision Making

However, as you will discover later, the analysis is based on a number of assumptions, the main one being that costs can be identified as being either fixed or variable. If you are given information about semi-variable costs you will therefore need to identify the fixed and variable elements.

Calculating the break-even point

Example

Lighting Limited manufacture table lamps. It presents you with the following information and asks you to calculate its break-even point (the volume of sales required at a given sales price in order to break even, i.e. in order to cover total costs (fixed and variable)).

Selling price per unit	£50
Direct material per unit	£20
Direct labour per unit (assume paid piece rate, therefore variable)	£10
Variable overheads per unit	£5
Fixed costs per annum	£15,000

We can calculate the break-even point a number of ways. Here is the easiest method:

Step 1 – calculate the contribution per unit,

This is simply:

$$\text{CONTRIBUTION} = \text{Sales} \\ \underline{\text{less variable costs}} \\ \underline{\text{Contribution}}$$

Table 10.1: Lighting Limited — *Per unit*

	£	£
Sales		50
less variable costs		
Direct material	20	
Direct labour	10	
Variable overheads	<u>5</u>	<u>35</u>
Contribution per unit		<u>15</u>

Therefore every table lamp we sell will contributes £15.

But contributes £15 towards what?

Towards eliminating the fixed costs of £15,000 which we have yet to consider. Once we have enough £15s to eliminate the fixed costs, we can start to make a profit.

Structure of Accounts

Step 2 – calculate the break-even point.

$$\text{Break-even point (units)} = \frac{\text{Total Fixed costs}}{\text{Contribution per unit}}$$

$$\frac{£15,000}{£15} = 1,000 \text{ units}$$

Therefore we need to sell 1,000 units in order to break even (cover total costs) which in terms of sales revenue equals:

1,000 units x £50 selling price per unit = £50,000

Table 10.2: Break-even point

	£ per unit					
Sales	50	x	1,000	=		£50,000
less variable costs						
Direct material	20	x	10,000	=	£20,000	
Direct labour	10	x	10,000	=	£10,000	
Variable overheads	5	x	10,000	=	£50,000	£35,000
Contribution	15	x	10,000	=		15,000
less fixed costs						15,000
Profit/loss						0

At 1001 units of sales, the additional unit creates an additional contribution of £15 and therefore a profit of £15. But at 999 units of sales, we lose £15 of contribution, therefore fixed costs are not eliminated and we have a loss of £15.

Let us look at another method of calculating the break-even point.

Step 1 – calculate the contribution/sales ratio

Sales	£50	100%
less Variable cost	£35	70%
Contribution	£15	30%

$$\text{Contribution/sales ratio} = \frac{\text{Contribution}}{\text{Sales}} \times 100$$

$$\frac{15}{50} \times 100 = 30\%$$

10 – Decision Making

i.e. every £1 of sales will provide 30p contribution.

Step 2 – Calculate the break-even point in terms of sales revenue

We can calculate the break-even point in terms of revenue by calculating how many 30ps, and hence £1 of sales, are required to cover fixed costs of £15,000 and therefore break even.

$$\text{Break-even point (£)} = \frac{\text{Total fixed costs}}{\text{Contribution/sales ratio}}$$

$$\frac{15000}{0.30} = £50,000$$

$$\text{Therefore, the break-even point in terms of units} = \frac{£50,000}{£50} = 1000 \text{ units}$$

Margin of safety

Having calculated the break-even point, the directors of Lighting Limited may wish to calculate the *margin of safety*. This is the amount by which forecast sales exceed the break-even point.

Lighting Limited

Forecast sales	2,000 units	100%
Break-even point	1,000 units	50%
Margin of safety	1,000 units	50%

In the case of Lighting Limited, sales can drop by 50% before a loss will result.

The margin of safety allows a company to assess its degree of risk. For example, a margin of safety of only 1% would indicate that if sales fell by more than 1% of the budgeted figure a loss would result.

We can also calculated the *margin of safety* as follows:

$$\frac{\text{Margin of safety}}{\text{Forecast sales}} \times 100$$

$$\frac{1,000}{2,000} \times 100 = 50\%$$

10.3 Break-even charts

The break-even point can also be found, or presented, by means of a break-even chart or graph (Figure 10.1).

Structure of Accounts

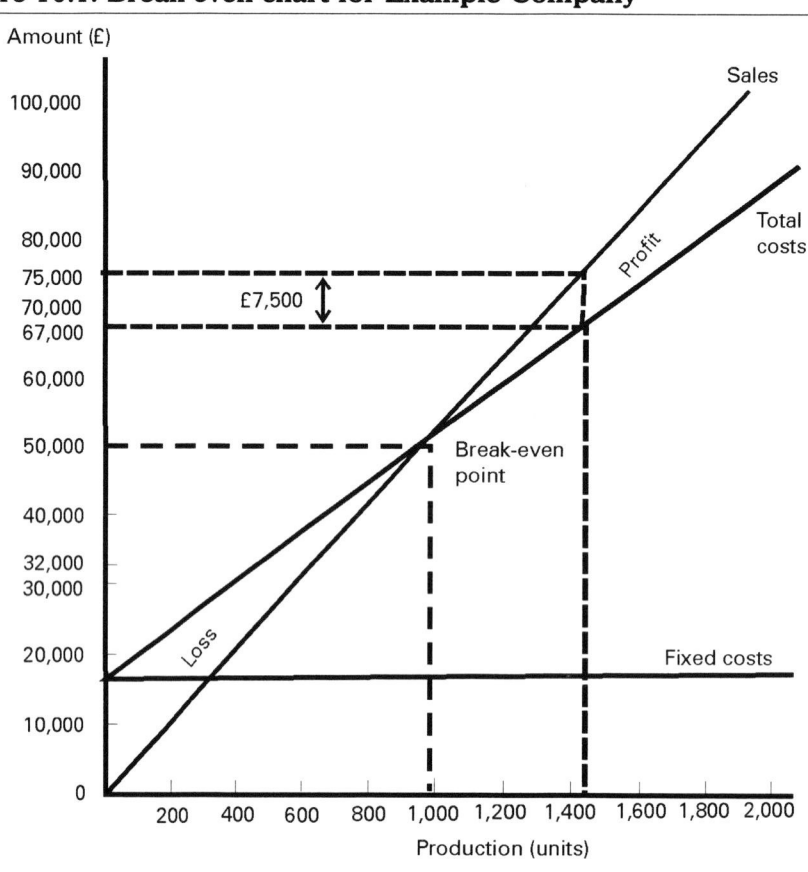

Figure 10.1: Break-even chart for Example Company

[Break-even chart showing Amount (£) on vertical axis from 0 to 100,000 and Production (units) on horizontal axis from 0 to 2,000. Lines shown: Sales, Total costs, Fixed costs. Break-even point marked. Profit of £7,500 indicated between £75,000 and £67,500 levels. Loss region shown on left of break-even point.]

Procedure/hints

a) Label each axis:

- horizontal axis – units of production
- vertical axis – amount (£)

b) As fixed costs are £15,000, we can draw this as a straight horizontal line.

c) The variable costs are then built on the fixed cost line to form the *total cost line*, e.g.

Production 0 units	Fixed cost	= £15,000	
	Variable cost	= 0	
	Plot at	£15,000	
Production 500 units	Fixed cost	= £15,000	
	Variable cost	= £17,500	(500 x £35)
	Plot at	£32,500	

10 – Decision Making

As we assume that variable costs vary in proportion to output (i.e. a linear relationship), the line will be a straight line, therefore you will need to work out only two points.

d) Plot the sales revenue line.

e) The point where the sales revenue and the total cost lines cross is the break-even point, which you can then read off in terms of units or £.

f) *Do not forget* a title.

The chart can also be used to calculate the profit or loss at various levels of sales, e.g.

At sales of 1,500 units –	Sales	£75,000
	Total costs	£67,500
	Profit	£7,500

10.4 The implications of increasing or reducing output

Reduction in output

A reduction in sales volume will affect every business unless it is able to reduce its costs proportionately. Unfortunately, a company may not be able to reduce its fixed costs, e.g.

Table 10.3: High Fixed Limited

	10,000 units	8,000 units
Sales (at £10 per unit)	£100,000	£80,000
less variable costs (£5 per unit)	£50,000	£40,000
Contribution	£50,000	£40,000
less Fixed costs	£40,000	£40,000
Net profit	£10,000	Nil

As a result companies with a high proportion of fixed costs will be badly affected by a *reduction* in volume, whereas those with mainly variable costs will be less affected.

The opposite, however, is also true.

Increase in output

Where a company has a high proportion of fixed costs it will benefit more than those with high variable costs if sales volume can be *increased*, e.g.

Table 10.4: High Fixed Limited

	10,000 units	12,000 units
Sales (at £10 per unit)	£100,000	£120,000
less Variable costs (at £5 per unit)	£50,000	£60,000
Contribution	£50,000	£60,000
less Fixed costs	£40,000	£40,000
	£10,000	£20,000

Table 10.5: High Variable Limited

	10,000 units	12,000 units
Sales (at £10 per unit)	£100,000	£120,000
less Variable costs (at £7 per unit)	£70,000	£84,000
Contribution	£30,000	£36,000
less Fixed costs	£20,000	£20,000
	£10,000	£16,000

Therefore:

Reduction in output

Company cost structure	Effect	Reason
High proportion of fixed costs	Badly affected	Costs remain high (fixed) but output has reduced
Mainly variable costs	Less affected	Costs reduce in line with output

Increase in output

Company cost structure	Effect	Reason
High proportion of fixed costs	Benefit more than those with mainly variable costs	Costs do not increase but output has
Mainly variable costs	Benefit less from increases in output	While output has increased so too have costs

10 – Decision Making

10.5 The use of break-even analysis as a decision-making tool and planning aid

In this section we shall use break-even analysis as a decision-making tool and planning aid, addressing the following issues:

- whether or not to accept new orders at reduced rates
- the maximum profit with limited resources (e.g. limited supply of material)
- the sales necessary to achieve a target profit
- whether to manufacture or buy goods for resale

Deciding whether or not to accept new orders at reduced rates

Example

Lighting Limited have been asked to supply one of the top hotel groups, Mansion plc, with 500 table lamps. While management feel this order may lead to further business, they are not sure whether to accept it, as Mansion plc are prepared to pay only £40 per lamp (£10 less than normal selling price).

Provided that there is spare capacity and that the only additional costs to be incurred from accepting this order are variable costs, the order can be accepted because it will still produce a positive contribution (albeit a reduction on the normal contribution):

Selling price	£40
less variable costs	£35
Contribution	£5

Fixed costs are covered by the normal production and therefore any contribution will be welcome.

Achieving maximum profit with limited resources

While a detailed examination of 'how to achieve maximum profit with limited resources using break-even analysis' may be going beyond the requirements of the syllabus, it is worthwhile considering in order to fully understand the use of break-even analysis.

Example

Lighting has now developed a range of products (Traditional, European and High Tech), all of which use the same basic materials but vary slightly in design and quantity of material.

Unfortunately, Lighting has insufficient material to manufacture the anticipated (budgeted) sales of all the products and ask your help in deciding the optimum level of production, i.e. which designs to produce with the limited resources available (in this case material).

Structure of Accounts

Table 10.6

	Price/Cost per unit			
	Traditional	European	High Tech	Total
Sales		50	60	65	175
less variable costs				
Direct material	20		30		25	
Direct labour	15	35	10	40	23	48	123
Contribution		15		20		17	52
Budgeted sales		2,000		2,000		2,000	6,000

In this example raw material is limited to £120,000 worth, which is insufficient to manufacture the anticipated sales of all the products (i.e. this is the *limiting factor*). In other questions cash or labour could be the limiting factor.

Total fixed costs = £50,000

Calculating the optimum level of production with a limiting factor

Step 1 – Calculate the contribution for each product (Sales less variable costs)

	Traditional	European	High Tech
Contribution per unit	15	20	17

If there were no limiting factors we could say that the European designs are more valuable to the company as they contribute more.

But in our case, they also use more of the limiting factor (raw material).

	Traditional	European	High Tech
Raw material per unit	20	30	25

Step 2 – calculate the contribution per £1 of limiting factor

	Traditional	European	High tech
Contribution	15	20	17
Raw material	20	30	25
Contribution per £1 of limiting factor	15/20	20/30	17/25
	0.75	0.66	0.68

We can now see that for every £1 of raw material used, Traditional lamps will provide £0.75p of contribution, whereas European lamps will provide only £0.66p of contribution

10 – Decision Making

and High Tech lamps £0.68p of contribution.

Therefore, Traditional makes best use of the scarce resource (or limiting factor as it is known), and we should therefore:

- use the raw material to first produce Traditional lamps, then
- High Tech lamps (which makes second best use of the limiting factor)
- finally, if we have any material left, we should produce European lamps.

If you find this difficult to accept and feel that a greater profit could be achieved by producing in order of the highest contribution per unit, consider the next example.

	Product A	Product B
Contribution per unit	£20	£200
Kg required to produce 1 unit	1	1,000

On the face of it, Product B is of greater benefit to the company (it has a higher contribution per unit), but imagine if the total stock of material was 1,000 kg, then:

	Product A	Product B
Contribution per unit	£20	£200
Kg required per unit	1 kg	1,000 kg
Maximum production	1,000 units	1 unit
Total contribution at maximum production	£20,000	£200

So, one unit of Product B contributes more than one unit of Product A but with the limited raw material available we can produce far more units of Product A and the total contribution of these units is greater than producing one unit of Product B.

In conclusion, we calculate and produce in order of *contribution per £1 of limiting factor*:

- Traditional   £0.75
- High tech   £0.68
- European   £0.66

Step 3 – Calculate the production levels

a) *Traditional:*

Material required = budgeted sales x raw material per unit
  = 2,000   x £20
  = £40,000

this leaves £80,000 of raw material to produce High Tech and European:

Structure of Accounts

Total material available	£120,000
less used re Traditional	£40,000
Left	£80,000

b) *High Tech:*

Material required = budgeted sales x raw material per unit

= 2,000   x £25

= £50,000

Therefore we now have only £30,000 of material left with which to produce High Tech lamps:

Total material available	£120,000
less used re Traditional	£40,000
Left	£80,000
less used re High Tech	£50,000
	£30,000

c) *European:*

As we only have £30,000 worth of material left we can only make:

$$\frac{\text{Stock of raw material}}{\text{Raw material per unit}} = \text{Production}$$

$$\frac{£30,000}{£30} = 1000 \text{ units}$$

Step 4 – Calculate the profit based on the identified levels of production

	Traditional	European	High Tech	Total
Contribution (unit)	£15	£20	£17	
Production	2,000	2,000	1,000	
Total contribution	£30,000	£40,000	£17,000	£87,000
less				
Fixed costs				£20,000
Profit				£67,000

You could have calculated the contribution for each product as follows, but I think you will agree that the above calculation is far easier.

10 – Decision Making

Traditional

Sales	(2,000 x £50)		£100,000
less variable costs			
Direct material	(2,000 x £20)	£40,000	
Direct labour	(2,000 x £15)	£30,000	£70,000
Contribution			£30,000

Calculating the sales necessary to achieve target profits

If we were asked to calculate the number of units required to achieve a profit of say £300,000, this could be found as follows:

$$\text{sales (units)} = \frac{\text{Fixed costs} + \text{required profit}}{\text{contribution per unit}}$$

In other words, there needs to be sufficient contribution in order to:

- cover the fixed costs, and
- to achieve the required profit.

Example

Sales per unit	20
Variable costs per unit	10
Contribution per unit	10
Fixed costs =	£200,000
Required profit =	£300,000

$$\text{sales required units} = \frac{£200,000 + £300,000}{£10}$$

50,000 units

Make or buy decisions

Companies may be faced with a decision of whether to continue making certain components or to buy them in. Break-even analysis can assist this decision by analysing the costs saved as a result of stopping production compared with the extra costs incurred resulting from buying the components. The study text provides a number of numerical examples for your consideration.

Apart from purely financial considerations, the company would need to consider whether they can be sure of delivery, quality and continued supply if they decide to purchase the components.

Structure of Accounts

Assumptions/limitations

At the start of this chapter I stated that break-even analysis is based on a number of assumptions which we must consider when assessing its value:

a) Costs can be defined as fixed or variable.

   As we have seen, some costs are semi-variable and management will therefore need to assess the fixed and variable elements.

b) Fixed costs will remain constant.

   Fixed costs may, in fact, increase at certain levels of output, e.g. at 80 per cent capacity more factory space may be required. This can, however, be built into the break-even analysis, giving a stepped fixed cost line (Figure 10.2).

Figure 10.2: Stepped fixed cost line

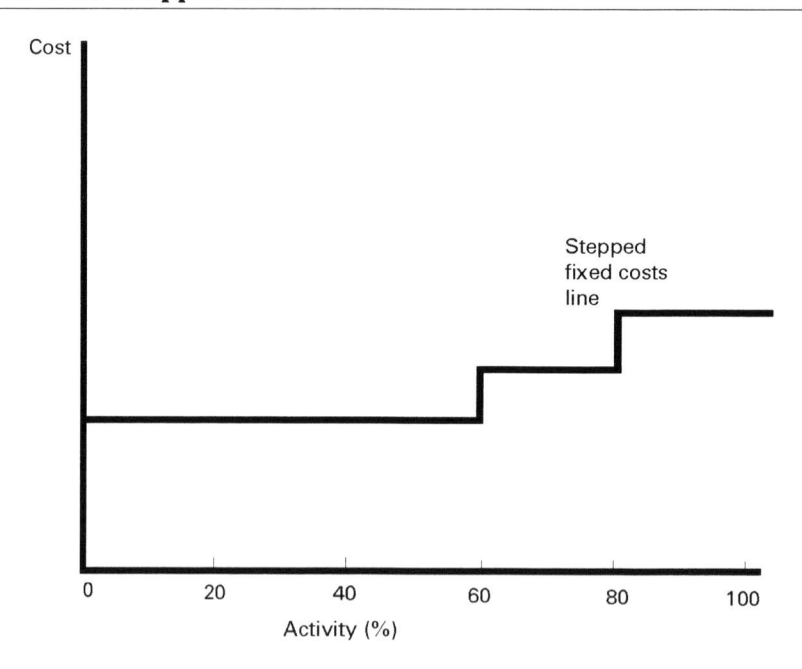

c) Variable costs vary proportionally with output (linear relationship).

   At certain levels of production additional costs may be incurred, e.g. factory workers (*direct labour*) paid on piece rate (so much per unit produced) may be paid a bonus at certain levels of production.

   At certain levels of production savings may be made, e.g. *direct material*; at low levels of production you may pay £10 per unit but at higher levels of production you may be able to get a discount for bulk buying.

10 – Decision Making

In addition, some costs are semi-variable, which as you know do not vary in direct proportion to output.

c) The only factor affecting costs and revenue is volume. In practice managerial decisions can alter costs, e.g. they can replace a small labour team (variable cost) with an automatic machine (fixed cost).

d) Technology and production methods remain unchanged.

e) Price stability.

f) The analysis relates to one particular product or a constant product mix.

g) No stock level changes.

Structure of Accounts

Summary

1 *Break-even analysis is* a method of identifying the volume of sales required at a given sales price in order to break even.

2 The *main assumption* on which the analysis is based is that costs can be identified as either fixed or variable.

3 *Fixed costs* are costs that are unaffected by changes in the volume of output, e.g. rates. Fixed costs may, however, alter in the future, but not as a result of changes in output.

4 *Variable costs* are costs that vary in proportion to the level of output.

5 *Semi-variable costs* are costs that have a fixed and variable element.

6 *Calculating the break-even point*

   a) Calculate the *contribution* per unit

   $$\text{Contribution} = \text{sales} - \text{variable costs}$$

   b) Calculate the break-even point

   $$\text{Break-even point} = \frac{\text{Total fixed costs}}{\text{Contribution per unit}}$$

7 *Contribution/Sales ratio indicates* how much the sale of each unit contributes towards eliminating fixed costs.

   $$\text{Contribution/Sales ratio} = \frac{\text{Contribution}}{\text{sales}} \times 100$$

   This indicates the amount of contribution for every £1 of sales.

8 $$\text{Break-even point (£)} = \frac{\text{Total fixed costs}}{\text{contribution/sales ratio}}$$

9 *Break-even charts* can also be used to find or represent the break-even point.

   Procedure

   a) Label axes;

   b) Plot fixed cost line;

   c) Build the variable cost line on to the fixed cost line to form *total costs*;

   d) Plot the sales revenue;

   e) Where the sales revenue and total cost lines cross is the break-even point;

   f) Do not forget a title.

10 *Margin of safety* is the amount by which forecast sales exceed the break-even point, which allows the company to assess its degree of risk

10 – Decision Making

$$\frac{\text{Margin of safety}}{\text{Forecast sales}} \times 100$$

11 *Use of break-even analysis as a decision-making tool and planning aid;*

   a) deciding whether or not to accept new orders at reduced rates;

   b) achieving maximum profit with unlimited resources;

      Step 1 – calculate the contribution for each product;

      Step 2 – calculate the contribution per £1 of limiting factor;

      Step 3 – calculate the production levels, producing those with the highest contribution per £1 of limiting factor first;

      Step 4 – calculate the profit.

   c) Calculating the sales necessary to achieve target profits;

$$\text{Sales (units)} = \frac{\text{Fixed costs} + \text{required profit}}{\text{contribution per unit}}$$

   d) make or buy decisions.

12 Assumption of break-even analysis

   a) cost can be defined as fixed or variable;

   b) fixed cost will remain constant and variable costs vary proportionally with output;

   c) the only factor affecting costs and revenue is volume;

   d) technology and production methods remain unchanged;

   e) price stability;

   f) the analysis relates to one particular product or a constant product mix;

   g) no stock level changes.

Structure of Accounts

SECTION C
CASH AND LIQUIDITY

So far we have concentrated on preparing the final accounts of:

- Sole traders;
- Partnerships;
- Limited companies and
- Manufacturing companies

in order to determine their profitability.

Clearly it is important for a business to be profitable. No business would survive long if it bought goods costing £5 per unit and sold them for £3 per unit.

However it is just as important to be able to pay your bills as they fall due. Consider the following company:

Day 1 purchase 1000 units at £10 per unit *in cash*

Day 2 sell 1000 units at £20 per unit *on 3 months credit*

After Day 2 the trading profit and loss account would be as follows:

Sales		20,000
less cost of goods sold		
opening stock	Nil	
+ purchases	10000	
	10000	
Closing stock	Nil	10,000
Gross profit		10,000
– expenses		Nil
Net profit		10,000

The company *appears* extremely profitable, it sells goods at 100% mark up and *appears* to have relatively cheap sources of supply and/or an ability to market its goods effectively while also keeping expenses under control.

Structure of Accounts

But how will the company pay its bills – wages, rent light, heat, etc. before it receives payment in three months time and how will it buy new stock? Many companies do so by borrowing from their bank, though at a cost – interest.

In addition what happens if:

- it incurs bad debts?
- the cost of supplies (purchases) goes up?
- competition moves into the market, forcing its sale price (sales) down?

And what if the bank refuses to provide the necessary finance?

The answer is, the company may have to cease trading, not because it is not profitable but because it cannot pay its bills as they fall due – put simply it lacks liquidity.

Over the next four chapters we will turn our attention to the subject of – cash and liquidity:

Chapter 11   Analysing our **Cash and Working Capital** needs

Chapter 12   Reconciling the bank balance – **Bank Reconciliation Statements**

Chapter 13   Preparing and interpreting **Cash Flow Statements (FRS 1)**

Chapter 14   Forecasting *future* cash requirements – **Cash Forecasts**

11
CASH AND WORKING CAPITAL

Syllabus Objectives
4.1 Buying and selling in a trading context

4.2 Working capital/Liquidity

   Its importance and matching long-term uses with long-term sources of cash.

Learning Objectives
After studying this chapter you should be able to:

1   Define working capital;

2   Appreciate the importance of working capital;

3   Describe the flow of funds cycle;

4   Calculate working capital and the flow of funds cycle;

5   State ways in which working capital can be kept to a minimum.

11.1   Introduction – What is working capital?

In the introduction to this section we saw the need for cash and liquidity. An examination of a company's working capital position will help us to determine the present and future level of liquidity required.

Working capital is often described as the blood flowing through a business; without an *adequate* supply the business will cease trading.

It is calculated in the following manner:

Current Assets	less	Current Liabilities
(Cash or items that can		(Amounts owed and due for
be converted into cash)		repayment within 12 months)

This is often expressed in the form of a ratio, e.g.

Structure of Accounts

Current Assets	–	Current Liabilities	=	Working Capital
£10,000	–	£5,000	=	£5,000
2	:	1		

You should always indicate how many times current liabilities are covered. In the last example they were covered twice. However, the situation may be as follows:

Current Assets	–	Current Liabilities	=	Working Capital
£5,000	–	£10,000	=	£5,000

Current assets cover only half of the current liabilities and the ratio will, therefore, be expressed as:

0.5 : 1

11.2 Assessing a company's working capital position

So which company has an *adequate* level of working capital, the one with a ratio of 2:1 or the one with a ratio of 0.5: 1?

From what we have said so far you might well assume that it is the company with the ratio of 2:1. After all *current assets* (cash or items that can be converted into cash) are twice as much as *current liabilities* (amounts owed and due for repayment within 12 months).

Unfortunately it is not that simple, we must consider:

a) The components of the calculation, i.e. the specific Current Assets and Current Liabilities;

b) The nature of the company's industry, i.e. whether it is in an industry where cash flows through the business quickly or not.

The components of the calculation

Consider the position of Hi-Fi Equipment:

11 – Cash and Working Capital

Table 11.1: Balance sheet extract of Hi-Fi Equipment Ltd as at 31.12.Y0

	£	£
Current assets		
Stock		100,000
Debtors		100,000
Bank		12,000
Cash		579
		212,579
less current liabilities		
Taxation	9,000	
Creditors	70,000	
Accrued expenses	298	79,298
Working capital		133,281

On the face of it its working capital position would appear to be satisfactory. Cash or items that can be converted into cash cover amounts due for repayment within 12 months almost 2.7 times:

$$\frac{\text{Current assets}}{\text{Current liabilities}} \quad \frac{212579}{79298} \quad = \quad 2.7 \text{ times}$$

Current assets	:	Current liabilities
2.7	:	1

But what if:

i) *Stock* includes bad stock of £80,000 which needs to be written off;

ii) *Debtors* includes bad debts of £70,000 which, once again, need to be written off and other debtors who were not due to pay for over 3 months;

iii) *Creditors* were all pressing for payment in the next day or so.

The true position is really:

Structure of Accounts

Current assets

Stock	(100,000 - 80,000)	20,000
Debtors	(100,000 - 70,000)	30,000
Bank		12,000
Cash		<u>579</u>
		62,579

less current liabilities

Taxation	9,000	
Creditors	70,000	
Accrued expenses	<u>298</u>	<u>79,298</u>
Working capital		(<u>16,719</u>)

$$\frac{\text{Current assets}}{\text{Current liabilities}} \quad \frac{62579}{79298} = 0.8 \text{ times}$$

Current assets : Current liabilities
0.8 : 1

As you can see, the balance sheet can be misleading and we must, therefore, consider the *components of the working capital calculations* and, in particular, when payments and receipts are due.

One component we have not yet considered is the bank.

Bank

A balance sheet is only a photograph of a company *as at* a particular date (the balance sheet date). As a result the balance sheet as at 31.12.Y0 may record bank as a current asset of £12,000, even though the position has since changed, possibly to an overdraft!

Look at the effect that spending cash can have.

What effect will there be on the working capital position if a cheque for £15,000 was written:

a) *to buy fixed assets and*

b) *to buy additional stock?*

a) The purchase of fixed assets will affect the balance sheet as follows:
- Fixed assets   increase by £15,000
- Current assets (bank)   reduce by £15,000

The reduction in liquidity will therefore be reflected in their working capital figure and ratio.

11 – Cash and Working Capital

b) The purchase of additional stock will affect the balance sheet as follows:
- Current assets (stock)   increase by £15,000
- Current assets (bank)   reduce by £15,000

The calculation of working capital and the working capital ratio will therefore be the same as before – *but* it should be clear that the company is less liquid. If the bank is unwilling to extend the overdraft further and creditors press for payment and/or if bills need to be paid, the company would first need to sell its stock and, if selling on credit, wait for its debtors to pay, before the company could generate cash.

The nature of the company's industry

As we have seen, Hi-Fi's apparently satisfactory ratio of 2.7:1 can, in reality, be worse. Does this mean that a company with a ratio of only 0.5:1 will, in reality, be in an even worse position, if in fact 0.5:1 is a bad position?

The answer is *'No, not necessarily'*.

An examination of the component parts may not reveal the problems encountered by Hi-Fi Equipment Ltd. It may even reveal that 0.5:1, is satisfactory due to the nature of its industry.

Imagine the company with a ratio of 0.5: 1 was a supermarket. Will it need a higher level of working capital?:

Stock   A lot of stock is sold every day which therefore generates a lot of cash. In addition stock must be kept low otherwise goods will go off.

Debtors   Most customers pay by cheque or cash which means that cash is generated quickly. (Note that even when customers pay by credit card, this generates cash immediately for the store.)

Creditors   Supermarkets have strong buying power and are usually able to negotiate good credit terms. As a result creditors may be large but may not be due for payment for some time.

In other words, 0.5:1 *can be* satisfactory, provided the 0.5 flows in quicker than the 1 flows out.

However, it is important to remember that many expenses need to be paid in advance, such as rent and rates. Therefore, even if a customer sells on cash terms and is able to secure long credit terms for suppliers, he or she will still need to pay these items in advance. Similarly, he or she will also need to maintain a cash float for day-to-day use.

As a result, working capital may still be required by food retailers, although the published accounts of the large superstores (e.g. Tesco) demonstrate their ability to operate profitably on working capital ratios of considerably less than 1:1.

Let us take a closer look at a company's working capital position and in particular how quickly cash does flow into and out of the business by examining its *cash cycle/flow of funds*.

Structure of Accounts

11.3 Cash cycle/flow of funds

The cash cycle of many companies follows the pattern below (*see* Figure 11.1):

- they buy goods or material on credit;
- with the material they manufacture stock for resale;
- they make sales on credit to debtors;
- they receive cash from their debtors at a later date; which
- enables them to repay their creditors.

There may also be breaks in the cycle for:

- Bad stock, and
- Bad debts.

Figure 11.1: Cash cycle/flow of funds

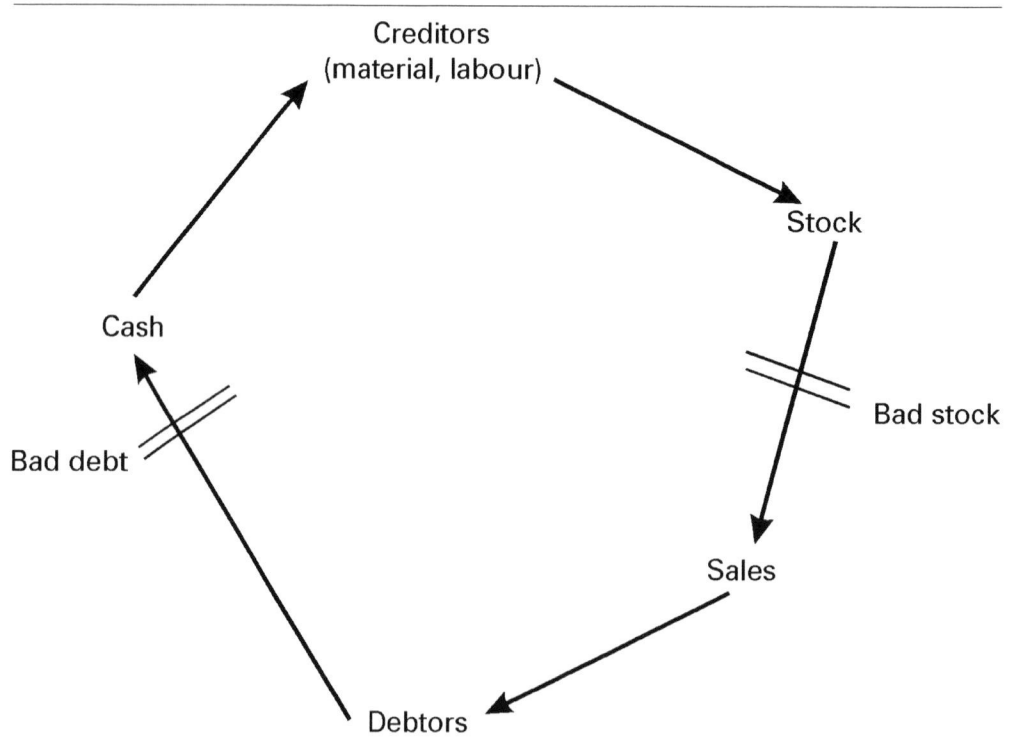

We can calculate the company's cash cycle using the following ratios:

11 – Cash and Working Capital

a) *Average stock turnover*

$$\frac{\text{Average stock}}{\text{Cost of goods sold}} \times 365 = \text{average number of days to turn stock}$$

N.B.: Average Stock $= \dfrac{\text{Opening stock} + \text{closing stock}}{2}$

If you are not given sufficient information to calculate average stock, it is quite acceptable to use the stock figure you have been given.

b) *Average debtors' settlement period*

$$\frac{\text{Debtors}}{\text{Sales}} \times 365 = \text{average number of days before debtors settle their debts}$$

c) *Average creditors' settlement period*

$$\frac{\text{Creditors}}{\text{Purchases}} \times 365 = \text{average number of days before we pay our creditors}$$

What does the following information tell you about the working capital position and cash cycle of Grassington Ltd?

	£
Sales	2 700
Purchases	1 800
Cost of goods sold	1 830
Average trade debtors outstanding	300
Average trade creditors outstanding	160
Average stocks held	305

All purchases and sales are made on credit, and trading transactions are expected to occur at an even rate throughout the year.

Assuming Grassington Ltd has no other current assets or current liabilities, its working capital is, *on average*:

Structure of Accounts

Current assets	£
Stock	305
Debtors	300
	605
less current liabilities	
Creditors	160
Working capital	**445**

$$\frac{\text{Current assets}}{\text{Current liabilities}} \quad \frac{605}{160} = 3.8 \text{ times}$$

Current assets : Current liabilities
3.8 : 1

Using the above ratios we can see whether this level of working capital is *adequate* given the company's current cash flow cycle:

a) *Average stock turnover*

$$\frac{\text{Average stock}}{\text{Cost of goods sold}} \times 365 = \text{average number of days to turn stock}$$

$$\frac{305}{1830} \times 365 = 60.83 \text{ days}$$

Note: This is an average, some stock may be sold on Day 1, other stock may take 120 days.

b) *Average debtors' settlement period*

$$\frac{\text{Debtors}}{\text{Sales}} \times 365 = \text{average number of days before debtors settle their debts}$$

$$\frac{300}{2700} \times 365 = 40.55 \text{ days}$$

Note: This is an average, some debtors may pay cash on Day 1, other debtors may pay after 80 days.

c) *Average creditors' settlement period*

$$\frac{\text{Creditors}}{\text{Purchases}} \times 365 = \text{average number of days before we pay our creditors}$$

$$\frac{160}{1800} \times 365 = 32.44 \text{ days}$$

Note: This is an average, some creditors may allow us 64 days credit, others may want paying now.

11 – Cash and Working Capital

Therefore *on average*, Grassington take:

	60.83	days to turn (sell) their stock
plus a further	40.55	days before the debtors settle their debts,
	101.38	days from sale to payment.
	32.44	days before they pay their creditors
	68.94	days working capital required

As a result Grassington must maintain a level of working capital in order to meet its debts as they fall due and to ensure adequate levels of stock.

If current assets were equal only to current liabilities it would, therefore, be unable to pay its creditors when requested to do so, and may also need to pay certain expenses in advance.

With a working capital ratio of 3.78:1 it would appear that Grassington has an *adequate* level of working capital, although we must consider:

- What we said about the component parts; do the stock and debtors figures include bad stock and bad debts that need writing off?
- The fact that the ratios are only averages.

We also need to consider whether it is too high! Maintaining working capital is expensive.

11.4 The cost of maintaining working capital

Having money tied up in working capital is expensive, e.g.

Stock — This will have cost money to buy or produce and earns the company nothing 'sitting on the shelf'. It may even cost the company money storing it – warehouse costs, staff, etc.

Debtors — If you allow your debtors too much credit, you may need to turn to the bank for an overdraft.

Bank — Balances should be kept to a minimum. While it can earn you interest, the return is likely to be less than if it were invested long term or in new machinery which could improve your business.

Cash — Once again, your cash float should be kept to a minimum. Cash will not give you a return and is also a security risk.

Companies should, therefore, keep working capital to a minimum, while ensuring an adequate level.

How do you keep working capital to a minimum and ensure an adequate level of working capital?

1 Monitor *stock* levels and try to predict future demand so that stock is kept to a minimum.

2 Chase *debtors* who fail to pay on time. Obviously, you could demand payment in cash but this may lose you sales.

3 Keep *bank* and *cash* balances to a minimum.

4 Take advantage of *credit* offered, i.e. let your creditors finance your operations although, obviously, you will need to be able to pay them when payment is due.

11.5 Conclusion – The importance of working capital

Working capital could be described as the 'blood' of the business; once it stops *flowing* the business is dead.

As we have seen, it is important for companies to ensure an adequate level of working capital and at the same time that they do not have excessive amounts tied up in working capital.

In addition they must realize that the situation requires constant management; in business nothing is static. If a company wishes to expand it may need to purchase/manufacture more stock, all of which requires money, not only to buy but also to store, pending sale. The additional sales may need to be on credit terms, which will increase debtors and, therefore, investment in working capital may be vital. Many companies forget this when trying to expand too quickly – a problem described as overtrading.

Similarly, companies may need to invest in working capital simply to maintain existing levels of operations, i.e. to meet bills, operate a cash float, or simply due to their cash cycle, as in the case of Grassington Ltd.

11 – Cash and Working Capital

Summary

1. *Working capital = Current Assets – Current Liabilities.*
2. It is often expressed as a *ratio*, in order to reflect how many times current assets cover current liabilities, e.g. 2:1 or 0.5:1.
3. Many companies can operate on ratios of *less than 1:1*.
4. Where the ratio is less than 1:1 it means that, on the face of it, cash or items which can be easily converted into cash do not cover amounts owing and due for repayment within 12 months. This can, obviously, be a problem but may not be.
5. In assessing a company's working capital position we must consider:
   a) *the components of the calculation;*
   b) *the nature of the company's industry.*
6. Even where current assets cover current liabilities companies can be in difficulty if current assets include bad stock/bad debts and/or if creditors are pressing for payment.
7. Although superstores can operate on ratios of less than 1:1 we must not forget that some bills must be paid in advance.
8. *Average stock turnover*

   $$\frac{\text{Average stock}}{\text{Cost of goods sold}} \times 365 = \text{average number of days to turn stock}$$

   N.B.: average stock $= \dfrac{\text{Opening stock + closing stock}}{2}$

9. *Average debtors' settlement period*

   $$\frac{\text{Debtors}}{\text{Sales}} \times 365 = \text{average number of days before debtors settle their debts}$$

10. *Average creditors' settlement period*

    $$\frac{\text{Creditors}}{\text{Purchases}} \times 365 = \text{average number of days before we pay our creditors}$$

11. The *cash operating cycle* examines how quickly a company turns its stock, receives payment from debtors and pays creditors.
12. Working capital is *expensive* and should be kept to a workable minimum.
13. In order to *keep working capital to a minimum* we must:
    - monitor stock levels and predict future demand;
    - chase debtors;
    - keep cash and bank balances to a minimum;
    - take advantage of credit.
14. Working capital is vital for the operation of a business and, particularly, if the company decides to expand.

12

BANK RECONCILIATION STATEMENTS

Syllabus Objectives
4.3 Cash

- Recording and bank reconciliation
- Adjusting for debtors and creditors

Learning Objectives
After studying this chapter you should be able to:
1 Explain the nature and purpose of reconciliation statements;
2 Produce reconciliation statements;
3 Outline what action, if any, should be taken following the production of such statements.

12.1 Introduction – What are reconciliation statements?

In the last chapter we assessed a company's working capital position by examining the company's current assets and current liabilities; after all, working capital = current assets less current liabilities.

One of the difficulties we discovered is that the balance sheet figures may not reflect a true picture:

i) *Stock* may include bad stock which needs to be written off;

ii) *Debtors* may include bad debts which need to be written off

iii) *Creditors* may be pressing for payment in the next day or so.

In addition the bank balance may have changed considerably since the balance sheet date.

I receive such bank statements every month. My statement tells me I am in credit yet I know that when all the cheques I have written are presented my account will be overdrawn!

Personally I am not too concerned about the false credit balance, in fact I would probably be more concerned if I knew the truth!

12 – Bank Reconciliation Statements

Companies on the other hand need to know their correct position at any moment in time, otherwise they may have surplus cash sitting idle or go overdrawn without notice, risking bank charges and/or having their cheques returned unpaid which would harm their ability to secure credit terms in the future.

As a result a company will need to reconcile its position by preparing a *bank reconciliation statement*.

Reconciliation statements

Reconciliation statements are statements drawn up to confirm whether or not the entries in two separate records, which relate to the same transaction, are consistent, for example:

- does the bank "T"account kept by the company agree with the bank statement?
- does the purchase account relating to an amount owed to a supplier agree with the statement of account received from the supplier?

In this chapter we are concerned with *bank reconciliation statements*.

12.2 Bank reconciliation statements

A bank reconciliation statement will indicate why the bank statement does not agree with the company's own record.

If you think about it there can be only four reasons why the bank statement and the company's own record do not agree *(in points a - d the terms debit and credit refer to their traditional usage in banking)*:

a) The bank has not recorded/received certain credits that the company has recorded/received, e.g. cheques received and about to be banked

b) The bank has not recorded/deducted certain debits that the company has recorded, e.g. the company has issued a cheque and therefore deducted the amount from its records yet the payee has not presented the cheque to the bank for payment, i.e. unpresented cheques

c) The company has not recorded/deducted certain debits that the bank has deducted, e.g. bank charges or items deducted in error

d) The company has not recorded certain credits that the bank has recorded, e.g. credits going direct to the bank or items credited in error

Example

Hughes Supplies Ltd has, today, received its bank statement which shows the balance at the close of business on 31.1.Y0 as £4,290. It cannot understand this because its own records indicate the balance should be only £2,700.

Draw a bank reconciliation statement to explain the difference:

Structure of Accounts

Table 12.1:   **Bank account**

01.1.Y0	Balance b/f	£2,000	02.1.Y0 Purchases chq 01233		£400
08.1.Y0	V Brown	£1,000	06.1.Y0 Purchases chq 01234		£200
11.1.Y0	D Firth	£750	10.1.Y0 Wages chq 01235		£500
28.1.Y0	I Hardy	£600			
			30.1.Y0 Electricity DD		£200
			30.1.Y0 Purchases chq 01236		£350
			31.1.Y0 Balance c/d		**£2,700**
		£4,350			£4,350

Table 12.2: Bank statement

Date		Payments	Receipts	Balance
01.1.Y0	Opening balance			2,000 Cr
08.1.Y0	Cheque 01234	200		1,800 Cr
10.1.Y0	Cheque 01235	500		1,300 Cr
12.1.Y0	Direct debit Pacific Ins Co	300		1,000 Cr
13.1.Y0	Credit		1,750	2,750 Cr
15.1.Y0	Cheque 01233	400		2,350 Cr
25.1.Y0	Credit		2,150	4,500 Cr
30.1.Y0	Direct debit: Electricity	200		4,300 Cr
31.1.Y0	Charges	10		**4,290 Cr**

Procedure

1   Check that the opening balance of both the cash book and the bank statement agree. If the opening balances do not agree, the reason for the difference in the closing balances may be due to a difference in the previous bank statement and as a result no matter how hard we try to reconcile the two records we will never be successful. We shall look at an example where the balances do not agree later.

In our examples the opening balances agree:

12 – Bank Reconciliation Statements

- bank "T" account   Bal b/f   £2,000
- bank statement   Opening bal   £2,000

We can, therefore, go on to look for the difference between the two records.

2 Tick off the entries which are common to both records,

    e.g. the opening balances as discussed above.

    e.g. Bank "T" account   02.01.Y0   Purchases   £400

          Bank statement   15.01.Y0   Cheque 01233   £400

Table 12.3: Bank account

Date	Description	Amount	Date	Description	Amount
01.1.Y0	Balance b/f	£2,000√	02.1.Y0	Purchases	£400√
08.1.Y0	V Brown	£1,000√	06.1.Y0	Purchases	£200√
11.1.Y0	D Firth	£750√	10.1.Y0	Wages	£500√
28.1.Y0	**I Hardy**	**£600a**	30.1.Y0	Electricity DD	£200√
			30.1.Y0	**Purchases**	**£350b**
			31.1.Y0	Balance c/d	£2,700
		£4,350			£4,350

Table 12.4: Bank statement

Date		Payments	Receipts	Balance
01.1.Y0	Opening balance			2,000 Cr√
08.1.Y0	Cheque 01234	200√		1,800 Cr
10.1.Y0	Cheque 01235	500√		1,300 Cr
12.1.Y0	Direct debit			
	Pacific Ins Co	**300c**		1,000 Cr
13.1.Y0	Credit		1,750√	2,750 Cr
15.1.Y0	Cheque 01233	400√		2,350 Cr
25.1.Y0	**Credit**		**2,150d**	4,500 Cr
30.1.Y0	Direct debit:			
	Electricity	200√		4,300 Cr
31.1.Y0	**Charges**	**10c**		4,290 Cr

181

Structure of Accounts

Note: A credit on the bank statement may be made up of a number of cheques received from various customers, e.g. we can assume that the credit of £1,750 banked on 13.01.Y0 was made up of cheques received from:

V Brown	£1,000
A Firth	£750
	£1,750

Cheques are not necessarily presented in the order they were issued so you may have to search for the entries.

3   At most, you will be left with the 4 sets of unmatched items we spoke of earlier, which I have labelled in the records above **(a) – (d)**:

   a) The bank has not recorded/received certain credits that the company has recorded/received

   I Hardy   £600

   b) The bank has not recorded/deducted certain debits that the company has recorded

   Purchases   £350

   c) The company has not recorded/deducted certain debits that the bank has deducted

   Direct debit   £300

   Charges   £10

   d) The company has not recorded certain credits that the bank has recorded,

   Credit   £2,150

   Items (c) and (d) may need entering in the company's records to bring them up to date, which we shall consider later.

   As it is also possible, that (c) and (d) represent items credited or debited in error by the bank. These would need to be brought to the bank's attention.

4   Draw up a bank reconciliation statement, i.e. start with the bank statement balance and work towards the cash book balance (or vice versa) by entering the unmatched items.

Note: Be careful when dealing with overdrawn accounts.

12 – Bank Reconciliation Statements

Table 12.5: Bank reconciliation statement as at 31.1.Y0

		£	£
	Balance as per bank statement		4,290
a)	add banking/lodgements not credited		600
			4,890
b)	less unpresented cheques – 01236		350
			4,540
c)	add outgoings not entered in the "T" account		
	Direct debit: Pacific Ins Co	300	
	Charges	10	310
			4,850
(d)	less receipts not entered in the "T" account		
	balance as per bank statement		2,150
	Balance as per cash book		2,700

(a) and (b) are straightforward – they have been entered in the cash book but not in the statement, therefore add or deduct them from the bank balance as if they were presented at the bank.

(c) and (d) are more difficult. The statement balance we are working from already includes these items so we must *cancel out their effect*, hence outgoings are added back and receipts are deducted.

As stated earlier, you could start with the cash book balance and work towards the bank statement balance; both are acceptable, but be careful the additions and subtractions are not the same.

Structure of Accounts

Table 12.6: Bank reconciliation statement as at 31.1.Y0

	£	£
Balance as per company records		2,700
less Outgoings not entered in the "T" account		
Direct debit Pacific Ins Co	300	
Bank charges	10	310
		2,390
add receipts not entered in the "T" account		2,150
		4,540
less Banking/lodgements not credited		600
		3,940
add Unpresented cheques		350
Balance as per bank statement		4,290

5 Outline any action you might take to investigate the validity of certain items, e.g. contact the bank. Remember the reason for your difference may be due to items debited or credited in error by the bank.

Updating the cash book

Let us go back to Hughes Supplies Ltd. If the items entered on the bank statement belong to the company, then Hughes Supplies will need to bring its bank "T" account up to date, e.g.

Table 12.7: Bank account

	£		£
Balance b/f	2,700	Direct debit	
		Pacific Ins Co	300
Credit	2,150	Bank charges	10
		Balance c/d	**4,540**
	4,850		4,850

We can then produce a bank reconciliation statement using the updated cash book balance.

12 – Bank Reconciliation Statements

Table 12.8: Bank reconciliation statement as at 31.1.Y0

	£
Balance as per company records	**4,540**
less bankings (lodgements) not credited	600
	3,940
add unpresented cheques	350
Balance as per bank statement	4,290

12.3 Dealing with different opening balances

Let us now look at an example where the opening balances of the two statements do not agree. As we stated earlier, if they do not agree, the reason for our difference in the closing balance may be due to a difference in the previous bank statement and no matter how hard we try to reconcile the two statements to hand we will never be successful.

Example

West Bank Ltd has received its bank statement for the month ending 28.2.Y0 but cannot reconcile this with its accounts.

Table 12.9: Bank statement

	Payments	Receipts	Balance
Feb 1 Opening balance			2,551.88 Cr
2 Credit		136.79	2,688.67 Cr
5 Credit		121.10	2,809.77 Cr
6 Cheque 1042	50.00		2,759.77 Cr
15 Bank giro credit		400.00	3,159.77 Cr
17 Direct debit. Water	40.00		3,119.77 Cr
20 Cheque 1047	51.11		3,068.66 Cr
22 Standing order. Rent	30.00		3,038.66 Cr
27 Credit		360.00	3,398.66 Cr
28 Credit		120.00	3,518.66 Cr
28 Cheque 1051	20.00		3,498.66 Cr

Structure of Accounts

Table 12.10:   **Bank Account**

		£			£
Feb 1	Balance c/f	2 638.67	Feb 6	Electricity	50.00
2	Sales B Black	121.10	17	Purchases	51.11
10	Sales K Allan	200.00	22	Rent	30.00
12	Sales A Burke	175.00	28	Cash	20.00
14	Sales P Platt	25.00	28	Fixtures	1,500.00
22	Sales V Gardner	120.00			
26	Sales J Mannion	240.00			
			28	Balance c/d	1,868.66
		3,519.77			3,519.77

At first sight we cannot tick off the opening balances because they do not agree:

    Bank statement   £2551.88
    Bank "T" account   £2638.67

When faced with this problem, find the difference – in our case £86.79 (£2638.67 – £2551.88).

Then look to see if there are any items in one record that might have appeared in the other record for the previous period.

In this example it *would seem* that the following entries on the bank statement appeared in the "T" account in the previous period, i.e. they are part of the balance b/f £2,638.67:

    Feb 2   Credit   £136.79
    Feb 6   Cheque   – £50.00
    Net   £86.79

In the real world, the company would verify this by checking their records for the previous period, clearly we cannot do this and therefore we have to make the assumption that they have appeared in the company's accounts.

We can, therefore tick off:

- the bank statement   Opening balance   2,551.88
                                     Feb 2 credit   136.79
                                                                 2,688.67
                                     Feb 6 cheque   – 50.00
                                                                  2638.67
- the opening balance of the bank "T" account   2638.67

12 – Bank Reconciliation Statements

We can then proceed as normal, following steps 2 – 5 above:

2) Tick off all common items (remember a credit on the bank statement may be made up of many entries in the company's records);

3) Identify those items not ticked off;

4) Draw up the reconciliation statement;

5) Outline any action you might take to investigate the validity of certain items of difference.

Structure of Accounts

Summary

1. *Reconciliation statements* are statements drawn up to confirm whether or not the entries in two separate records, which relate to the same transaction, are consistent, for example:
   - is the bank "T"account kept by the company consistent with the bank statement?
   - is the purchase account relating to an amount owed to a supplier consistent with the statement of account received from the supplier?

2. A *bank reconciliation statement* will indicate why the bank statement does not agree with the company's own record.

3. There can be only *4 reasons why the bank statement and the company's own record do not agree:*
   a) the bank has not recorded/received certain credits that the company has recorded/received, e.g. credits received and about to be banked
   b) the bank has not recorded/deducted certain debits that the company has recorded, e.g. the company has issued a cheque and therefore deducted the amount from its records yet the payee has not presented the cheque to the bank for payment, i.e. unpresented cheques
   c) the company has not recorded/deducted certain debits that the bank has deducted, e.g. bank charges or items deducted in error
   d) the company has not recorded certain credits that the bank has recorded, e.g. credits going direct to the bank or items credited in error

4. In *drawing a reconciliation statement* you should:
   a) Check that the opening balances agree. If they do not, find the difference and look to see if there are any items on the bank statement that might have appeared in the company's records for the previous period, or vice versa;
   b) Tick off all common items (remember a credit on the bank statement may be made up of many entries in the company's account);
   c) Identify those items not ticked off;
   d) Draw up the reconciliation statement;
   e) Outline any action you might take to investigate the validity of certain items of difference.

5. If requested to do so, the bank "T" account should be *brought up to date* by inserting the entries that appear on the statement but not in the bank "T" account.

6. *Where the opening balances of the two statements do not agree* the reason for our difference in the closing balance may be due to a difference in the previous bank statement and no matter how hard we try to reconcile the two statements to hand we will never be successful.

7. *When the opening balances do not agree* find the difference by looking for any items in one record that might have appeared in the other record for the previous period, then proceed as normal.

13

CASHFLOW STATEMENTS (FRS 1)

Syllabus Objectives

4.4 The cashflow statement (FRS 1)

- Sources of cash (long-term and short-term)
- Uses of cash
- Construction of statement based on final accounts and the adjustments given in Section 1.4 of the syllabus
- Overtrading
- Interpretation of statement (including the use of ratios)

Learning Objectives

After studying this chapter you should be able to:

1. Outline the purpose of a cashflow statement;
2. Identify inflows (sources) and outflows (applications) of cash;
3. Produce cashflow statements that deal with the sale or purchase of assets.

Introduction

In Chapter 11 we discovered that cashflow is as important as profit. Without cash flowing through the business, a company will be unable to pay its debts as they fall due, even if they are able to sell goods at a profit.

As a result the published trading profit and loss account and balance sheet of a company may show a profit but hide a cashflow problem.

Financial Reporting Standard 1 (FRS 1) (one of the accounting rules) makes it obligatory for most businesses to publish what is known as a Cashflow Statement.

13.1 Cashflow statements

The objective of the statement is to show:

- where cash has come from *(INFLOWS)*, and
- where cash has gone *(OUTFLOWS)*.

FRS 1 calls for the *inflows* and *outflows* to be presented under the following seven headings.

1 *Operating activities*

2 *Returns on investment and servicing of finance*

3 *Taxation*

4 *Capital expenditure*

5 *Equity dividends paid*

6 *Management of liquid resources*

7 *Financing*

   Total of inflows less outflows

The total of the seven sections *(inflows less outflows)* should then equal the *analysis of changes in cash/bank during the year*, as illustrated in the example statement below. After all, the company must have got the money to buy or pay for the items listed under the headings from its cash holding or from its bank account.

Example presentation

The cashflow statement opposite shows the various items that may appear under each of the seven headings. This form of presentation is acceptable in the examination, although in practice published statements normally show only the totals for each heading followed by a series of *notes* below the statement detailing the various items under each heading.

13 – Cashflow Statements (FRS 1)

Table 13.1: Cashflow statement for year ended 31 March 19X3

	£	£
Operating activities		
Net profit before tax and interest	11,600	
Depreciation for year	3,800	
Gain on sale of equipment	(400)	
Increase in stock	(1,400)	
Increase in debtors	(400)	
Increase in creditors	1,000	
Net cash inflow from operating activities		14,200
Returns on investments and servicing of finance		
Interest paid	(1,600)	
Interest received	NIL	
Dividends and interest received	NIL	
Net cash outflow from returns on investments and servicing of finance		(1,600)
Taxation		
Tax paid		(6,000)
Capital expenditure		
Purchase of fixed assets	(9,000)	
Sale of fixed assets	1,400	
Net cash outflow from investment activities		(7,600)
Equity dividends paid		
Equity dividends paid		NIL
Management of liquid resources		
Purchase of treasury bills	NIL	
Sale of treasury bills	NIL	NIL
Financing		
New capital/issue of shares/loans	NIL	
Repayment of shares/loans	NIL	
Net cash inflow/outflow from financing		NIL
Decrease in cash/bank		(1,000)
Analysis of changes in cash/bank during year		
Bank balance at start of year		3,000
Net cash outflow		(1,000)
Bank balance at end of year		2,000

Structure of Accounts

Note: The items marked 'NIL' are shown here for illustrative purposes, and would not be shown as such in an examination answer.

Here is a closer look at each of the seven headings, detailing the items that might fall under each one and whether the items are *inflows* or *outflows* of cash.

1 Operating activities.

- What we need to establish is the cash generated from operating activities and this can be derived from operating profit
- *items not involving the flow of cash* (i.e. bookkeeping or non-cash items which have already been deducted from profit or added to profit and which we therefore need to add back or deduct from profit as we need to determine the *cashflow*)
  - e.g. *depreciation for the year* – this has already been deducted from profit but as it did not involve cash we add it back to the profit figure
  - e.g. *book profit on sale of assets* – this has already been added to profit but it did not involve cash so it is deducted from the profit figure
- *plus/minus changes in working capital items, excluding cash* – in other words, stock, debtors and creditors.
  - *Stock* – an *increase* in stock was obviously financed from an *outflow* of cash, whereas a *decrease* in stock will have resulted in an *inflow* of cash.
  - *Debtors* – an *increase* in debtors (giving more credit to customers) is the same as an *outflow* and a *decrease* in debtors is an *inflow*
  - *Creditors* – an *increase* (taking more credit) is an *inflow* and a *decrease* is an *outflow*

2 *Returns on investment and servicing of finance.*

- Returns on your investments will include interest received and/or dividends received. Clearly these are *inflows*.
- The payments or servicing of finance will include interest paid and/or dividends paid. These are *outflows*.

  BUT please note you *do not* include *equity dividends paid* (i.e. the dividends paid to ordinary shareholders) under this heading; they are listed under a separate heading.

  so this section is made up of any:

- *interest paid or received*; and
- *dividends paid (though not equity dividends) or received.*

3 *Taxation.*

- *corporation tax paid* – which is clearly an *outflow* of cash.

13 – Cashflow Statements (FRS 1)

4 *Capital expenditure.*

- *purchase of fixed assets, tangible and intangible (outflow)*
- *sale of fixed assets (inflow).*

5 *Equity dividends paid.*

- the *equity dividends paid* (i.e. the dividends paid to ordinary shareholders) is clearly an *outflow*

6 *Management of liquid resources.*

- *purchase of financial assets (outflow)*, e.g. Treasury bills. These are like shares issued by the government, which you buy and hold as an investment.
- *sale of financial assets (inflow).*

7 *Financing.*

i.e. amounts paid (*outflow*) and received (*inflow*) in respect of the raising of finance, for example:

- *share issues/repaid* (as we are examining cashflow we are concerned only with shares issued for cash and therefore not bonus issues)
- *long-term loans paid/received.*

13.2 Preparing a cashflow statement

Having looked at a specimen cashflow statement and some examples of inflows and outflows, see if you can prepare such a statement for Rampgill Ltd.

Structure of Accounts

Table 13.2: Balance sheet for Rampgill Ltd as at ...

	31.12.X0	31.12.X1		31.12.X0	31.12.X1
	£	£		£	£
Fixed assets at cost	390,000	426,000	Ordinary share capital	200,000	220,000
less depreciation	52,000	62,000	General reserve	5,000	10,000
	338,000	364,000	Profit and loss a/c	175,000	200,000
				380,000	430,000
			10% debenture	30,000	15,000
				410,000	445,000
Current assets			*Current liabilities*		
Stock	80,000	100,000	Taxation	20,000	30,000
Debtors	30,000	50,000	Creditors	20,000	30,000
Bank	15,000	10,000	Proposed dividend	15,000	20,000
Cash	2,000	1,000			
	465,000	525,000		465,000	525,000

*Profit before taxation = £80,000

Step 1

When you are asked to provide a cashflow statement, I would suggest that you calculate the changes in cash/bank first, because this is easy and gives you something to aim at. However, you should present your final answer with the "Analysis of changes in cash/bank" at the bottom of your statement as shown in the example above.

We do this by looking at the changes in the cash and bank balance stated in the balance sheets, i.e:

	31.12.X0	**31.12.X1**	**Changes**
Bank	15,000	10,000	(5,000)
Cash	2,000	1,000	(1,000)
			(6,000)

So, we should find that the *inflows* less *outflows* of our seven headings equals (6000).

Step 2

Complete the cashflow statement starting with the first heading, operating activities. In order to do this you are basically looking for changes in the balance sheet items between 31.12 X0 and 31.12.X1. However be careful: some items do not follow this rule. Watch out for dividends, taxation and depreciation, and the sale/purchase of Fixed Assets.

13 – Cashflow Statements (FRS 1)

Here is my explanation of how to complete the cashflow statement followed by the answer.

Explanation
Operating Activities

a) *Profit before taxation*

You must always start with profit before taxation and interest, because this is the major source of funds. In this question this figure was given as a note, but in other questions you will need to calculate it from the balance sheets. The easiest way to do this is to think of the layout of a limited company profit and loss account and work backwards, filling in the figures until you arrive back at profit before taxation. In the example above, we would have done this as follows.

Table 13.3: Trading profit and loss account extract of Rampgill Ltd for the year ending 31.12.X1

	£	
Profit before taxation and interest	80,000	
less taxation	30,000	
Profit after taxation	50,000	*Work*
less proposed dividend	20,000	*Backwards*
	30,000	
less transfer to general reserve	5,000	
Retained profit for the year	25,000	
Retained profit c/d	175,000	
Balance of profits	200,000	

Many students find this difficult, so let us just look at what happened by referring to Rampgill's balance sheets for 19X0 and 19X1.

The retained profit as at 31.12.X1 is £200,000, whereas it was only £175,000 as at 31.12.X0. We can, therefore, conclude that this year's trading has achieved a profit of £25,000. But remember, this is after making certain appropriations. In our example, these are:

- *Transfer to reserves* of £5,000 because general reserves have grown from £5,000 (19X0) to £10,000 (19X1)
- *Proposed dividend* of £20,000. *Note*: This is one of those items I warned you about. It is *not* the difference between the two years that we add back. It is the amount that we have proposed to pay to shareholders this year, 31.12.X1, £20,000 as we are

Structure of Accounts

reconstructing the profit and loss for this year in order to get back to the profit before taxation.

- *Taxation of £30,000.* Once again we add back the amount outstanding as at 31.12.X1 and *not* the difference between the two years.

b) *Add back items not involving cash*
In this example we have one such item, depreciation, since this is a bookkeeping entry and not a cash item. The cumulative depreciation in the balance sheets has grown from £52,000 to £62,000. The depreciation for the year, to be added back to profit, is therefore £10,000.

c) *Increases and decreases in working capital: items excluding cash*
The figures are obtained by looking at the movements in the items of working capital over the two years. But remember: in doing so you must ask yourself, has this caused an increase or decrease in cash? For example, the increase in stock of £20,000 will have resulted in an outflow of cash but the increase in creditors of £10,000 will have saved cash flowing out of the business.

Returns on investments and servicing of finance

d) *Dividends.* The amount that has been *paid* is £15,000, the amount outstanding as at 31.12.X0. The proposed dividend of £20,000 as at 31.12.X1 has not yet been paid. *But remember* under this heading we are not concerned with *equity dividends paid* (i.e. dividends paid to ordinary shareholders). These go under a heading of their own.

Taxation

e) As we are trying to identify the amount which has been *paid*, the figure we use is £20,000 – the amount outstanding as at 31.12.X0. The amount outstanding at 31.12.X1 is still outstanding and due for payment in the future, hence it is an outstanding current liability.

Capital expenditure

f) We can see from the difference between the two balance sheets that £36,000 of Fixed Assets have been purchased.

Equity dividends paid

g) As discussed above (d) the equity dividend actually paid (not proposed) is £15,000, the amount outstanding as at 31.12.X0. The proposed dividend of £20,000 as at 31.12.X1 has not yet been paid.

Management of liquid resources

h) In this example we have not purchased or sold any financial assets.

Financing

i) These items are found by looking at differences between the two balance sheets. But remember we are concerned with cashflow and not movements in reserves.

13 – Cashflow Statements (FRS 1)

Table 13.4: Cashflow statement of Rampgill Ltd for year ended 19X1

		£	£
Note	Operating activities		
a)	Net profit before tax and interest	80,000	
b)	Depreciation for year	10,000	
c)	Increase in stock	(20,000)	
c)	Increase in debtors	(20,000)	
c)	Increase in creditors	<u>10,000</u>	
	Net cash inflow from operating activities		60,000
	Returns on investments and servicing of finance	NIL	NIL
	Taxation		
e)	Taxation paid	<u>(20,000)</u>	
			(20,000)
	Capital expenditure		
f)	Purchase of fixed assets	<u>(36,000)</u>	
			(36,000)
	Equity dividends paid		
g)	Ordinary dividend paid	<u>(15,000)</u>	
			(15,000)
h)	**Management of liquid resources**		NIL
	Financing		
i)	Issue of shares (i.e. Cash received from issue)	20,000	
	Repayment of debenture	<u>(15,000)</u>	
	Net cash inflow from financing		<u>5,000</u>
	Decrease in cash/bank		<u>(6,000)</u>
	Analysis of changes in cash/bank during year		
	Balance at start of year		
	Cash	2,000	
	Bank	<u>15,000</u>	
			17,000
	Balance at end of year		
	Cash	1,000	
	Bank	<u>10,000</u>	
			<u>11,000</u>
	Net cash outflow		<u>(6,000)</u>

Structure of Accounts

13.3 The purchase and sale of fixed assets during the year

In the last example, Rampgill's fixed assets increased from £390,000 (31.12 X0) to £426,000 (31.12.X1) and we therefore stated that there had been a purchase of fixed assets worth £36,000 (*capital expenditure*).

It may be that they bought fixed assets worth £46,000 and also sold fixed assets worth £10,000. However, if that were the case, we would have been told about the sale in a note at the foot of the question.

Let us examine such a situation now:

Table 13.5: Balance sheet of Wire Mesh Ltd as at 31.12.X7 and X8

	19X7	19X8		19X7	19X8
	£	£		£	£
Fixed assets					
– cost	40,000	70,000	Share capital	20,000	25,000
– depreciation	10,000	15,000	Profit and loss a/c	8,000	5,000
	30,000	55,000		28,000	30,000
Current assets			Loan	5,000	10,000
Stock	10,000	20,000		33,000	40,000
Debtors	5,000	1,000			
Bank	6,000	1,000	Creditors	8,000	32,000
			Proposed dividend	10,000	5,000
	51,000	77,000		51,000	77,000

Notes:

1. Profit before taxation £2,000

2. Fixed assets which had cost £3,000, and which had been depreciated by £1,000, were sold during the year for £2,500.

13 – Cashflow Statements (FRS 1)

Procedure

1 Calculate the profit or loss on sale.

	£
Cost	3,000
– depreciation	1,000
Book value	2,000
Sale proceeds	2,500
– book value	2,000
Book profit	500

This is only a bookkeeping profit (i.e. the amount we received over the book value). It is, therefore, *an item which does not involve cash*.

On this occasion, it is a bookkeeping item that we will *deduct* from profit before tax under our calculation of net cash inflow/outflow from 'operating activities'. In the cashflow statement for Rampgill we *added* back depreciation because this is a bookkeeping item which has been previously deducted. Here the book profit on the sale of the fixed asset has already been included in our profit figure and we must therefore *deduct it*, when examining cashflow.

2 The actual proceeds received £2,500 (and, therefore, an inflow) are included under the heading *Capital expenditure*.

3 Calculate the movement in fixed assets.

	Cost	Depreciation	Book value
	£	£	£
Balance sheet 19X7 (see above)	40,000	10,000	30,000
less sale (as per note 2)	3,000	1,000	2,000
	37,000	9,000	28,000
add additions	**33,000**	**6,000**	**27,000**
Balance sheet 19X8 (see above)	70,000	15,000	55,000

We are given the balance sheet figures for 19X7 and 19X8 and also information relating to the sale. We can therefore calculate the purchases and depreciation for the year.

4 Construct the cashflow statement using the information calculated in stages 1–3, above. They are highlighted in bold in the answer that follows.

Structure of Accounts

Table 13.6: Cashflow statement of Wire Mesh Ltd for year ended 31.12.X8

	£	£
Operating activities		
Net profit before tax and interest	2,000	
Depreciation for year	**6,000**	
Profit on sale of fixed asset	**500**	
Increase in stock	(10,000)	
Decrease in debtors	4,000	
Increase in creditors	24,000	
Net cash inflow from operating activities		25,500
Returns on investments and servicing of finance		NIL
Taxation		
Taxation	NIL	
		NIL
Capital expenditure		
Purchase of fixed assets	(33,000)	
Sale of fixed assets	2,500	
Net outflow from investing activities		(30,500)
Equity dividends paid		
Dividend paid		(10,000)
Management of liquid resources		NIL
Financing		
Cash received from issue of shares	5,000	
Cash received from loan	5,000	
Net inflow from financing		10,000
Decrease in cash/bank		**(5,000)**
Analysis of changes in cash/bank during year		
<u>Balance at start of year</u>		
Cash	—	
Bank	6,000	
		6,000
<u>Balance at end of year</u>		
Cash	—	
Bank	1,000	
		1,000
Net cash outflow		**(5,000)**

13 – Cashflow Statements (FRS 1)

13.4 Analysis of the cashflow statement

Financial policy

As we have stated, the cashflow statement provides the reader with an indication of the financial policy adopted by the company and its effect on the company's financial position, e.g. financing long-term investments and overtrading.

Financing long-term investments

Analysis of the cashflow statement will reveal how the company has financed its long-term investments, such as the purchase of fixed assets.

The purchase of long-term investments should be financed by the raising of long-term finance, such as share issues, retained profits or loans.

In the case of Wire Mesh Ltd above, we can clearly see that the purchase of £33,000 fixed assets has *not* been financed by the raising of long-term finance (profits, share issues and loans only equal £17,500 when added together).

The purchase has, obviously, been achieved by reducing the period available to debtors, reducing the bank balance and, in particular, by increasing the credit from suppliers.

Unless it has changed its pattern of trading this situation can continue for only so long, as debtors may begin to look elsewhere, the bank may refuse to extend the overdraft and creditors may demand repayment.

Overtrading

Many companies, and this may go for Wire Mesh Ltd, suffer from overtrading, i.e. from attempting to expand too quickly by accepting large, or additional, orders which require additional working capital and leave little resources for the day-to-day business.

For example, suppose the level of production in Year 1 was 1,000 mattresses per week, which it sold to bed manufacturers on cash terms. In Year 2, however, it accepted an order for 2,000 mattresses per week from one of the brand leaders, with payment on credit terms of 2 months. The acceptance of this order may result in:

a) the need for new machinery;

b) an increase in stock;

c) a reduction in the bank balance, and

d) an increase in the supply of raw materials (creditors).

What also tends to happen in such situations is that the normal business is neglected in an attempt to satisfy the large order, which may then lead to the loss of 'bread and butter' business, making the company dependent on the large contract.

Structure of Accounts

Summary

1 *FRS 1* makes it obligatory for all companies above a certain size to publish a cashflow statement.

2 This statement shows *where cash has come from and where cash has gone.*

3 Examples of *inflows* are:
- the cash generated from profits;
- proceeds of sale of fixed assets;
- issue of shares;
- borrowing long term.

4 Examples of *outflows* are:
- the cash flow associated with losses;
- purchase of fixed assets;
- repaying loans;
- paying taxation;
- paying dividends.

5 Adjustments must be made for *items not involving cash*, e.g. depreciation, which is merely a bookkeeping entry, and book profits, e.g. a disposal of fixed assets.

6 In working back towards profit before taxation, add back the taxation and proposed dividends of Year 2.

7 The *tax and dividends that have been paid* are an outflow of funds, and are the amounts in the balance sheet for Year 1.

8 Where the company has purchased and sold assets during the year you will need to:
   a) calculate the profit on sale (which is a book profit);
   b) calculate the movements in fixed assets.

9 The cashflow statement provides *an indication of the financial policy adopted by the company and its effects on the company's financial position.*

10 Analysis will reveal *how the company finances its long-term investments.*

11 The purchase of long-term investments should be financed by the raising of long-term finance, such as share issues, retained profits or loans, otherwise the company may be short of working capital for its day-to-day business.

12 *Overtrading* occurs where companies attempt to expand too quickly.

13 – Cashflow Statements (FRS 1)

13 *Overtrading may result in:*

   a) an increase in fixed assets;

   b) an increase in stock;

   c) reduction in credit given to debtors;

   d) reduction in the bank balance;

   e) increase in credit taken from suppliers.

14
CASH FORECASTS

Syllabus Objectives

4.5 Forecast results

- The cash forecast
- Forecast trading profit and loss account and balance sheet

Learning Objectives

After studying this chapter you should be able to:

1 Outline what is meant by a cashflow forecast;

2 Appreciate that profit and cash are not the same thing;

3 Produce a cashflow forecast that deals with the giving and receiving of credit;

4 Produce forecast trading profit and loss accounts and balance sheets from a cashflow forecast;

5 Explain how business plans can be adapted to provide an acceptable cashflow, having regard to resources;

6 Appreciate the importance of such forecasts.

14.1 Introduction – What is a cashflow forecast?

In the last chapter we examined cashflow statements, which record the cash that **has** come into and gone out of a business in the ***past***.

Cashflow forecasts, as you might suspect, are a forecast of the cash which ***will*** flow into and out of a business in the ***future***.

14.2 How are cashflow forecasts constructed?

The cashflow forecast is a financial summary of the sales and production budgets together with all other financial data, e.g. interest charges.

14 – Cash Forecasts

The marketing/sales director will predict his or her sales turnover for the year ahead, based on past performance, recent events and economic/market trends.

Similarly the production director will forecast the expected production levels, together with the associated costs, e.g. wages, electricity, etc.

The bringing together of these two budgets is not as easy as it sounds. It is not uncommon for a sales director to be forecasting sales far in excess of what the production director feels can be produced.

Example cashflow forecast

Let us look at an example, which provides a considerable amount of information about the *predicted* inflows and ouflows of a business.

Susan is starting a dress shop. She has £15,000 capital in her bank account and her bank has agreed to grant her a £5,000 loan which shall be repayable over two years by quarterly installments of £625 starting in March, her third month of business. Her bank manager also agrees an overdraft facility of £1,000.

She obtains a leasehold shop without premium, the rent on which is £4,000 per annum payable quarterly in advance. Rates are £600 per annum which she elects to pay by twelve monthly instalments. She buys a motor car for £3,000 which she thinks will depreciate to £1,800 over the next year. She also buys £6,000 worth of carpets and shop fittings: these she expects to last for five years, after which she will discard them and refurbish the shop.

She purchases an initial stock of £10,000. On this, as with all her purchases, she imposes a mark-up of 100 per cent. As stock is sold, she replaces it in the same month. For the first six months she has to pay cash on delivery for her stock. After that, she gets one month's credit.

All her sales are for cash or on credit card. Her monthly operating expenses (other than any identified above) are £500 per month for the first four months and £750 per month thereafter.

She expects her sales in her first year to be:

January	£2,000	July	£6,000
February	£2,000	August	£8,000
March	£3,000	September	£9,000
April	£3 500	October	£12,000
May	£4,000	November	£10,000
June	£6,000	December	£12,000

The June sales figure includes £3,000 for goods sold at cost in a summer sale. The October sales figure included £4,000 for goods sold at cost in an autumn sale.

She will draw £500 per month for personal living expenses.

Structure of Accounts

Table 14.1: Specimen layout
Cashflow forecast of Expectations Ltd for 12 months ending 31.12.Y0

	1	2	3	4	5	6	7	8	9	10	11	12	Dr/Cr	Total
Income														
Sales: Cash														
1 month credit														
2 months credit														
Total income														
Expenditure														
Initial stock														
Purchases														
Wages														
Electricity														
Insurance														
Premises														
Motor vehicles														
Equipment														
Interest charges														
etc.														
Total expenditure														
Income – expenditure														
Opening balance (capital)														
Other injections (e.g. loans)														
Cumulative balance														

14 – Cash Forecasts

Required:

a) A monthly cashflow forecast for Susan's first year. Ignore bank interest, credit card charges and taxation.

b) In the light of this forecast, can you offer any advice to Susan?

So, how do we go about preparing a cashflow forecast for Susan's first year?

Step 1

Clearly we need to sort all the predicted inflows and outflows of *cash* into some sort of meaningful order, so that we can easily see how much is coming in and going out of the business.

Here is a blank layout which I would suggest you adopt (*see* Table 14.1 on previous page).

Step 2

Insert all the **cash** inflows and outflows into the table, recording **when** the cash is received and paid.

In other words:

1 Cashflow forecasts are concerned only with **cash**. Therefore depreciation and other non-cash items or bookkeeping entries, such as book profit on the sale of assets, do not appear.

2 The cashflow forecast is concerned with **when** cash is received or paid, not the date of sale or purchase. For example, sales in January on one month's credit would be recorded as an anticipated cash receipt in February.

Here is a copy of Susan's cashflow forecast, together with notes explaining the various entries. See Table 14.2 on page 204.

Notes:

1	*Sales*	Simply insert the figures given in the appropriate month, because all of her sales are for cash or on credit card. (In future questions watch out for sales on credit.)
2	*Bank loan*	The question states "quarterly instalments of £625 starting in March". Therefore simply insert these amounts
3	*Rent*	The question states "£4,000 p.a. payable quarterly in advance". Therefore insert £1,000 per quarter starting in January.
4	*Rates*	The question states "£600 p.a. in 12 monthly instalments". Therefore insert £50 per month.
5	*Motor car*	The question states "£3,000 with depreciation of £1,800 in the first year". We can assume Susan pays for the car immediately (January). As for depreciation – we can forget it, cashflow forecasts are concerned with cash; depreciation is a non-cash item.

Structure of Accounts

Table 14.2: Cashflow forecast for Susan's first year

	Jan £	Feb £	Mar £	Apr £	May £	Jun £	Jul £	Aug £	Sep £	Oct £	Nov £	Dec £	Dr/Cr £	Total (6)
Income														
Sales:	2,000	2,000	3,000	3,500	4,000	6,000	6,000	8,000	9,000	12,000	10,000	12,000		77,500
Total income	2,000	2,000	3,000	3,500	4,000	6,000	6,000	8,000	9,000	12,000	10,000	12,000		77,500
Expenditure														
Bank loan			625			625			625			625		2,500
Rent	1,000			1,000			1,000			1,000				4,000
Rates	50	50	50	50	50	50	50	50	50	50	50	50		600
Motor car	3,000													3,000
Carpets/Shop fittings	6,000													6,000
Initial stock	10,000													10,000
Purchases	1,000	1,000	1,500	1,750	2,000	4,500		3,000	4,000	4,500	8,000	5,000	6,000	42,250
Operating expenses	500	500	500	500	750	750	750	750	750	750	750	750		8,000
Personal living expenses	500	500	500	500	500	500	500	500	500	500	500	500		6,000
Total expenditure	22,050	2,050	3,175	3,800	3,300	6,425	2,300	4,300	5,925	6,800	9,300	6,925	6,000	82,350
Income less expenditure	(20,050)	(50)	(175)	(300)	700	(425)	3,700	3,700	3,075	5,200	700	5,075		
Opening balance (capital)	15,000	(5)	(100)	(275)	(575)	125	(300)	3,400	7,100	10,175	15,375	16,075		
Other injections (loan)	5,000													
Cumulative balance	(50)	(100)	(275)	(575)	125	(300)	3,400	7,100	10,175	15,375	16,075	21,150		

208

14 – Cash Forecasts

6 *Fittings*   The question states "£6,000 with depreciation of....". Once again assume an immediate purchase and forget the depreciation

7 *Initial stock*   The question states "She purchases an initial stock of £10,000". We can assume it is paid for immediately unless we are told anything to the contrary.

8 *Purchases*   *Let me come back to this one as it takes a little explaining.*

9 *Operating expenses* Simply insert the monthly figures given in the question.

10 *Drawings*   Again, simply insert £500 per month as per question.

Note 8: purchases throughout the year

As promised, we will now go back to the purchases of stock. The question states that:

"She purchases an initial stock of £10,000. On this, as with all her purchases, she *imposes a mark-up of 100 per cent. As stock is sold, she replaces it in the same month. For the first six months she has to pay cash on delivery for her stock. After that, she gets one month's credit.*

All her sales are for cash or on credit card. Her monthly operating expenses (other than any identified above) are £500 per month for the first four months and £750 per month thereafter.

She expects her sales in her first year to be:

January	£2,000	July	£6,000
February	£2,000	August	£8,000
March	£3,000	September	£9,000
April	£3 500	October	£12,000
May	£4,000	November	£10,000
June	£6,000	December	£12,000

The June sales figure includes £3,000 for goods sold at cost in a summer sale. The October sales figure included £4,000 for goods sold at cost in an autumn sale."

The important points to note, (*highlighted above*) are:

- Susan imposes a 100% mark-up on purchases.
- As stock is sold she will purchase enough stock in the same month to replace it.
- In the first six months she will pay cash on delivery for purchases and thereafter get one month's credit.
- June and October sales include £3,000 and £4,000 respectively for goods sold at cost in the summer and autumn sales.

Structure of Accounts

What do we mean by mark-up?

Mark-up is the amount by which the purchase price is increased to arrive at the selling price.

e.g. 50% mark-up

Purchase price *plus* 50% of the purchase price = selling price

Purchase price per unit	=	£100
plus mark-up	= 50% of purchase price	£50
Selling price per unit	= £100 + 50%, i.e. £50	£150

It is very easy to increase the cost of purchases by the mark-up in order to arrive at the selling price. But if we are given the selling price and a mark-up of 50% we have to work backwards in order to arrive at the cost of purchases.

Purchase price	+ 50% of the purchase price	= selling price
the whole purchase price, 100% +	50% of P	= £150

therefore: 150P = £150

P   = £100

In some questions you may be given the *margin* rather than the *mark-up*.

A *margin* is the amount by which selling price exceeds the purchasing cost.

e.g. 50% margin

*Selling price **less** 50% of the selling price = purchase price*

Selling price per unit	=	£150
less margin	= 50% of selling price	£75
Purchasing price per unit	= £150 − 50% i.e. £75 =	£75

It is very easy to reduce the selling price by the margin in order to arrive at the purchasing price. But if we are given the cost of purchases and a margin of 50% we have to work backwards in order to arrive at the selling price.

Selling price	− 50% of the selling price	= purchases price
the whole selling price, 100% −	50% of S	= £75

therefore: 50% of S   = £75

S   = £150

Note:

Despite the same selling price (£150), a mark-up of 50% and a margin of 50% arrive at different purchasing costs, because we have taken 50% of different items.

Let us now return to Susan. In Susan's case she has imposed a *mark-up of 100 %*. *Mark-up* you will recall is the amount by which purchases are increased to arrive at the selling price.

14 – Cash Forecasts

A 100% mark-up means that she has doubled her purchase costs to arrive at her selling price or that purchases (replacement costs) are half the selling price.

	Sales	Replacement cost /Purchases
January	£2,000	£1,000
February	£2,000	£1,000
March	£3,000	£1 500
April	£3 500	£1 750
May	£4,000	£2,000
June	**£6,000**	**£4 500**
July	£6,000	£3,000
August	£8,000	£4,000
September	£9,000	£4 500
October	**£12,000**	**£8,000**
November	£10,000	£5,000
December	£12,000	£6,000

If replacement cost is half the selling price then why do purchases for June and October not equal £3,000 and £6,000 respectively?

The reason is that June and October sales include £3,000 and £4,000 respectively for goods sold at cost in the summer and autumn sales. Therefore the replacement cost of the goods sold in June and October equal:

June			Replacement cost
Total sales	£6,000		
Sales at cost	£3,000		£3,000
Sales at mark-up	£3,000		£1 500, i.e. 50%
			£4,500
October			
Total sales	£12,000		
Sales at cost	£4,000		£4,000
Sales at mark-up	£8,000		£4,000, i.e. 50%
			£8,000

Structure of Accounts

One of the most important points to realize, however, is that while Susan will replace stock which is sold in the same month *she does not necessarily pay for it that month*.

In Susan's case, in the first six months she will pay cash on delivery for purchases and thereafter get one month's credit. Therefore purchases are made as follows:

Table 14.3: Purchases

	Sales	Replacement cost /Purchases	Payment Date
Cash on delivery			
January	£2,000	£1,000	January
February	£2,000	£1,000	February
March	£3,000	£1 500	March
April	£3 500	£1 750	April
May	£4,000	£2,000	May
June	£6,000	£4 500	June
1 month credit			
July	£6,000	£3,000	August
August	£8,000	£4,000	September
September	£9,000	£4 500	October
October	£12,000	£8,000	November
November	£10,000	£5,000	December
December	£12,000	£6,000	**January**

Cash to be paid after the final month represents a *creditor*, because the cash is still due to be paid at the end of the accounting period in question, e.g. the goods Susan purchased in December will not be paid for until January of next year, hence we have a *creditor*.

Cash to be received after the final month, for goods sold on credit, represents a *debtor*, because it is cash owed to you at the end of the accounting period in question.

You will see that the specimen layout and Susan's cashflow forecast includes a column for debtors and creditors, which should ease your recording of such items.

Step 3

Once you have inserted all the cash inflows and outflows total the budget both across (including any debtors or creditors) and down, calculating the income less expenditure for each month and the cumulative balance (or running total), revealing how much you anticipate being in credit or overdrawn each month

14 – Cash Forecasts

Totalling the budget across and down allows you to check the accuracy of your addition, e.g. total expenditure should equal £82,350 both across (Jan – Dr/Cr inclusive) and down. If not, you need to check your addition.

The total column also has another use. It is a summary of each account which we can use like a trial balance when one is asked to produce a forecast trading profit and loss account and balance sheet from a cashflow forecast.

Before we produce Susan's forecast trading profit and loss account and balance sheet, let us consider what the cashflow forecast tells us, after all the question did ask us to advise Susan.

The forecast tells us that:

a) Susan will have a credit balance of £21,150 by the end of the year (the cumulative balance or running total);
b) Susan will need overdraft facilities only for January–April and for June;
c) Her maximum overdraft will be £575.

Provided the bank can rely on Susan's estimates (i.e. that sales are not overestimated and that items of expenditure have not been overlooked) and that they trust Susan they can safely provide the required overdrafts.

With such a large credit balance building up she should be advised to consider the investment of these funds, or consider paying off the loan in order to avoid further interest charges.

14.3 Producing a forecast trading profit and loss account and balance sheet from a cashflow forecast

Once you have produced a cashflow forecast, producing forecast accounts is very simple. Let us look back at Susan's cashflow forecast and see exactly how it is done.

As I stated earlier, the *total column* can be used like a *trial balance*. It is therefore a case of rearranging the items. Unfortunately it does not list every item we need. We must also include:

a) *Depreciation* which you will recall was not included in the cashflow forecast because it is a *non-cash item*, i.e.

$$\text{Motor car} = £1,800 \text{ (given in the question)}$$

Fittings = Cost £6,000
Life 5 years
Residual value Nil

$$\frac{£6,000}{5} = £1,200 \text{ p.a.}$$

Structure of Accounts

Be careful; in some questions the cashflow forecast is for only a six-month period, and you should therefore only include depreciation for six months.

b) Stock. If stock has remained constant, the closing stock will be same as the opening stock – £1,000.

c) The cash balance as at the end of the period, as a current asset, i.e. £21,150.

d) The total outstanding *debtors* and *creditors*, i.e. creditors, £6,000.

e) The outstanding loan as a current or long-term liability,

i.e. loan	£5,000	
less repayments	£2,500	(4 x £625)
	£2,500	

f) The capital amount = £15,000

You should use every item in the total column plus those mentioned above, therefore if your balance sheet does not balance, quickly check that you have not missed an item.

Here is a copy of Susan's forecast trading profit and loss account of Susan for the year ending – –

Trade 14.4: Forecast trading profit and loss account of Susan for the year ending – –

	£	£
Sales		77,500
less cost of goods sold		
Opening stock	10,000	
+ purchases	42,250	
	52,250	
– closing stock	10,000	42,250
Gross profit		35,250
less expenses		
Rent	4,000	
Rates	600	
Operating expenses	8,000	
Depreciation: Motor car (a)	1,800	
Fittings (a)	1,200	15,600
Net profit		19,650

14 – Cash Forecasts

Table 14.5: Forecast balance sheet of Susan as at – –

Fixed assets

Motor car		3,000
– depreciation (a)		**1,800**
		1,200
Fittings	6,000	
– depreciation (a)	**1,200**	4,800
		6,000

Current assets

Stock (b)	**10,000**	
Debtors		
Bank/Cash (c)	**21,150**	
	31,150	

less current liabilities

Creditors (d)	**6,000**	25,150
		31,150

Long-term liabilities

Loan (e)		**2,500**
		28,650

Financed by

Capital (f)		15,000
and Net Profit		19,650
		34,650
– Drawings		6,000
		28,650

14.4 The benefits of cashflow forecasts

As we have seen throughout this chapter cashflow forecasts have a number of benefits.

1. They act as an early warning system and enable companies to determine whether or not the business will be able to meet its financial commitments as they fall due. Remember just because a company can buy goods at £5,000 and sell them for £10,000 does not

mean it is destined for success. If it can only sell the goods on three months' credit, it must have sufficient cash to initially purchase the goods and also finance wages, light, heat, etc. until cash comes in from sales.

2. Companies are able to assess whether or not they will need financial assistance (overdrafts or loans) and, if so, how much and for how long.

3. If companies do need financial assistance, a well-prepared cashflow forecast will assist it in obtaining the finance required – provided of course, that it shows the bank that it will eventually be repaid!

4. They enable companies to assess whether or not the company will be profitable.

5. They provide financial discipline and targets to be reached.

6. Forecasts act as a guide for management decisions.

7. Companies are able to measure their performance by comparing the actual results to the budget and analyse significant variances.

14 – Cash Forecasts

Summary

1 A cashflow forecast is a forecast of the cash that will flow into and out of the business in the future.

2 Cashflow forecasts are constructed from the sales and production budgets, together with all other financial data, e.g. interest charges.

3 Cashflow forecasts are concerned only with *cash*; therefore do *not include* depreciation and other bookkeeping entries.

4 Cashflow forecasts reflect *when* cash is received and paid, *not* the date of sale or purchase.

5 Cash to be received after the final month represents a *debtor*.

6 Cash to be paid after the final month represents a *creditor*.

7 If stock is to be kept at the same level, purchases must replace stock sold.

8 Mark-up is the amount by which purchases are increased to arrive at the selling price, e.g. purchase price plus 50% of the purchase price = selling price.

9 Margin is the amount by which selling price exceeds the purchasing costs, e.g.

Selling price less 50% of the selling price   = purchase price

10 Cashflow forecasts reveal:
- the forecast cash balance at the end of the accounting period;
- the maximum overdraft requirement;
- the period over which overdraft facilities are required.

11 Forecast trading profit and loss accounts and balance sheets can be drawn from cashflow forecasts. *But* you must include:

a) depreciation;

b) closing stock;

c) the closing cash balance;

d) the total outstanding debtors and creditors;

e) outstanding loans;

f) capital.

12 It enables a company to determine whether or not the business will be able to meet its financial commitments as they fall due.

13 Other uses are:

a) it allows you to assess whether or not you will need financial assistance, and if so, how much and for how long;

Structure of Accounts

b) it enables you to assess your profitability;

c) it enables you to measure performance by comparing actual results with forecast results and analysing significant variances;

d) it acts as a guide for management decisions;

e) it provides financial discipline and targets.

Section D

THE REGULATORY REGIME AND THE INTERPRETATION OF ACCOUNTS

This section focuses on two issues:

1. The regulatory regime, i.e. the regulations governing the way in which accounts are prepared and presented

   and

2. The interpretation of accounts, i.e. the assessment of a company's performance over time or in comparison to another company

At first sight you may feel that they are two unrelated issues, but you would be wrong.

Consider the following two clothes retailers for a moment; which one has performed better over the last year?

Accounting policies	Company A		Company B	
Depreciation policy	Reducing balance		Straight line	
Provision for bad debt policy	5% of debtors		2% of debtors	
Profit and loss account				
	£	£	£	£
Gross profit on trading		20,000		20,000
less expenses				
Provision for depreciation	2,000		1,000	
Provision for bad debts	500		200	
Trading expenses	10,000	12,500	10,000	11 200
Net profit on trading		7,500		8,800

At first sight you may be tempted to say Company B because it has the greater net profit, but a closer look at the accounts reveals that both companies have achieved the same gross profit

Structure of Accounts

and incurred the same trading expenses. Company B appears more profitable simply because it has adopted different accounting policies, *not* because it trades more effectively.

The method of depreciation adopted will affect the amount of depreciation charged to each year's accounts, and as a result the profit calculation for the year, as well as the reported value of the fixed asset in the balance sheet. In addition the bad debt provision will also affect the charge for the year and hence the profit calculation as well as the debtors' figure in the balance sheet.

So, how can we interpret the accounts and the performance of companies unless we fully understand the regulatory regime and in particular the accounting policies adopted by the company under examination?

This section therefore starts with an examination of the regulatory regime:

Chapter 15 **The Regulatory Regime and Accounting Concepts**

Chapter 16 **Asset Valuation and Profit Measurement**

  before concluding with

Chapter 17 **Interpretation of Accounts and Ratio Analysis**

15

THE REGULATORY REGIME AND ACCOUNTING CONCEPTS

Syllabus Objectives

5.1 Regulatory regime, including audit as an external check

5.2 Sources of authority
- Legislation
- ASB – SSAPs and FRSs

5.3 Accounting concepts
- Entity
- Money measurement
- Matching
- Realization
- Accruals
- Historical cost
- Going concern
- Consistency
- Prudence and conservatism
- Materiality

5.4 FRS 18 – Accounting policies

Learning Objectives

After studying this chapter you should be able to:

1. Outline the various sources of regulations companies must observe.
2. Appreciate why accounts should show a "true and fair" view and explain what is meant by this term.

Structure of Accounts

3   Outline the Objectives of Statements of Standard Accounting Practice (SSAPs) and Financial Reporting Standards (FRSs) and the standard-setting process.

4   List the main users of accounts.

5   Explain how standards "narrow the range of permissible accounting treatments applicable to transactions or situation".

6   Outline the requirements of "FRS 18 – Accounting policies".

7   Appreciate the role played by international accounting standards, the stock exchange and non-mandatory recommendations in the regulatory regime.

15.1   Introduction – The regulatory regime

UK companies must observe regulations from various sources when preparing and presenting their accounts:

1. Legislation – UK and EU

2. Standards or statements of best practice, in particular Statements of Standard Accounting Practice (SSAPs) and Financial Reporting Standards (FRSs)

3. Stock Exchange rules (listed companies only)

4. Non-mandatory requirements

Let us examine each one in turn. However please note that this chapter goes beyond the requirements of your syllabus in order to give you a detailed look at the regulatory regime. The examination and syllabus will focus on

1.   Legislation, and

2.   The Accounting Standards Board (ASB) – SSAPs/FRSs

Legislation – UK and EU

Companies Act 1981

The UK implemented the EC Fourth Directive into the Companies Act 1981. EC directives are issued by the EU, and member states (of which the UK is one) then have a fixed time in which to incorporate the provisions into their own national legislation.

The Fourth Directive introduced a standard format for profit and loss accounts and balance sheets of companies.

Companies Act 1985

This Act brought together the acts of 1947, 1948, 1967, 1980 and 1981, setting out general rules and formats concerning the content and form of published company accounts.

15 – The Regulatory Regime and Accounting Concepts

The objective was to assist users to understand and evaluate a company's progress and to enable them to compare one company to another due to the standard form of presentation.

One important section worth noting is Section 226, which states that:

> *The balance sheet shall give a **true and fair view** of the state of affairs of the company as at the end of the financial year, and the profit and loss account shall give a **true and fair view** of the profit or loss of the company for the financial year.*

The Act also stated that companies with a turnover of more than £350,000 (since raised to £1m) must have an independent examination of their records and financial statement to ensure they reflect a "true and fair view", i.e. the accounts need to be *audited*.

But what exactly is a true and fair view?

The companies acts did not define what was meant by a true and fair view.

However legal opinion suggests that:

> *Accounts will not be true and fair unless the information they contain is sufficient in quality and quantity to satisfy the reasonable expectations of the readers to whom they are addressed.*
>
> *…the courts will treat compliance with accepted **accounting principles (discussed below)** as prima facia evidence that the accounts are true and fair.*

Directors are also obliged to depart from the requirements of other legislation in order to ensure that the accounts show a "true and fair view". The reason for the departure and its effects should also be shown as a note accompanying the accounts.

The act also recognized ***accounting standards* (discussed below)**, and made it law for companies to disclose whether the accounts have been prepared in accordance with the standards, any material departure from the standards and the reason for departure.

Companies Act 1989

This Act amended the 1985 Act, implemented the EC Seventh and Eighth Directives and introduced regulations relating to small companies and directors.

The EC Seventh Directive is mainly concerned with the preparation of consolidated accounts, i.e. the accounts of a group of companies, with a holding company and a number of subsidiaries. You will study consolidated accounts when you go on to study for the Associateship.

The EC Eighth Directive concerns the regulation of auditors. On the whole, the Companies

Structure of Accounts

Acts say 'what to report' and SSAPs and FRSs (see 15.2 below) say 'how to measure and disclose items'.

15.2 Standards or statements of best practice – Statement of Standard Accounting Practice (SSAPs) and Financial Reporting Standards (FRSs)

What are SSAPs and FRSs?

SSAPs and FRSs are statements of required accounting practice to be followed when producing the final accounts of a business.

The original objectives of these rules or standards were to:

1. Recommend disclosure of accounting bases (discussed below);
2. Narrow the areas of difference and variety in accounts;
3. Require disclosure of departure from standards;
4. Introduce a system of wide standard setting;
5. Seek improvements in existing disclosure requirements of company law and stock exchange.

What is the standard-setting process?

The process has undergone many changes over the years. While this is unlikely to be examined, here is a brief history of the process:

1960s	The major impetus for standards of best practice and uniformity came in the 1960s following a number of scandals where companies were seen to publish accounts which were incorrect and lacked uniformity.
Jan 1970	The Accounting Standards Steering Committee (ASSC) was formed by the Council of the Institute of Chartered Accountants in England and Wales with the objective of removing subjectivity from the way in which accounts were prepared and presented by developing statements and standards of best practice and by encouraging disclosure of the accounting policies adopted.
Feb 1976	By February 1976 other accounting bodies had joined the ASSC and on 1 Feb 1976 the ASSC became the *Accounting Standards Committee (ASC)* responsible for preparing draft standards, which, if approved by all the accounting bodies, would be issued as a *Statement of Standard Accounting Practice (SSAP)* to be observed by the members.

15 – The Regulatory Regime and Accounting Concepts

SSAPs were said to have the following advantages:

- they reduced confusion over the methods to adopt
- they provided a focal point for debate about best practice
- they encouraged disclosure of accounting policies used
- they were less rigid than legislation

The ASC also developed and issued *Statements of Recommended Practice (SORPs)*. These were not mandatory and were concerned with issues of a non-general nature. However, like SSAPs, they were issued to encourage standardization of the issues concerned.

Jan 1986 — The ASC became a Committee of the Consultative Committee of Accounting Bodies Limited (CCAB Limited).

Sept 1988 — Following criticisms, the Dearing Committee was established to review the standard-setting process. It presented its findings in 1988 to the CCAB.

Its recommendations included:

- Observance of accounting standards should remain as far as possible the responsibility of auditors, preparers and users of accounts and there should not be a general move to incorporate them into law.
- A financial reporting council should be created covering at high level a variety of interests, with the chairman appointed by the Secretary of State for Trade and Industry and the Governor of the Bank of England, to guide standard-setting in the public interest.
- Devising standards should be carried out by an expert accounting standards board with a full-time chairman and technical director and salaried staff. The board would issue standards on its own authority by a two-thirds majority.
- A review panel should be established to examine contentious departures from accounting standards by large companies.

1990 — The government announced the establishment of the Financial Reporting Council under the chairmanship of Sir Ron Dearing.

Aug 1990 — The ASC was replaced by the *Accounting Standards Board (ASB)* following a number of criticisms of the ASC and SSAPs. Criticisms included:

- The ASC was too open to political lobbying
- CCAB approval was required for SSAPs
- Too many detailed rules led to rigidity rather than flexibility, although

Structure of Accounts

at times SSAPs were also seen to allow more than one way of preparing the accounts

- There was no conceptual framework established for the development and issue of standards
- SSAPs were reactive rather than proactive
- SSAPs were inappropriate in some circumstances
- User groups were not directly involved in the creation of SSAPs

Despite the criticisms, the ASB agreed to adopt the SSAPs issued by the ASC, although a number have since been superseded by *Financial Reporting Standards (FRSs)* issued by the ASB.

Adoption by the ASB gave the SSAPs the status of "accounting standards" within the meaning of the Companies Act 1985. In addition the government has indicated that it would provide statutory backing for specific standards if necessary.

15 – The Regulatory Regime and Accounting Concepts

The present standard-setting regime

Financial Reporting Council
The Council guides the ASB

Accounting Standards Board (ASB)
The ASB develops; issues and withdraws standards, **as outlined below**.

Financial Reporting Review Panel (FRRP)
The FRRP will enquire into accounts, e.g. if the accounts have been qualified by an auditor for non-compliance with the companies act, or following media comment, or following a complaint by an individual or a referral from the Stock Exchange.

*It will gather evidence enabling the court to determine whether the accounts show a "**true and fair view**". Under Section 245B of the Companies Act 1985 the courts have powers to order a company to rectify its accounts if they are found to be defective.*

At the time of writing, the FRRP has not yet invoked S245B.

Urgent Issues Task Force (UITF)
The UITF assist the ASB in areas where an Accounting Standard or Companies Act provision exists but where unsatisfactory or conflicting interpretations exist or seem likely to develop.

The UITF then issues abstracts giving guidance on how standards should be interpreted. If a company fails to comply with an abstract, it is required to give adequate disclosure of the fact in its accounts. Abstracts might then become part of an FRS.

Let us take a closer look at the role of the ASB.

The Accounting Standards Board (ASB)

The aim of the ASB is to:

Establish and improve standards of financial accounting and reporting, for the benefit of users, preparers, and auditors of financial information.

The aim will be achieved by:

1 Developing *principles* to guide it in establishing standards and to provide a framework within which others can exercise judgement in resolving accounting issues.

2 *Issuing new standards, or amending existing ones*, in response to evolving business practice, new economic developments and deficiencies being identified in current practice.

3 *Addressing current issues promptly.*

Let us examine each aim in a little more detail.

The development of a Statement of Principles to guide the ASB in establishing standards

The Statement of Principles for Financial Reporting was published in December 1999.

The purpose of the statement is to:

- Guide the ASB in the development and review of accounting standards.

- Provide a basis for choosing between alternative accounting treatments.

- Provide those interested – in particular, *users, preparers and auditors* – with an understanding of the approach adopted and how to apply standards.

The statement consists of eight chapters discussing:

1 The objective of financial statements.

2 The reporting entity.

3 The qualitative characteristics of financial information.

4 The elements of financial statements.

5 Recognition in financial statements.

6 Measurement in financial statements.

7 Presentation of financial information.

8 Accounting for interests in other entities.

At this stage of your studies you do not need to know about the Statement of Principles in great detail. However please be aware of its existence and purpose.

It is also worth reminding ourselves of the major users of accounts, who were identified in the

15 – The Regulatory Regime and Accounting Concepts

statement of principles. The major uses are defined as those groups that have a reasonable right to information about the reporting entity and include:

- *Investors (shareholders), existing and potential,* who need to decide whether to buy or sell the company's shares or to subscribe for new shares when a rights issue is made.
- *Employees* to assess the stability and profitability of the company and its ability to provide pay, retirement benefits and employment opportunities.
- *Lenders* to determine whether their loans and interest will be repaid on time.
- *Suppliers* to determine whether they will be paid on time.
- *Customers* need information concerning the continuance of the company.
- *Government and government agencies,* e.g. the Inland Revenue for tax purposes.
- *The general public* (taxpayers, ratepayers, environmentalists) to determine the effect on the local economy.

Previously the *Corporate Report*, commissioned by the ASC in 1975, identified seven user groups which included those groups outlined above as well as analysts and advisers, for example financial advisers, financial journalists, economists, etc.:

Issuing new standards, or amending existing standards

FRSs (which are now issued rather than SSAPs) are issued following a period of investigation, discussion and consultation as follows:

- The board or other interested parties identify areas that are suitable subjects for FRSs.
- The board and its staff then carry out research and consultation, examining the relevant issues, existing practice and the implications (e.g. legal and economic) of introducing particular accounting requirements.
- A Discussion Paper (DP) may then be produced and circulated to interested parties.
- A Financial Reporting Exposure Draft (FRED) is then published to allow interested parties the opportunity to comment on the proposals and to allow the board to judge the appropriateness of the proposal and the level of acceptance.
- The issue of a Financial Reporting Standard (FRS) will then follow.

But why do we need accounting standards?

Without them companies would be free to draw up their final accounts in any manner they desired. You may recall that in the introduction to this section we examined the performance of two clothes retailing companies whose accounts were identical, except that they adopted different accounting policies relating to depreciation and the provision for bad and doubtful debts.

The result was that one company was able to show a higher profit figure and also greater assets values as a result of using lower charges for depreciation and provision for bad and doubtful debts.

FRSs (and formerly SSAPs) are therefore developed with the primary aim of narrowing and regularizing the range of permissible accounting treatments applicable to transactions or situations.

How do SSAPs and FRSs solve the problem?

The standards could simply state that all companies must adopt exactly the same policies, e.g.

- account for depreciation using straight line depreciation at x%;
- provide for doubtful debts at a rate of 5 per cent of debtors.

The Accounting Standards Board (ASB) and their predecessors the Accounting Standards Committee (ASC) recognize that not all companies or industries are the same and therefore not all companies can adopt exactly the same policies, e.g.

- It may be more realistic for one company to adopt the reducing balance method of calculating depreciation due to the nature of their assets.
- Bad debts may be higher in one industry or company than another and hence their provision for doubtful debts should be higher.

Therefore:

- Standards outline the recommended practice to be followed in the case of specific transactions or situations, while allowing companies a degree of flexibility to interpret the standards in a way most suitable for their company and industry. Two companies may therefore still report different profit figures, simply because of the way they have interpreted the accounting standard.
- Companies are also free to follow a different policy/practice from that recommended by the relevant standard, but only in exceptional circumstances.

Given this flexibility, what have SSAPs and FRSs achieved?

FRS 18 – Accounting Policies is a particularly important standard in this respect in that it imposes an obligation to disclose the assumptions upon which the financial statements are based. It also sets out the principles to be followed in selecting accounting policies.

Here is a look at FRS 18 in more detail.

FRS 18 Accounting Policies

FRS 18 defines two important terms:

- Accounting policies;
- Estimation techniques.

FRS 18 requires that accounting policies should be consistent with accounting standards,

15 – The Regulatory Regime and Accounting Concepts

Urgent Issues Task Force (UITF) Abstracts and companies legislation. Where this requirement allows a choice, the FRS requires an entity to select those accounting policies judged to be most appropriate to its particular circumstances for the purpose of giving a true and fair view.

The Statement of Principles sets out four objectives for accounting information and accounting policies have to be selected to help achieve those objectives.

The objectives are:

- *Relevance* – information is relevant if it has the ability to influence the economic decisions of users and is provided in time to influence those decisions.
- *Reliability* – is achieved where information faithfully represents what it claims to represent, is free from bias and material error and is materially complete. (Materiality is discussed below.)
- *Comparability* – is achieved by a combination of consistency of treatment and disclosure.
- *Understandability* – is achieved through the way the information is presented and by reporting the substance of the transaction. It is assumed that users of the accounts will have a reasonable knowledge of business and economic activities and accounting and a willingness to study the information provided.

Accounting Policies

Accounting policies are defined by FRS 18 as:

Those principles, bases, conventions, rules and practices applied by an entity that specify how the effects of transactions and other events are to be reflected in its financial statements through

(i) recognizing

(ii) selecting measurement bases for, and

(iii) presenting

assets, liabilities, gains, losses and changes in shareholders' funds

Recognizing means reporting the transaction in either the profit and loss account or balance sheet.

Selecting measurement bases means, for example, deciding between FIFO and AVCO for stock valuation.

Presenting involves deciding exactly where the transaction will be reported, e.g. whether the item is a fixed or current asset.

Estimation Techniques

These are the methods used to apply the measurement basis. The commonest estimation

Structure of Accounts

technique encountered is the selection of the method of depreciation, i.e. reducing balance and straight line are estimation techniques.

Key Accounting Concepts

Going concern

This means that the accounts are drawn up on the basis that the business is a going concern and will continue to trade for the foreseeable future. The accountant preparing the accounts will, of course, need to satisfy himself or herself that this is the case.

If the business was not a going concern the balance sheet would alter significantly, e.g.

- *Assets* may lie idle and therefore lose their value; stock may have to be sold at reduced prices.
- *Liabilities* may increase, such as penalty payments under contracts.

Consistency

Companies are expected to adopt the same accounting treatment of items each year. A change in the way we treat certain items can have a dramatic effect on the profit figure and it would be unfair to increase profits by simply changing the way in which we draw up the accounts. That does not mean that changes are not allowed, but that any changes must be clearly stated. The effect on the year's results should also be identified and the previous year's figure restated to provide a comparison.

Accruals (or matching concept)

A trading profit and loss account reflects a company's performance for a particular account period, e.g. for the year ending 31.12.01.

We are required us to match all income relating to a particular period with the expenditure incurred which relates to that period and not the cash receipts and payments of that period. You will recall from Chapter 4 that this will mean that the company will have to make adjustments for items prepaid and owing (accruals) when preparing their accounts.

Prudence and conservatism (see Chapter 4)

This means that companies should take account of all foreseeable losses, while only recognizing profits when realization is reasonably certain. Profits should not be taken into account if there is any doubt they will be realized.

The Companies Act 1985 recognized the above four concepts and added a fifth:

Separate valuation principle

In determining the amount to be attributed to an asset or liability in the balance sheet each component item must be determined separately and the separate valuations must then be added up to arrive at the balance sheet figure. A loss on one stock line cannot therefore be covered by unrealized profits on another stock line.

15 – The Regulatory Regime and Accounting Concepts

Although not covered by the Companies Act there are a number of other important concepts:

Business entity

The accounts show the activities of the *business* not the owner. The organization should be seen as a separate business entity. You will remember from our studies so far that we have ignored the owner's personal assets when preparing the accounts of the business.

Historical cost

The accepted basis for recording goods or services acquired by the business is to record them at historical cost, i.e. their cost price, not their estimated value today. This is the most objective method of valuation, but has led to problems in periods of high rates of inflation.

Materiality

Materiality is defined as "an expression of the relative significance or importance of a particular matter in the context of the financial statement as a whole". When deciding on how to treat an item of expenditure you therefore need to consider the significance or importance of the item. For example, most companies will treat the purchase of a stapler (even though it may last for several years) as an expense (revenue expenditure) and therefore write it off profits in the period in which it was purchased, rather than treat it as the purchase of an asset (capital expenditure) because of its relatively low cost. Only companies buying and selling staplers or manufacturing staplers are likely to treat them as assets.

Money measurement

All items must be expressed in terms of money values. Accounting reports deal only with aspects of business that can be reduced to monetary terms. For example, one cannot record the values that a business may place on the skills of its workforce, even though this may affect the results of the business.

Realization

Revenue is recognized when the goods or services concerned have been transferred to the customer, or the right to receive it has been established. For example, when selling goods on credit we record the sale even though we will not receive payment for some time. You may not feel that this is very *prudent*, after all we might not get paid. You are quite right, which is why the *prudence concept* requires us to make provision for doubtful debts.

15.3   International Accounting Standards (IASs)

Since 2001 IASs have been developed and issued by the International Accounting Standards Board (IASB). The IASB replaced the International Accounting Standards Committee (IASC) which was set up in June 1973 under an agreement by the accounting bodies of Australia, Canada, France, Germany, Japan, Mexico, the Netherlands, the USA and the UK and Ireland. However there are now over 100 members in over 80 countries.

The objectives of the IASC were:

- to formulate and publish, in the public interest, accounting standards to be observed in the presentation of financial statements and to promote their worldwide acceptance and observance
- to work generally for the improvement and harmonization of regulations, accounting standards and procedures relating to the presentation of financial statements.

The change from the IASC to the IASB was necessary because the structure of the former was unwieldy and made the development of various standards difficult.

The effects of the IASs on UK regulation

Before the ASB came into existence the effect of IASs on UK standard setting was limited – some SSAPs and IASs were in agreement, some were not and some covered different issues.

However the IASC's Framework for the Preparation and Presentation of Financial Statements changed matters. The ASB based its own Statement of Principles (highlighted earlier) on the IASC's framework and FRSs issued by the ASB also state their compliance with IASs or IAS exposure drafts.

It is intended that all listed companies within the EU will comply with IASs by 2005 and the ASB have stated that they see convergence with the IASs as one of their primary aims.

15.4 Stock Exchange rules

In order for a company to receive a listing for its shares on the Stock Exchange or the Alternative Investment Market, it must conform with Stock Exchange regulations contained in the listing rules issued by the Council of the Stock Exchange.

The company thereby agrees to certain procedures and standards, including the disclosure of accounting information.

Many of the requirements do not have legal backing but the possibility of the Stock Exchange withdrawing the company's securities from the Stock Exchange list, meaning that the company's shares would no longer be traded on the market, ensures compliance by companies.

15.5 Non-mandatory recommendations

There are a number of non-mandatory (non-compulsory) codes of conduct or statements of best practice to which companies should refer when preparing and presenting their accounts:

- Recommendations from the accounting bodies
- The Cadbury Report 1992

15 – The Regulatory Regime and Accounting Concepts

- The Operating and Financial Review 1993
- The Greenbury Report 1995
- The Hampel Report 1998
- The Combined Code 1998

These are mainly concerned with the way in which companies are governed (controlled) by the directors, i.e. corporate governance.

The Cadbury Report 1992

The Cadbury Committee was set up by the Financial Reporting Council, the Stock Exchange and the accounting profession to report on financial aspects of corporate governance.

The committee produced a *voluntary* code of best practice. Although voluntary, the board of directors is responsible for applying its provisions and must state whether or not the accounts comply with the code.

The code examines four areas:

- *Board of directors*

    Which should:
    - meet regularly
    - retain full control over important decisions such as capital expenditure
    - monitor the executive management
    - have clear and acceptable divisions of responsibility to ensure a balance of power and authority
    - include executive and non-executive directors

- *Executive directors*

    Should
    - not have contracts that exceed three years without shareholder approval
    - fully disclose their total emoluments, including pension and share options
    - be paid on the basis of recommendations from a remuneration committee made up wholly or mainly of non-executive directors

- *Non-executive directors*

    Should be
    - able to exert significant influence by virtue of number and experience and thereby bring independent judgement on issues of importance
    - appointed for specific terms and selected through a formal process

Structure of Accounts

- *Controls and reporting*

    It is the board's duty to

    - present a balanced and understandable assessment of the company's position
    - ensure that an objective and professional relationship is maintained
    - establish an audit committee
    - explain their responsibilities for preparing the accounts next to a statement by the auditors
    - report on the effectiveness of the company's internal control system
    - report that the company is a going concern

The Operating and Financial Review 1993

Listed companies are encouraged to develop and present an operating and financial review detailing:

- the main factors and uncertainties that will affect the business in the future, outlining the *principal risks* and how the company intends to manage those risks
- the reason for and the effect of changes in accounting policies
- good and bad aspects of the business
- comments on trends
- an explanation of the capital structure and financial position

Its principal aim is to assist investors.

The Greenbury Report 1995

This report dealt with the specific issue of directors' remunerations. It identified best practice and issued a Code of Best Practice.

The Hampel Report 1998

The main provisions are:

- Chairman and chief executives should have separate roles.
- Directors should be on contracts of one year or less.
- The remuneration committee should be made up of independent non-executive directors.
- Non-executive directors may be paid in shares although this is not recommended.
- A senior non-executive director should be nominated to deal with the concerns of shareholders.
- Directors should be trained in their role.

15 – The Regulatory Regime and Accounting Concepts

The Combined Code 1998

In 1998 the Stock Exchange issued the final version of the Principles of Good Governance and Code of Best Practice, known as The Combined Code. This brings together the key elements of the Cadbury Report, the Greenbury Report and the Hampel Report.

15.6 Conclusion

Before moving onto the next chapter which examines a number of SSAPs and FRSs in more detail, here is a comprehensive list of all the SSAPs and FRSs issued to date, together with a note of those which have been superseded by others or withdrawn. Fortunately you do not need to know about all of them. The list is provided to enable you to see the extent of work carried out by the ASB and ASC and to see how standards have evolved.

Standard

SSAP 1	Accounting for associate companies	Superseded by FRS 9
SSAP 2	Disclosure of accounting policies	Superseded by FRS 18
SSAP 3	Earnings per share	Superseded by FRS 14
SSAP 4	Accounting for government grants	
SSAP 5	Accounting for VAT	
SSAP 6	Extraordinary items and prior year adjustments	Superseded by FRS 3
SSAP 7		Withdrawn
SSAP 8	Taxation under the imputation system	Superseded by FRS 16
SSAP 9	Stocks and long-term contracts	
SSAP 10	Statement of sources and application of funds	Superseded by FRS 1
SSAP 11		Withdrawn
SSAP 12	Accounting for depreciation	Superseded by FRS 15
SSAP 13	Accounting for research and development	
SSAP 14	Group accounts	Superseded by FRS 2
SSAP 15	Accounting for deferred taxation	Superseded FRS 19
SSAP 16	Current cost accounting	Withdrawn
SSAP 17	Accounting for post-balance sheet events	
SSAP 18	Accounting for contingencies	Superseded by FRS 12
SSAP 19	Accounting for investment properties	
SSAP 20	Foreign exchange translation	

Structure of Accounts

Standard *(continued)*

SSAP 21	Accounting for leases and hire purchase transactions	
SSAP 22	Accounting for goodwill	Superseded by FRS 10
SSAP 23	Accounting for acquisitions and mergers	Superseded by FRS 6
SSAP 24	Accounting for pension costs	Superseded by FRS 17
SSAP 25	Segmental reporting	
FRS 1	Cashflow statements	
FRS 2	Accounting for subsidiary undertakings	
FRS 3	Reporting financial performance	
FRS 4	Capital instruments	
FRS 5	Reporting the substance of transactions	
FRS 6	Acquisitions and mergers	
FRS 7	Fair values in acquisition accounting	
FRS 8	Related part transactions	
FRS 9	Associates and joint ventures	
FRS 10	Goodwill and intangible assets	
FRS 11	Impairment of fixed assets and goodwill	
FRS 12	Provisions, contingent liabilities and contingent assets	
FRS 13	Derivatives and other financial instruments	
FRS 14	Earnings per share	
FRS 15	Tangible fixed assets	
FRS 16	Current taxation	
FRS 17	Retirement benefits	
FRS 18	Accounting Policies	
FRS 19	Deferred taxation	

So which SSAPs and FRSs do we need to know about for the examination?

Standard

SSAP 9	Stocks and long-term contracts

15 – The Regulatory Regime and Accounting Concepts

FRS 1	Cashflow statements
FRS 3	Reporting financial performance
FRS 15	Tangible fixed assets
FRS 18	Accounting policies

Now that does look better! – particularly as we have already examined:

- FRS 18 above
- FRS 15 in Chapter 6 and
- FRS 1 in Chapter 13.

In the next chapter we will therefore examine:

- SSAP 9 and
- FRS 3

The *examination questions* will be concerned with:

1. An understanding of SSAPs, FRSs and accounting policies;
2. A discussion of their importance;
3. An ability to illustrate the impact of the above standards and policies on final accounts, in particular the reported profit.

Summary

1. *UK companies must observe regulations from various sources* when preparing and presenting their accounts:

   - Legislation – UK and EU
   - Standards or statements of best practice, in particular Statements of Standard Accounting Practice (SSAPs) and Financial Reporting Standards (FRSs)
   - International Accounting Standards (IASs)
   - Stock Exchange rules
   - Non-mandatory requirements

2. The Companies Act 1985 brought together the acts of 1947, 1948, 1967, 1980 and 1981, setting out general rules and formats concerning the content and form of published company accounts.

3. Section 226 Companies Act 1985, states that:

   *the balance sheet shall give a **true and fair view** of the state of affairs of the company as at the end of the financial year, and the profit and loss account shall give a **true and fair view** of the profit or loss of the company for the financial year.*

4. Legal opinion suggests that:

   *Accounts will not be **true and fair** unless the information they contain is sufficient in quality and quantity to satisfy the reasonable expectations of the readers to whom they are addressed.*

   *...the courts will treat compliance with accepted **accounting principles** as prima facia evidence that the accounts are true and fair.*

5. *Statements of Standard Accounting Practice (SSAPs) and Financial Reporting Standards (FRSs) are statements of recommended accounting practice to be followed when producing the final accounts of a business.*

6. *The original objectives of SSAPs and FRSs were to:*
   1. recommend disclosure of accounting bases;
   2. narrow the areas of difference and variety in accounts;
   3. require disclosure of departure from standards;

15 – The Regulatory Regime and Accounting Concepts

    4   introduce a system of wide standard setting;

    5   seek improvements in existing disclosure requirements of company law and stock exchange

7 *The present standard-setting regime*

- Financial Reporting Council (FRC)
- Accounting Standards Board (ASB)
- Financial Reporting Review Panel (FRRP)
- Urgent Issues Task Force (UITF)

8. *The Financial Reporting Review Panel (FRRP)* will enquire into accounts, e.g. if the accounts have been qualified by an auditor for non-compliance with the Companies Act, or following media comment, or following a complaint by an individual or a referral from the Stock Exchange.

9. *The Urgent Issues Task Force (UITF)* assists the ASB in areas where an accounting standard or Companies Act provisions exists but where unsatisfactory or conflicting interpretations exist or seem likely to develop.

10. *The accounting standards board (ASB)*

    The aim of the ASB is to "establish and improve standards of financial accounting and reporting, for the benefit of users, preparers, and auditors of financial information".

11. *The aim of the ASB will be achieved by*:

    1 Developing *principles* to guide it in establishing standards and to provide a framework within which others can exercise judgement in resolving accounting issues

    2 *Issuing new standards, or amending existing ones*, in response to evolving business practice, new economic developments and deficiencies being identified in current practice

    3 *Addressing current issues promptly*

12. The *major users of accounts* are defined as those groups that have a reasonable right to information about the reporting entity and include:

    - Investors (shareholders), existing and potential
    - Employees
    - Lenders
    - Suppliers
    - Customers
    - Government and government agencies
    - The general public

Structure of Accounts

13. The ASB and the ASC both *recognize that not all companies or industries are the same and therefore not all companies can adopt exactly the same policies.*

14. *SSAP 2 Disclosure of Accounting Policies,* defined three important terms:
    - Fundamental (essential) accounting concepts
    - Accounting bases
    - Accounting policies

15. *Fundamental accounting concepts*

    Going concern

    This means that the accounts are drawn up on the basis that the business is a going concern.

    Consistency

    Companies are expected to adopt the same accounting treatment of items each year.

    Accruals (or matching concept)

    SSAP 2 requires us to match all income relating to a particular period with the expenditure incurred which relates to that period and not the cash receipts and payments of that period.

    Prudence and conservatism

    This means that companies should take account of all foreseeable losses, while only recognizing profits when realization is reasonably certain.

16. *The Companies Act 1985 recognized the four fundamental concepts and added a fifth concept:*

    Separate valuation principle

    In determining the amount to be attributed to an asset or liability in the balance sheet each component item must be determined separately and the separate valuations must then be added up to arrive at the balance sheet figure.

17. While not covered by SSAP 2 there are a number of *other important concepts*:

    Business entity
    The accounts show the activities of the *business* not the owner.

    Historical cost
    The accepted basis for recording goods or services acquired by the business is to record them at historical cost, i.e. their cost price, not their estimated value today.

    Materiality
    When deciding on how to treat an item of expenditure we will consider the material needs of the organization.

15 – The Regulatory Regime and Accounting Concepts

Money measurement

All items must be expressed in terms of money values.

Realization

Revenue is recognized when the goods or services concerned have been transferred to the customer, or the right to receive them has been established.

18. *Accounting bases* are "the methods developed for expressing or applying fundamental accounting concepts to financial transactions or items.

19. *Accounting policies* are the specific accounting bases followed by a company.

20. *SSAP 2 and the Companies Act 1985 require that:*

    - the policies should be applied consistently from one year to the next
    - if the accounts are prepared on the basis of assumptions which differ in material respect from any of the generally accepted fundamental accounting concepts then:
    - details of the assumption must be stated
    - the reasons for making the assumption must be stated
    - the effect of the departure must be stated
    - the accounting policies adopted must be stated as a note to the accounts

21. *International Accounting Standards(IASs)* are developed and issued by the International Standards Board (IASB).

22. *The objectives of the IASB are:*

- to formulate and publish, in the public interest, accounting standards to be observed in the presentation of financial statements and to promote their worldwide acceptance and observance.
- to work generally for the improvement and harmonization of regulations, accounting standards and procedures relating to the presentation of financial statements.

23. The ASB based its own statement of principles (highlighted earlier) on the IASCs framework, and FRSs issued by the ASB also state their compliance with IASs.

24. *Stock Exchange rules*

    In order for a company to receive a listing for its shares on the Stock Exchange or the Alternative Investment Market, it must conform with stock exchange regulations contained in the listing rules or Yellow Book issued by the Council of the Stock Exchange.

25. *Non-mandatory recommendations*

    There are a number of non-mandatory (non-compulsory) codes of conduct or statements of best practice to which companies should refer when preparing and presenting their accounts:

Structure of Accounts

- Recommendations from the accounting bodies
- The Operating and Financial Review 1993
- The Combined Code 1998

These are mainly concerned with the way in which companies are governed (controlled) by the directors, i.e. corporate governance.

16

ASSET VALUATION AND PROFIT MEASUREMENT

Syllabus Objectives

6.1 The link between the valuation of assets and liabilities and profit measurement

6.2 SSAP 9 stock identification and valuation

   FIFO, lower of cost and net realizable value, full cost, and present location and condition

6.3 Depreciation

- The effect of straight line and reducing balance methods (FRS 18) on asset valuation and profit measurement

6.4 Goodwill

- The difference between the value of a business as a whole and the value of its net assets in the balance sheet

6.5 Asset revaluation and revaluation reserve

6.6 Non-recurrent transactions (FRS 3)

- Definition of exceptional items and prior year adjustments with simple examples

Learning Objectives

After studying this chapter you should be able to:

1 Outline the link between *profit measurement and asset valuation*

SSAP 9 Stock and Long-term Contracts

2 Define the normal basis for stock valuation, cost and net realizable value

3 Calculate closing stock using FIFO, LIFO and AVCO on a periodic and a perpetual basis

4 Appreciate the implication of different stock valuations

FRS 15 Tangible Fixed Assets

5 Outline the major recommendations for depreciation

Structure of Accounts

Goodwill
6 Define and calculate the value of goodwill

7 Provide reasons for goodwill

Asset revaluation
8 Appreciate the significance of asset revaluation and the accounting entries required

FRS 3 Reporting Financial Performance
9 Outline the major elements of FRS 3

10 Explain the important components of the profit and loss account

11 Define exceptional item, extraordinary item and prior period adjustment

12 Define and calculate earnings per share, commenting upon its significance.

Introduction

In the last chapter we saw that:

> *SSAPs and FRSs are developed with the primary aim being to narrow and regularize the range of permissible accounting treatments applicable to transactions or situations.*

However, we also saw that SSAPs and FRSs:

> *do not state that all companies must adopt exactly the same policies*

because the ASB (and ASC) recognize that not all companies or industries are the same and therefore not all companies can adopt exactly the same policies.

Therefore:

> *Standards outline the recommended practice to be followed in the case of certain transactions or situations, while allowing companies a degree of flexibility to interpret the standards in a way most suitable for their company and industry.*

Two companies may therefore report different profit figures and asset values simply because of the way they have interpreted the accounting standard.

But, *FRS 18 – Accounting Policies* imposes an obligation to disclose the assumptions upon which the financial statements are based.

In this chapter we will examine "Profit measurement and asset valuation", focusing on a number of the standards which are open to interpretation.

Profit measurement

Here is the profit and loss account of the limited company which we examined in detail in Chapter 8.

Which items will be affected by the policies adopted by the company and/or the interpretation of those policies when *measuring profit*?

16 – Asset Valuation and Profit Measurement

Table 16.1: Trading profit and loss account of Example Ltd for the year ending 31.12.X9

	£	£	£
Sales			500,000
Less cost of goods sold			
Opening stock		50,000	
+ purchases		250,000	
		300,000	
– closing stock		60,000	240,000
Gross profit			260,000
Less expenses			
Rent and rates		5,000	
Provision for bad and doubtful debts			3,000
Light and heat		6,000	
Wages		50,000	
Motor expenses		20,000	
Directors' remuneration		40,000	
Auditors' remuneration		3,000	
Debenture interest		2,000	
Amortization of goodwill		2,000	
Depreciation:			
Equipment		5,000	
Fixtures and fittings		5,000	141,000
Net profit for the year			119,000
before taxation			
Less corporation tax			40,000
Net profit for the year			79,000
after taxation			
Plus retained profits			
from previous year			72,000
			151,000
Less appropriation			
Transfer to general reserve		5,000	
Transfer to other reserves		6,000	
		11,000	
Preference dividends			
Final proposed		3,000	
Ordinary dividends:			
interim paid	2,000		
Final proposed	5,000	7,000	21,000
			130,000

Structure of Accounts

You may well have stated that the following items can be affected by the policies adopted and/or the interpretation of those policies when *measuring profit*.

Sales

The *prudence concept* states that companies should recognize profits only when realization is reasonably certain. Does the company recognize the sale (and profit) when customers place an order or when customers pay the cash amount due?

Stock (see below)

SSAP 9 suggests various methods for valuing *stock and long-term contracts*. If companies adopt inconsistent methods their calculation of opening and closing stock figures may be different and hence so too will the *profit measurement*. As you can see both opening and closing stock feature in the calculation of gross profit.

Expenses

The *accruals (or matching concept)* means that companies should match the income relating to a particular period with the expenditure incurred in that same period by accounting for prepayments and accruals (amounts owing). The techniques used to calculate/estimate prepayments and accruals will affect the expenses figures and hence the profit.

Provisions

The *provision for bad debts* may be different from one company to another depending upon their assessment of risk and their interpretation of the *prudence concept*.

Provision for Depreciation may also differ from company to company depending upon the method of calculation used.

Clearly the higher the provision the lower the *profit* for that particular year.

Appropriations

Although not affecting the net profit, the amount of appropriation will affect the retained profit at the end of the accounting period. For example:
- transfers to reserves
- dividends paid and proposed

Asset valuation

Now let us look at the balance sheet, which we also examined in detail in Chapter 8 in order to see how *asset values* are affected by the policies adopted and/or the interpretation of those policies.

16 – Asset Valuation and Profit Measurement

Table 16.2: Balance sheet of Example Ltd at 31.12.X8

	£	£	£
Fixed assets			
Intangible:			
Goodwill			6,000
less goodwill written off			2,000
			4,000
Tangible:			
Premises		160,000	
Equipment	30,000		
– depreciation	10,000	20,000	
Fixtures and fittings	18,000		
– depreciation	5,000	13,000	
Motor vehicles		21,000	214,000
			218,000
Current assets			
Stock		60,000	
Debtors	20,000		
– provision for bad debts	5,000	15,000	
Bank		20,000	
Cash		1,000	
		96,000	
less: Creditors: amounts falling due within one year			
Creditors	10,000		
Proposed dividends:			
Preference	3,000		
Ordinary	5,000		
Taxation	40,000	58,000	
Net current assets			38,000
			256,000

Structure of Accounts

less

Creditors: amounts falling due after more than one year

10% debenture 2006		20,000
		236,000

Capital and reserves

	Authorized	Issued
Capital		
Ordinary shares of £1 each fully paid	70,000	50,000
10% preference shares of £1 each	30,000	30,000
	100,000	80,000
Reserves		
General reserves	10,000	
Other reserves	16,000	
Retained profits	130,000	156,000
		236,000

The following items can be affected by the policies adopted and/or the interpretation of those policies when *valuing assets*.

Fixed assets

Goodwill

The calculation of goodwill which depends on the interpretation of *FRS 10 and 11 (although these standards are not within your syllabus)* and the amount of goodwill written off each year.

Tangible assets, e.g land and buildings
Whether they have been the subject of revaluation.

Current assets

Stock
As detailed above.

Debtors

The provision for bad and doubtful debts will clearly affect the outstanding debtors figure.

For the rest of this chapter, we will focus on a number of the areas we have identified in more detail:

16 – Asset Valuation and Profit Measurement

1. The valuation of stock and long-term contracts, SSAP 9
2. Depreciation, FRS 15 (recapping Chapter 6)
3. Goodwill
4. Asset revaluation and revaluation reserve
5. Non-recurrent transaction FRS 3 – Reporting Financial performance

16.1 SSAP 9 – Stock and work in progress

Stock

The 'normal basis for stock valuation is the lower of *cost* and *net realizable value*'.

But how do we calculate cost and net realizable value?

Cost

Cost is defined by SSAP 9 as being 'expenditure which *has been* incurred in the normal course on business in bringing the product or service *to its present location and condition*'. But how is cost calculated? A manufacturer may calculate his cost of stock in the following manner:

Raw materials	£500
Wages of manufacturing staff	£1,000
	£1,500

i.e. he has added together those costs involved in the items manufactured, which is known as *marginal cost basis*.

Alternatively, the manufacturer may add to this an amount in respect of overheads incurred in manufacturing the items, e.g. factory light and heat, but not salesman's salary. This is known as *total cost basis*. Cost can therefore be calculated differently depending upon the method adopted. SSAP 9 recommends 'total cost basis'.

Net realizable value

Net realizable value means the *estimated* selling price less any *further costs to be* incurred, on completion of product, e.g. advertising, selling or delivery costs. Once again one company may calculate it differently to the next. The difference in calculating the *cost* and the *net realizable value* can be represented as follows. As you will see it relies on your knowledge of their definitions.

Structure of Accounts

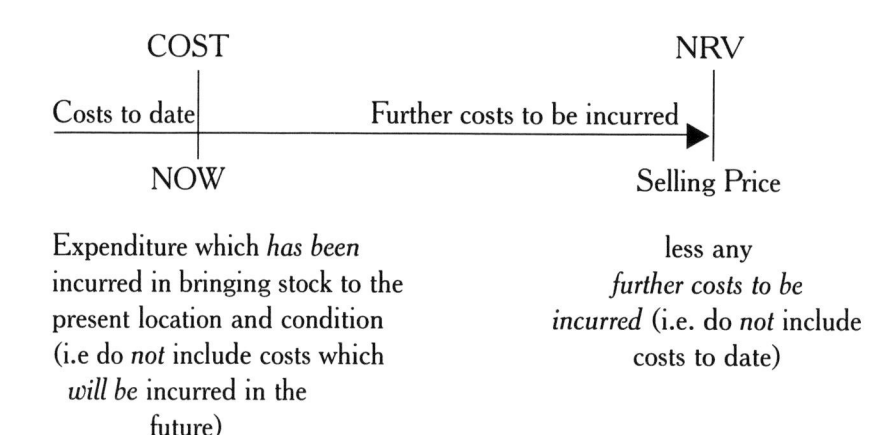

```
         COST                                    NRV
          |                                       |
Costs to date|     Further costs to be incurred   |
─────────────┼──────────────────────────────────► |
          |                                       |
         NOW                                Selling Price
```

Expenditure which *has been* incurred in bringing stock to the present location and condition (i.e do *not* include costs which *will be* incurred in the future)

less any *further costs to be incurred* (i.e. do *not* include costs to date)

Having calculated both the *Cost* and *Net realizable value*, the basis for valuing your stock is the *lower of* cost and net realizable value. Therefore, where the stock of a clothes shop consisted of unfashionable clothes which cost £5,000 but could only realize £2,000, they should be valued at the lower figure of £2,000.

This is because the *higher stock figure would overstate the asset figure and overstate the profit*.

We shall examine the effect on profit more clearly later, but for now, think about the relationship between closing stock and profit – how does a higher closing stock result in a higher profit figure?

Calculating the cost of closing stock

A shopkeeper will need to add up the number of items left on the shelves and then multiply this by the cost price or net realizable value of the items. This is known as *stocktaking*, and in many larger companies is done with the help of a computer.

It sounds very simple, but what is the valuation of the closing stock in this example?

DIY Stores Ltd

January	1	Purchased	10 units at £15 each = £150
	10	Purchased	20 units at £18 each = £360
	12	Sold	22 units at £25 each = £550
	15	Purchased	10 units at £20 each = £200
	26	Sold	6 units at £25 each = £150

Step 1 – calculate the closing stock (in units)

Purchases	40 units
less sales	28 units
Closing stock	12 units

16 – Asset Valuation and Profit Measurement

Step 2 – calculate the value of the closing stock.

But which 12 units are left in stock?

There are a number of methods which assist us in this matter:

a) FIFO,

b) LIFO,

c) AVCO.

As you will see once again, where there are a number of methods, there are a number of valuations we could arrive at.

FIFO (First in first out)

i.e. we assume that the first items purchased are the first to be sold. The 12 units left are therefore assumed to be those purchased last:

	10 purchased on 15 January at £20 each	= £200
and	2 of those purchased on 10 January at £18 each	= £36
		£236

LIFO (Last in first out)

i.e. we assume that the last items purchased are the first sold.

As a result the 12 units left in stock are:

	10 purchased on 1 January at £15 each	= £150
and	2 of those purchased on 10 January at £18 each	= £36
		£185

AVCO (Average cost)

i.e. we calculate the average price per unit purchased.

January	1	10 at £15 each =	£150
January	10	20 at £18 each =	£360
January	15	10 at £20 each =	£200
		40	£710

$\frac{710}{40}$ = £17.75 average price per unit

Closing stock = average price per unit   x   number in stock

£17.75   x   12   = £213

Structure of Accounts

The stock valuations above are known as *periodic valuations*, as they view the *period* as a whole, examining total purchases during the accounting period, i.e. we look back on the whole period (January) in order to value the closing stock of 12 units. Where companies are able to maintain detailed stock records they may choose to value stock on a *perpetual inventory basis*, valuing stock after each transaction.

FIFO (Perpetual inventory basis)

	Receipts			Issues			Stock		
Date	Quantity	Price	Value	Quantity	Price	Value	Quantity	Price	Value
Jan 1	10	£15	£150				10	£15	£150
Jan 10	20	£18	£180				10	£15	£150
							20	£18	£360
							30		£510
Jan 12				10	£15	£150	8	£18	£144
				12	£18	£216			
				22		£366			
Jan 15	10	£20	£200				8	£18	£144
							10	£20	£200
							18		£344
Jan 26				6	£18	£108	2	£18	£36
							10	£20	£200
							12		£236

Notes:

1 *Stock* — always list the items which make up the stock, making sure you keep them in date order.

2 *Issues* — by listing the stock in order of purchase it is a simple matter of looking at the list and under FIFO issue the *first (top)* items (see 12 January).

3 After each issue we can check we are correct.

    e.g.   Stock 10 January   = £510

           less issues 12 January = £366

           Stock 12 January   = £144

4 Sale price £25 *is not* part of the cost calculation.

16 – Asset Valuation and Profit Measurement

5   Using FIFO the *perpetual* valuation is always the same as the *periodic* valuation. Therefore, if the examiner asks you to calculate the closing stock using FIFO under the *perpetual basis*, you will be able to check your answer. The examiner will, however, expect to see a table similar to that above and not just the final figure, so use it only to check your result.

Although your syllabus concentrates on FIFO, we will complete our example with a look at LIFO and AVCO.

LIFO (Perpetual inventory basis)

| | Receipts ||| Issues ||| Stock |||
Date	Quantity	Price	Value	Quantity	Price	Value	Quantity	Price	Value
Jan 1	10	£15	£150				10	£15	£150
Jan 10	20	£18	£180				10	£15	£150
							20	£18	£360
							30		£510
Jan 12				20	£18	£360	8	£15	£120
				2	£15	£30	8		£120
						£390			
Jan 15	10	£20	£200				8	£15	£120
							10	£20	£200
							18		£320
Jan 26				6	£20	£120	8	£15	£120
							4	£20	£80
							12		£200

Note:

Unlike FIFO, LIFO can produce different results for *periodic* and *perpetual* basis.

Structure of Accounts

c) AVCO – Average cost (Perpetual inventory basis)

Stock

	Receipts			Issues			Average		
Date	Quantity	Price	Value	Quantity	Price	Value	Quantity	Price	Value
Jan 1	10	£15	£150				10	£15	£150
Jan 10	20	£18	£360				10		£150
							20		£360
							30		£510
							av. price = $\frac{£510}{30}$		
							30	£17	£510
Jan 12				22	£17	£374	8	£17	£136
Jan 15	10	£20	£200				8		£136
							10		£200
							18		£336
							av. price = $\frac{£336}{18}$		
							18	£18.66	£336
Jan 26				6	£18.66	£112	12	£18.66	£224

Note:

AVCO involves calculating the average price per unit after each transaction and issuing stock at the average price ruling at that time.

Calculation of closing stock summary

We have calculated the cost of closing stock using various methods and come up with the following values:

Periodic methods

a) FIFO   £236
b) LIFO   £185
c) AVCO   £213

Perpetual methods

a)   FIFO   £236

16 – Asset Valuation and Profit Measurement

b)   LIFO   £200
c)   AVCO   £224

So which valuation do we use?

As stated earlier, where companies are able to or need to maintain detailed stock records they may choose to value stock on a *perpetual inventory basis*, valuing stock after each transaction.

SSAP 9 does not ordinarily permit companies to use LIFO. As LIFO assumes that the last items in are the first out, the stock valuation may be based on items purchased a long time ago which may not reflect the current position, as prices tend to increase over a period of time.

What are the implications of different closing stock valuations?

Clearly the *asset values* will differ, but so too will the *profit measurement*.

Compare the profit calculations below:

Using FIFO:

Sales		200
Less cost of good sold		
Opening stock	50	
+ purchases	250	
	300	
– closing stock	**236**	**64**
Gross profit		136

Using LIFO:

Sales		200
Less cost of good sold		
Opening stock	50	
+ purchases	250	
	300	
– closing stock	**185**	**115**
Gross profit		85

As you can see the higher the closing stock figure, the lower the cost of goods sold and hence the higher the profit. High closing stock – high profit.

Let us now turn our attention to another area open to interpretation.

Structure of Accounts

16.2 Accounting for depreciation

Before reading further can you remember from Chapter 6:

- what FRS 15 recommends?
- the various methods you can use to calculate the depreciation charge for the year?
- the implications of different calculations of depreciation?

Here is a brief reminder; for full details please refer to Chapter 6.

FRS 15 requires that assets with a finite life should be depreciated *not* which method of calculation should be used. The most popular methods of calculating the depreciation charge for the year, and the two methods you need to be aware of for the examination, are:

- *Straight line* – the same amount for each year of the asset's life
- *Reducing balance* – a charge of say 50% of the balance each year

As a result two companies which have different method of calculating depreciation will arrive at a different profit figure.

	Company X	Company Y
Depreciation policy	Straight line	Reducing balance
	£	£
Net profit before depreciation	50,000	50,000
less depreciation	5,000	10,000
Net profit after depreciation	45,000	40,000

But FRS 15 and/or FRS 18 do require companies to disclose:

- the method they have adopted to calculate depreciation
- the useful economic life or depreciation rates
- the total depreciation charge
- the gross amount of depreciable assets and related accumulated depreciation
- any changes of methodology, the reasons for the change and the implications of the change

Therefore, those with a vested interest (e.g. shareholders, creditors, banks, etc.) can examine the accounting policies in order to understand how the profit has been determined and to appreciate the effect of the policies on the final accounts.

Now to the third area of interest – goodwill.

16 – Asset Valuation and Profit Measurement

16.3 Goodwill

What is goodwill?

According to your syllabus

> *Goodwill is the difference between the value of a firm as a whole and the value of its net assets in the balance sheet.*

Imagine you are buying a business, let us say a record shop. The net assets in the balance sheet are valued at:

	£
Premises	40,000
Equipment	5,000
Fittings	3,000
Stock	2,000
	50,000

The owner, however, feels that the value of the firm as a whole is £60,000, and therefore asks you to pay this amount for the business. But what are you buying for the extra £10,000 for?

The answer is "Goodwill".

> *Goodwill is the difference between the value of a firm as a whole and the value of its net assets in the balance sheet.*

Value of the business as a whole	60,000
Net assets in the balance sheet	50,000
Goodwill	10,000

Reasons for goodwill

You may be asked to pay £10,000 in excess of the asset value for a number of reasons:

1 *Trade under the same name*	You therefore inherit the trade and reputation of the old company, provided they have a good name! This is something you would need to consider before paying for goodwill or trading under the same name.
2 *Inherited skilled/trained staff*	This will save recruitment and training costs as well

Structure of Accounts

		as ensuring the business continues to operate smoothly.
3	*Location*	May be particularly advantageous and should therefore have a price as well as the individual assets of the business.
4	*Goodwill with suppliers*	
5	*Trade marks, patents and brands*	While the assets (chocolate-making machines etc.) of Nestle and another less well known confectionery company may be the same, you would be asked to pay more for Nestle, simply due to the value attached to the brand names you would purchase.
6	*Monopoly position.*	

All of the above features can make a significant contribution to a firm's profitability and as such are valuable assets. If you were buying the above business for £60,000 as a going concern your opening balance sheet would appear as follows:

Assets
Intangible assets

Goodwill		10,000
Tangible assets		
Premises	40,000	
Equipment	5,000	
Fittings	3,000	
Stock	<u>2,000</u>	<u>50,000</u>
		<u>60,000</u>
Capital		<u>60,000</u>

The goodwill you have purchased (*purchased goodwill*) should then be written off (amortized) over its useful life.

Although you would initially include purchased goodwill in your opening balance sheet, the previous owner should not have included the item in his or her balance sheet. It only derives its value when the business is purchased, i.e. *non-purchased goodwill* should not be included in the accounts of companies.

But how do you value goodwill?

As far as the examination is concerned you only need to be aware that:

16 – Asset Valuation and Profit Measurement

Goodwill is the difference between the value of a firm as a whole and the value of its net assets in the balance sheet.

In reality it is often calculated in accordance with the custom of the industry. For example:

1. Negotiation between the buyer and seller;
2. Sales x industry norm;
3. Profits x a number of years;
4. Average profit for x number of years x industry norm;
5. Super profits x a number of years, i.e. net profit less the amount the owner could have earned had he or she not worked in the business – wages, e.g.

		£
Net profit		20,000
less wages	10,000	
Interest (had capital been invested)	2,000	12,000
		8,000

6. Discounted momentum value method. While your first year's profits may owe much to the trade and reputation you have inherited, after say five years your customers will only be loyal because of your service and reputation, i.e. because of the goodwill you have put into the business. This method takes this into account by examining:

   a) estimated profits if the *existing business* is taken over, i.e. including inherited reputation;

   b) estimated profits if a new *identical business* starts (i.e. without the inherited reputation)

Year	Estimated profits of existing firm including goodwill £	Estimated profits of new firm excluding goodwill £	Excess £
1	20,000	10,000	10,000
2	23,000	14,000	9,000
3	25,000	18,000	7,000
4	26,000	22,000	4,000
5	26,000	26,000	—
			£30,000

The excess is therefore seen to be directly as a result of *goodwill*. So goodwill is the amount paid in excess of the asset value which, as we have seen, may be for a number of reasons and calculated in a number of ways.

Structure of Accounts

As goodwill can be calculated in a number of ways, one company may well adopt a different method from another, which will therefore result in a different asset valuation and indeed a different amount to be written off goodwill each year and hence a different profit.

FRS 10 and 11 are concerned with accounting for goodwill. You will be pleased to know that you do not need to be aware of these standards until you go on to study for the banking associateship. However here is a brief outline of the disclosure requirements which aid those with a vested interest (e.g. shareholders, creditors, banks, etc.) to understand how the assets have been valued and to appreciate the effect of the policies on the final accounts companies are required to disclose the following:

- the accounting policy adopted
- the goodwill acquired during the year
- the amortization policy adopted
- the movements during the year
- the amortization period (life)

16.4 Asset revaluation and revaluation reserve

We looked at the mechanics for dealing with the revaluation of assets in Chapter 8. Here is the example we considered. Fixed assets valued in the balance at £100,000 are found to have a true value of £150,000, how would you account for this revaluation?

There are of course two entries we need to make:

a) increase the fixed assets by £50,000, and

b) create a revaluation reserve of £50,000

The *double entries* makes sure the balance sheet balances!

FRS 11 – Impairment of Fixed Assets and Goodwill and *FRS 15 – Tangible Fixed Assets* deal with the valuation of assets in great detail. However knowledge of these standards is not required for your examination and we will therefore move onto our final item.

16.5 Non-recurrent transactions, FRS 3 – Reporting Financial Performance

The ASB issued FRS 3 for a number of reasons:

- organizations were becoming increasingly complex and therefore a *new format of the profit and loss account* was required to improve the quality of information
- *Earnings per share*, a figure used to assess a company's performance, was seen as too simplistic and the ASB wanted to move emphasis away from earnings per share

16 – Asset Valuation and Profit Measurement

The objective of FRS 3 is to:

> *require reporting entities within its scope to highlight a range of **important components** of financial performance to aid users in **understanding the performance achieved** by a reporting entity in a period and to **assist them in forming a basis for their assessment** of future results and cashflows*

i.e. to aid users in:

- understanding the performance achieved (*in the past*), and
- assist them in assessing *future* results and cashflows.

The main elements FRS 3 is concerned with are:

A A new format of the profit and loss account

B Statement of recognized gains and losses

C Reconciliation of movements in shareholders' funds

D Disclosure of profit based on historic cost

E Earnings per share and extraordinary items

F Prior year adjustments

Here is an outline of A to F. Please note your syllabus and examination are NOT concerned with B, C and D, or the calculation of earnings per share as outlined in E.

A – A new format of the profit and loss account

The new format shows a number of important components to aid the users' understanding and assessment of past and future performance:

- Results of continuing activities
- Results of discontinued activities
- Profit or loss on the sale or termination of an operation, costs of a fundamental reorganization or restructuring and profit and losses on the disposal of fixed assets
- Extraordinary items

Let us look at each one in turn.

Results from continuing activities (including acquired operations)

i.e. results from those activities which are likely to continue in the future, split between activities carried out in the previous year and acquired operations.

Results from discontinued activities

i.e. results from those activities which have been discontinued (sold or terminated) during the year, and which will therefore not be achieved in the future. It also alerts the user to the fact that significant changes have been made which will affect future performance.

Profit or loss on the sale or termination of an operation, costs of a fundamental reorganization or restructuring and profit and losses on the disposal of fixed assets

These items are unlikely to occur again in the future. By taking them out of normal profit and loss and showing them separately the user can see the normal position. Once again it also alerts the user to the fact that significant changes have been made which will affect future performance.

Extraordinary items

i.e. material, abnormal items which fall outside the ordinary activities of the business. As these are not likely to recur, they are shown separately from the results of ordinary activities.

Here is an example of a profit and loss account drawn in compliance with FRS 3.

16 – Asset Valuation and Profit Measurement

Table 16.3: Profit & loss account drawn in compliance with FRS 3

	Continuing Operations	Acquisitions	Discontinued Operations	Total Year 2	Total Year 1
Turnover	500	100	200	800	700
Cost of sales	350	80	190	620	550
Gross profit	150	20	10	180	150
Net operating expenses	50	10	20	80	70
Operating profit	100	10	(10)	100	80
Profit on sale of continuing operations	20			20	
Loss on disposal of discontinued operations			(30)	(30)	
Profit on ordinary activities before interest	120	10	(40)	90	80
Interest				5	3
Profit on ordinary activities before taxation				115	77
Taxation				40	35
Profit on ordinary activities after tax				75	42
Extraordinary items				(4)	2
Profit for the year				71	44
Dividend				3	2
Retained profit for the year				68	42

As you can see, the user can easily identify:

- turnover (sales);
- cost of sales;
- gross profit;
- operating expenses and
- operating profit

for continuing operations, acquired operations and discontinued operations.

In addition, the user can also identify

- Profit on ordinary activities and
- Profit including extraordinary items, which may be either positive or negative depending upon the nature of the extraordinary item.

Note: Unless asked to draw a profit and loss account in accordance with FRS 3 use the format we have used throughout the text. It may be useful however to draw a specimen profit and loss account similar to that above if asked to explain the objective and requirements of FRS 3.

B – Statement of recognized gains and losses

This is a new *primary* statement required by FRS3. By *primary* statement it means it is of equal prominence to the balance sheet, profit and loss account and cashflow statement.

Although the profit and loss account will include most of a company's gains and losses it will not include movements in reserves (other than by way of a note accompanying the accounts). FRS 3 makes it obligatory to reveal such gains and losses as follows:

Example:

Profit for the year (as per p and l)	x
Items taken directly to reserves:	
Revaluation of fixed assets	x
Revaluation of investment properties:	x
Total recognized gains and losses	x
Prior year adjustments	(x)
Total gains and losses since last report	x

An additional statement required by FRS 3 to be included in the notes to the accounts is the reconciliation of movements in shareholders funds.

C – Reconciliation of movements in shareholders' funds

The purpose of this note is to show clearly how shareholders' funds have changed during the year, which will depend on:

- the profit and loss account

16 – Asset Valuation and Profit Measurement

- other changes in shareholders' funds as shown in the statement of recognized gains and losses
- all other changes in shareholders funds not shown in the statement of recognized gains and losses, e.g. dividends paid and proposed, changes in capital (share issues and redemptions).

Example:

Profit for the year	x
Dividends	(x)
Other recognized gains and losses	x
New share capital	x
Net addition to shareholders' funds	x
Opening shareholders' funds	x
Closing shareholders' funds	x

D – Disclosure of profit based on historic cost

Accounts should be prepared on the basis of *historical cost*. However many companies prepare their accounts under the historical cost convention but as modified by the revaluation of fixed assets. Therefore because different approaches are being taken a note is needed to aid comparisons. The purpose of the note is to restate the profit to a historical cost basis, i.e. to eliminate the effect of revaluations on reported profit.

E – Earnings per share and extraordinary items

Earnings per share is a major measure of a company's performance:

$$EPS = \frac{Earnings}{Number\ of\ shares\ in\ issue}$$

But how do you calculate earnings?

- is it profit before tax or after tax?
- is it profit on ordinary activities or profit after extraordinary items, which may be either positive or negative depending upon the nature of the extraordinary item?

Prior to FRS 3 extraordinary items were excluded. Therefore if a company could include some expenses as extraordinary they would be excluded, which would boost earnings (profits) and boost earnings per share and hence the company would appear to be performing better.

Structure of Accounts

FRS 3 changed the definition of extraordinary item and the way in which earnings per share is calculated and thus restricted the ways companies could manipulate the figures. FRS 3 defines exceptional and extraordinary items as follows:

Exceptional items:

*Material items which derive from events or transactions that fall within the **ordinary activities** of the reporting entity and which individually or, if of a similar type, in aggregate, need to be disclosed by virtue of their size or incidence if the financial statements are to give a true and fair view.*

e.g.

- abnormal charges for bad debts
- abnormal provisions

Accounting treatment:

- generally exceptional items should be included in the relevant profit and loss account heading
- details and explanations of these items should be disclosed in the notes to the accounts

However there are exceptions to this treatment. The following items:

- Profit/loss on sale or termination of an operation
- Cost of fundamental reorganization
- Profit/loss on disposal of fixed assets

are shown separately on the face of the profit and loss account, after operating profit. This is because, although they are not expected to recur regularly, they are likely to be of such a size that readers of the accounts need to have these items highlighted to warn of their possible effects on the future results and cashflows.

Extraordinary items:

*Material items possessing a high degree of abnormality which arise from events or transactions that fall **outside the ordinary activities** of the reporting entity and which are not expected to recur.*

Accounting treatment:

- Shown on the face of the profit and loss account before dividends

However, FRS 3 makes it clear that such items are very rare if indeed they exist at all. Certainly no accounts in practice have included extraordinary items since FRS 3 was

16 – Asset Valuation and Profit Measurement

published. If such items were to exist, readers should be warned separately of their existence due to their material size and the effect they might have on future results and cashflows.

Earnings per share

FRS 3 and FRS 14 defines earnings per share as:

the profit in pence attributable to each equity share, based on the (consolidated) profit of the period after tax, minority interests, extraordinary items and preference dividends, divided by the number of equity shares in issue.

i.e.

$$\frac{\text{Profit after tax, minority interest, extraordinary items, preference dividend}}{\text{Number of equity shares}}$$

As stated earlier, prior to FRS 3 earnings were calculated before extraordinary items and hence the earnings per share figure could be manipulated by misuse of extraordinary items. FRS 3 gives a clear definition which all companies must abide by which therefore aids the comparison of:

- the performance of a particular company over a period of time (from year to year)
- the performance of one company in comparison to another company
- the returns from equity shares in the company compared to the returns available from other investments

For more details you may refer to *FRS 14, Earnings Per Share*. This may well form part of your later studies.

F – Prior year adjustments

When the final accounts are produced they may include estimates (e.g. provisions, accruals) that are found to be incorrect the following year. The question is, what do we do?

Do we deal with it in this year's accounts or make an adjustment to last year's accounts? If the error is small we will deal with it in this year's accounts, leaving last year's unchanged. But, if the error is:

- fundamental
- caused by a change in accounting policy

Then a *prior year adjustment* is necessary. The accounting treatment is as follows:

- restate the prior year profit and loss account and balance sheet
- restate the opening reserve balance
- include the adjustment in the reconciliation of movements in shareholders' funds
- include a note at the foot of the statement of total recognized gains and losses of the current period

Structure of Accounts

Summary

1 *Profit measurement* is affected by the policies adopted and/or the interpretation of policies affecting:

- Sales
- Stock
- Expenses
- Provisions, e.g. depreciation
- Appropriations; although not affecting the net profit the amount of appropriation will affect the retained profit.

2 *Asset valuation* can be affected by the policies adopted and/or the interpretation of those policies affecting

- Fixed assets
- Goodwill
- Tangible assets, e.g land and buildings
- Stock
- Debtors

SSAP 9 – Stock and work in progress

3 The '*normal basis for stock valuation is the lower of cost and net realizable value*'.

4 *Cost* is defined by SSAP 9 as being 'expenditure which *has been* incurred in the normal course of business in bringing the product or service to its present location and condition'.

5 *Net realizable value* means the estimated selling price less any further costs to be incurred on completion of the product, e.g. advertising, selling or delivery costs.

6 *Stock may be calculated* in the following manner:

- *marginal cost basis*
- *total cost basis*

    using:

- FIFO, i.e. we assume that the first items purchased are the first to be sold.
- LIFO, i.e. we assume that the last items purchased are the first sold.
- AVCO, i.e. we calculate the average price per unit purchased.

8 FIFO, LIFO and AVCO can all be calculated on either a periodic basis or on a perpetual inventory basis, valuing stock after each transaction.

9 *SSAP 9* does not ordinarily permit companies *to use LIFO*.

16 – Asset Valuation and Profit Measurement

10 *Different closing stock valuations will result in different asset values and profit figures.*

11 *The higher the closing stock figure, the lower the cost of goods sold and hence the higher the profit. High closing stock – high profit.*

Accounting for Depreciation

12 *FRS 15* requires that *assets with a finite useful life* be depreciated *not* which method of calculation should be used.

13 The most popular *methods of calculating the depreciation charge* for the year
- Straight line – the same amount for each year of the asset's life
- Reducing balance – a charge of say 50% of the balance each year

14 *FRS 15 requires companies to disclose*:
- the method they have adopted to calculate depreciation
- the useful economic life or depreciation rates
- the total depreciation charge
- the gross amount of depreciable assets and related accumulated depreciation
- any changes of methodology, the reasons for the change and the implications of the change

Goodwill

15 *Definition* 'Goodwill is the difference between the value of a firm as a whole and the value of its net assets in the balance sheet'.

16 *Reasons for goodwill*
- Trade under the same name
- Inherit skilled/trained staff
- Location
- Goodwill connections with suppliers
- Trade marks, patents and brands
- Monopoly position.

17 The goodwill you have purchased *(purchased goodwill)* should then be written off (amortized) over its useful life.

18 *Non-purchased goodwill* should not be included in the accounts of companies.

19 *Goodwill is often calculated in accordance with the custom of the industry.* For example:
- Negotiation between the buyer and seller;

Structure of Accounts

- Sales x industry norm;
- Profits x a number of years;
- Average profit for x number of years x industry norm;
- Super profits x a number of years, i.e. net profit less the amount the owner could have earned had he or she not worked in the business;
- Discounted momentum value method. This method compares:

  a) estimated profits if the *existing business* is taken over, i.e. including inherited reputation;

  b) estimated profits if a new *identical business* starts i.e. without the inherited reputation.

Asset revaluation and revaluation reserve

20 *When fixed assets are revalued* the accounting entries are as follows:

- increase the fixed assets in accordance with the revaluation, and
- create a revaluation reserve of a similar amount

Non-recurrent transaction, FRS 3 – Reporting Financial Performance

21 *The ADB issued FRS 3 for a number of reasons:*

- Organizations were becoming increasingly complex and therefore a new format of the profit and loss account was required to improve the quality of information
- Earnings per share, a figure used to assess a company's performance, was seen as too simplistic and the ABS wanted to move emphasis away from earnings per share

22 *The objective of FRS 3 is to:*

require reporting entities within its scope to highlight a range of important components of financial performance to aid users in understanding the performance achieved by a reporting entity in a period and to assist them in forming a basis for their assessment of future results and cashflows.

23 *The main elements of FRS 3 are*

- A new format of the profit and loss account
- Statement of recognized gains and losses
- Reconciliation of movements in shareholders' funds
- Disclosure of profit based on historic cost
- Earnings per share and extraordinary items
- Prior year adjustments

16 – Asset Valuation and Profit Measurement

24 *The new format shows* a number of important components to aid the users' understanding and assessment of past and future performance:

- Results of continuing activities
- Results of discontinued activities
- Profit or loss on the sale or termination of an operation, costs of a fundamental reorganization or restructuring and profit and losses on the disposal of fixed assets
- Extraordinary items

25 *Results from continuing activities (including acquired operations)*

i.e. results from those activities which are likely to continue in the future, split between activities carried out in the previous year and acquired operations.

26 *Results from discontinued activities*

i.e. results from those activities which have been discontinued (sold or terminated) during the year, and which will therefore not be achieved in the future. It also alerts the user to the fact that significant changes have been made which will affect future performance.

27 *Profit or loss on the sale or termination of an operation, costs of a fundamental reorganization or restructuring and profit and losses on the disposal of fixed assets*

These items can be significant. By taking them out of operating profit or loss and showing them separately the user can see the underlying position. Once again it also alerts the user to the fact that significant transactions have happened which may affect future performance.

28 *Extraordinary items*

i.e. material, abnormal items which fall outside the ordinary activities of the business. As these are not likely to recur, they are shown separately from the results of ordinary activities.

29 *Statement of recognized gains and losses* shows movements in reserves, i.e. *recognized* as opposed to *realized* gains and losses.

30 *Reconciliation of movements in shareholders' funds* shows how shareholders' funds have changed during the year, which will depend on:

31 *Disclosure of profit based on historic cost* – the purpose of the note is to restate the profit on a historical cost basis, i.e. to eliminate the effect of revaluations on reported profit.

32 *Exceptional items:*

Material items which derive from events or transactions that fall within the **ordinary activities** of the reporting entity and which individually or, if of a similar type, in aggregate, need to be disclosed by virtue of their size or incidence if the financial statements are to give a true and fair view.

Structure of Accounts

Accounting treatment:

- generally exceptional items should be included in the relevant profit and loss account heading
- details and explanations of these items should be disclosed in the notes to the accounts

33 *Extraordinary items:*

*Material items possessing a high degree of abnormality which arise from events or transactions that fall **outside the ordinary activities** of the reporting entity and which are not expected to recur.*

Accounting treatment:

- Shown on the face of the profit and loss account before dividends.

34 *Earnings per share*

the profit in pence attributable to each equity share, based on the (consolidated) profit of the period after tax, minority interests, extraordinary items and preference dividends, divided by the number of equity shares in issue.

i.e.

$$\frac{\text{Profit after tax, minority interest, extraordinary items, preference dividend}}{\text{Number of equity shares}}$$

35 *Prior year adjustments* – The accounting treatment is as follows:

- restate the prior year profit and loss account and balance sheet
- restate the opening reserve balance
- include the adjustment in the reconciliation of movements in shareholders' funds
- include a note at the foot of the statement of total recognized gains and losses of the current period

17

INTERPRETATION OF ACCOUNTS AND RATIO ANALYSIS

Syllabus Objectives

7.1 The effect of profit on financial position

Profit as an increase in capital and net assets

7.2 The comparability of accounting information and its strengths and limitations

7.3 Interpretation of accounts

Between companies and over time, using cash flow and ratio analysis

7.4 Ratios
- Gross profit
- Net profit
- Costs
- Gearing
- Return on capital employed
- Turnover of debtors, creditors, stock and assets
- Working capital
- Liquidity

7.5 Corporate development

Its reflection in the accounting statements

Learning Objectives

After studying this chapter you should be able to:

1 Explain the use of accounting ratios;

2 Calculate the various accounting ratios;

The Structure of Accounts

3   Analyse a company's performance using ratio analysis;

4   Outline the limitations of ratios and consider such limitations when analysing company performance.

Introduction

Finally we come to our last chapter. By now you should be able to:

- prepare the accounts of various types of businesses (Sections A and B)
- analyse a company's cash position (Section C) and
- outline the regulatory regime and appreciate the implications of companies adopting different accounting policies (Section D)

But what do the accounts mean and how do we interpret the accounts?

We can interpret the accounts using *ratio analysis*.

17.1   What is ratio analysis?

Ratio analysis is a method which can be used to assess a company's performance over a period of time or to compare the performance of two companies. In comparing the performance of two companies you must consider the nature of each company's business because the ratios of a supermarket will be significantly different from those of an engineering company, simply because of the nature of their business.

Ratio analysis can be extremely useful to both the management of the company and bank managers when faced with loan requests. As a bank clerk, you may in the future be asked by your bank manager to calculate various ratios in respect of a customer's account and to discuss your findings before he or she meets the customer to discuss the loan request.

In order to prepare for this task and the more immediate task of the examination you will need to be able to:

- calculate accounting ratios, using various formulas, and
- interpret the results of your calculations (the ratios)

17.2   Calculating accounting ratios

In order to do this in the examination you will need to:

- learn the formulas for the ratios
- extract the necessary information from the final accounts in order to calculate the ratios

Here is a list of the accounting ratios and formulas which you will need to learn for your

17 – Interpretation of Accounts and Ratio Analysis

examination. There are more, but we will leave these until later in your studies.

A. *Profitability ratios*

1 Return on total capital employed $\quad \dfrac{\text{Net profit before interest and tax}}{\text{Total capital employed}} \times 100 = \%$

2 Gross margin $\quad \dfrac{\text{Gross profit}}{\text{Sales}} \times 100 = \%$

3 Net margin $\quad \dfrac{\text{Net profit}}{\text{Sales}} \times 100 = \%$

4 Cost ratio $\quad \dfrac{\text{Expense}}{\text{Sales}} \times 100 = \%$

Note: You may be asked to calculate particular expenses as a percentage of sales,

e.g. *Staff costs, etc.*

B. *Operating ratios*

5 Rate of stock turnover $\quad \dfrac{\text{Average stock}}{\text{Cost of goods sold}} \times 365 = \text{days}$

Note: Average stock = $\dfrac{\text{Opening stock} + \text{Closing stock}}{2}$

If you are not given a full trading profit and loss account showing the opening and closing stock, simply use the closing stock figure shown in the current assets.

6 Debtors' settlement period $\quad \dfrac{\text{Debtors}}{\text{Sales}} \times 365 = \text{days}$

7 Creditors' settlement period $\quad \dfrac{\text{Creditors}}{\text{Purchases}} \times 365 = \text{days}$

Note: If you are not given a full trading profit and loss account showing the figure for purchases simply use the cost of goods sold.

C. *Liquidity ratios*

8 Working capital ratio $\quad$ Current Assets: Current Liabilities $\quad = \quad$ x: 1

9 Liquidity ratio $\quad$ Liquid Assets: Current Liabilities $\quad = \quad$ x: 1

Note: $\quad$ Liquid Assets = Current Assets less stock

The Structure of Accounts

D. Gearing ratios

10 Gearing percentage $\quad \dfrac{\text{Long-term Liabilities}}{\text{Total Capital Employed}} \times 100 = \%$

11 Equity: Debt   Shareholders' Capital Employed: Long-term Liabilities = x: 1

Having learnt the formulas the next step is to extract the necessary information from the final accounts and calculate the ratios. Here are the final accounts of Poynton Ltd, followed by my calculations for 19Y0.

Table 17.1: Trading profit and loss account of Poynton Ltd for the years ending 31.12.Y0 and 31.12.Y1

	31.12.Y0 £	31.12.Y0 £	31.12.Y1 £	31.12.Y1 £
Sales		200,000		400,000
less cost of goods sold				
Opening stock	30,000		15,000	
+ purchases	85,000		165,000	
	115,000		180,000	
− closing stock	15,000	100,000	30,000	150,000
Gross profit		100,000		250,000
less expenses		80,000		215,000
Net profit before tax		20,000		35,000
less taxation		7,000		12,000
Retained profit for the year		13,000		27,000
+Balance of profits		27,000		40,000
Retained profits		40,000		67,000

17 – Interpretation of Accounts and Ratio Analysis

Table 17.2: Balance sheet of Poynton Ltd as at 31.12.Y0 and 31.12.Y1

	31.12.Y0		31.12.Y1	
	£	£	£	£
Fixed assets		250,000		250,000
Current assets				
Stock	15,000		30,000	
Debtors	30,000		65,000	
Bank	1,000		4,000	
Cash	1,000		—	
less	47,000		99,000	
Current liabilities				
Taxation	7,000		12,000	
Creditors	30,000		50,000	
	37,000	10,000	62,000	37,000
		260,000		287,000
Share capital		200,000		200,000
and retained profits		40,000		67,000
Shareholders' capital employed		240,000		267,000
Long-term liabilities				
Loan		20,000		20,000
Total capital employed		260,000		287,000

Look at the ratios I have calculated on the next page for 19Y0, then have a go at calculating the ratios for the year 19Y1.

The Structure of Accounts

19Y0

A. *Profitability ratios*

1 Return on total capital employed

$$\frac{\text{Net profit before interest and tax}}{\text{Total capital employed}} \times 100 \quad \frac{20{,}000}{260{,}000} \times 10 = 7.69\%$$

2 Gross margin

$$\frac{\text{Gross profit}}{\text{Sales}} \times 100 \quad \frac{100{,}000}{200{,}000} \times 100 = 50\%$$

3 Net margin

$$\frac{\text{Net profit}}{\text{sales}} \times 100 \quad \frac{20{,}000}{200{,}000} \times 100 = 10\%$$

4 Cost ratio

$$\frac{\text{Expense}}{\text{Sales}} \times 100 \quad \frac{80{,}000}{200{,}000} \times 100 = 40\%$$

B. *Operating ratios*

5 Rate of stock turnover

$$\text{Average stock} \quad \frac{30{,}000 + 15{,}000}{2} = 22{,}500$$

$$\frac{\text{Average stock}}{\text{Cost of goods sold}} \times 365 \quad \frac{22{,}500}{100{,}000} \times 365 = 82 \text{ days}$$

6 Debtors' settlement period

$$\frac{\text{Debtors}}{\text{Sales}} \times 365 \quad \frac{30{,}000}{200{,}000} \times 365 = 55 \text{ days}$$

7 Creditors' settlement period

$$\frac{\text{Creditors}}{\text{Purchases}} \times 365 \quad \frac{30{,}000}{85{,}000} \times 365 = 129 \text{ days}$$

C. *Liquidity ratios*

8 Working capital ratio

Current assets: current liabilities $\quad 47{,}000 : 37{,}000 = 1.27 : 1$

9 Liquidity ratio

Liquid assets: current liabilities $\quad 32{,}000 : 37{,}000 = 0.86 : 1$

17 – Interpretation of Accounts and Ratio Analysis

D. *Gearing ratios*

10 Gearing percentage

$$\frac{\text{Long-term liabilities}}{\text{Total capital employed}} \times 100 \quad \frac{20,000}{260,000} \times 100 = \quad 7.69\%$$

11 Equity: Debt

Shareholders' capital employed: Long-term liabilities   240,000: 20,000 =   12: 1

Here are the results for 19Y0 together with the ratios you should have calculated for 19Y1.

	19Y0	19Y1
A. *Profitability ratios*		
1 Return on capital employed	7.69%	12.20%
2 Gross margin	50%	62.5 %
3 Net margin	10%	8.75%
4 Cost ratios	40%	53.75%
B. *Operating ratios*		
5 Rate of stock turnover	82 days	55 days
6 Debtors' settlement period	55 days	59 days
7 Creditors' settlement period	129 days	111 days
C. *Liquidity ratios*		
8 Working capital ratio	1.27: 1	1.60: 1
9 Liquidity ratio	0.86: 1	1.11: 1
D. *Gearing ratios*		
10 Gearing percentage	7.69%	6.97%
11 Equity: Debt	12: 1	13.35: 1

17.3   Interpretation of account ratios

Having calculated the ratios we must now look at the results and consider what they mean. Take each ratio in turn and comment briefly on:

The Structure of Accounts

- What the ratio is designed to show.
- The *trend*, i.e. the direction in which the company is going, by comparing the results of 19Y0 with those of 19Y1. For large loans you may need to assess three or even five years accounts.
- Whether the *trend* shows an improvement or decline in performance.
- Why performance has improved or declined.

Here are some comments on the performance of Poynton Ltd, together with some points of explanation where appropriate.

Profitability

1 *Return on capital employed*

- This ratio measures the return on the long-term funds employed in the business and is an indication of whether the company has successfully utilized its assets during the period.
- Poynton's return has increased from 7.69% to 12.20%.
- This shows an improvement in return, indicating that Poynton has successfully utilized its assets.

2 *Gross profit margin*

- This ratio measures gross profit as a percentage of sales.
- Poynton's return has increased from 50% to 62.5% of sales. In addition, it is worth noting that not only has the return increased but the volume of sales (£200,000 – £400,000) has also doubled.
- This shows a considerable improvement in performance; Poynton is selling twice as much at a better gross profit margin
- It indicates that Poynton has either effectively controlled its cost of goods sold (purchasing costs or manufacturing costs) and/or managed to increase its sales price, maybe due to better marketing without a corresponding increase in the cost of goods sold.

		19Y0		*19Y1*	
	Sales	£200	100%	£400	100%
less	Cost of goods sold	£100	50%	£150	37.5%
	Gross profit	£100	50%	£250	62.5%

A decrease in the gross margin may be due to a reduction in the selling price against stable costs, although one would hope that the reduced price would bring greater volume of sales.

17 – Interpretation of Accounts and Ratio Analysis

3 *Net profit margin*

- This measures net profit as a percentage of sales.
- Poynton's return has reduced from 10% – 8.75% of sales.
- This shows a decline in performance.
- A declining net margin indicates that Poynton has been unable to control *all of its costs*. But which costs in particular (purchasing/manufacturing or expenses)? Given the considerable improvement in the gross margin we know it is not purchasing/manufacturing costs and can therefore conclude that the reduction in net margin was due to the company's failure to control expenses.

		19Y0		19Y1	
		£		£	
	Sales	200,000	100%	400,000	100%
less	Cost of goods sold	100,000	50%	150,000	37.5%
	Gross profit	100,000	50%	250,000	62.5%
less	Expenses	80,000	40%	215,000	53.75%
	Net profit	20,000	10%	35,000	8.75%

4 *Cost ratios*

- This measures the particular expense (in this case total expenses) as a percentage of sales.
- Poynton's total expenses have increased from 40% – 53.75% of sales.
- This shows a decline in performance.
- A declining ratio indicates that Poynton has been unable to control its expenses.
- If we were give details of the expenses we could look to see which particular expenses have not been controlled and then ask why not. It may be for reasons beyond its control, e.g. a rates increase, but it may also be due to poor management control.

Operating performance

5 *Average rate of stock turnover*

- This measures how quickly (*on average*) a company is turning its stock.
- Poynton's stock is now turning every 55 days instead of every 82 days.
- This is clearly an improvement. The quicker the turnover the better, because this will speed up the cashflow cycle and ensure that expensive stock is not sitting idle on the shelves.

The Structure of Accounts

- As stated earlier, sales volume has doubled, leading to improvement in stock turnover.

6 *Average debtors' settlement period*

- This ratio measures how long (*on average*) it takes for debtors to settle their debts.
- Poyntons debtors now settle their debts every 59 days rather than every 55 days.
- An increased settlement period may be the reason for increased sales, however in our case, the change is not dramatic. It is certainly no cause for concern; Poynton appears to be controlling its debtors effectively.

    If the debtors are taking considerably longer to pay companies may need to chase their debtors. You must also remember that the ratio indicates only the *average* settlement period. If some of the sales are on cash terms, then some debtors are outstanding for longer than 59 days and the debtors' figure may even include bad debts. As a result an *aged analysis of debtors*, showing how much is outstanding between various periods, would prove useful.

    Aged analysis of debtors

Period	Amount outstanding
0–7 days	£15,000
over 7–14 days	£10,000
over 14–21 days	£6,000
over 21–28 days	£2,000

    etc.

7 *Average creditors' settlement period*

- This ratio measures how long (*on average*) Poynton takes to pay its creditors.
- Poynton used to take 129 days credit but now takes only 111 days.
- Again not a dramatic change and no cause for concern.
- We might ask why it is paying its bills quicker. If the period is getting longer it may be because management is taking full advantage of credit facilities, or it could be that it has a cashflow problem. We should therefore compare this result with our liquidity ratios.

Liquidity

8 *Working capital*

- This shows whether cash and items that can be converted into cash adequately cover amounts due for repayment within the next 12 months.
- Our ratio has increased from 1.27: 1 to 1.6: 1.

17 – Interpretation of Accounts and Ratio Analysis

- There is therefore more cover on the amounts due for repayment. (We will discuss whether this is an improvement or not in a moment.)
- Although creditors have increased from £30,000 to £50,000 this is more than matched by an increase in debtors, stock and bank.

9 *Liquidity ratio*

- By deducting stock from the Current Assets we are able to compare the most liquid Current Assets with Current Liabilities to gain a more critical assessment of liquidity.
- Cover has increased from 0.86: 1 to 1.11: 1.
- The company is therefore more liquid.

You will no doubt recall from our look at the cashflow cycle that we need to consider the operating ratios and the nature of the industry in order to determine whether the situation is good or bad. Even cover of 3:1 can be insufficient if stock includes unsaleable stock, debtors includes bad debts and creditors are pressing for payment. In our case, we can see that:

- Stock is turning faster (55 days), and volume of sales is increasing;
- Debtors are settling around about the same time (59 days) and
- Poynton is still enjoying long periods of credit, although slightly less than before (111 days);
- Cash therefore comes in (on average) every 55 + 59 = 114 days and goes out every 111 days;
- The creditors are financing the business and hence Poynton would be foolish to maintain a large amount of working capital
- Their cover would therefore appear adequate, if not a little high.

Capital adequacy

10 *Gearing percentage*

- This examines the extent to which the company relies on borrowed funds.
- Borrowed funds now account for 6.97% of the total capital employed, compared to 7.69% the previous year.
- From the bank's point of view this is an improvement. Where companies are highly geared (e.g. above, say, 55%) they are relying heavily on borrowed funds and will be faced with high interest charges and may find it difficult to raise further finance.
- The improvement comes from generating profits without increasing long-term liabilities (loans).

11 *Debt: Equity*

- This ratio also examines the extent to which the company relies on borrowed funds

The Structure of Accounts

by comparing debt (funds borrowed long term) with equity (shareholders' funds).

- The shareholders' funds employed in the business are now 13.35 times bigger than borrowed funds employed in the business, compared to 12 times bigger the previous year.
- From the bank's point of view this is good because Poynton's stake in the business is substantial.

Summary

Profitability

- Improved return on capital employed, indicating the company has successfully utilized its assets during the period.
- Gross margin has increased from 50% to 62.5% and sales volume has doubled; this shows that Poynton has either effectively controlled its cost of goods sold (purchasing costs or manufacturing costs) and/or managed to increase its sales price maybe due to better marketing without a corresponding increase in the cost of goods sold.
- Despite the improvement in the gross margin the net margin has reduced from 10% – 8.75%, indicating that Poynton has been unable to control its expenses, which must be investigated.

Operating performance and liquidity

- Stock is turning faster (55 days), and volume of sales is increasing.
- Debtors are settling around about the same time (59 days); and
- Poynton is still enjoying long periods of credit, although slightly shorter than before (111 days).
- Cash therefore comes in (on average) every 55 + 59 = 114 days and goes out every 111 days.
- The creditors are financing the business and hence Poynton would be foolish to maintain a large amount of working capital.
- Its cover would therefore appear adequate.

Capital adequacy

- There is little reliance on borrowed funds, which account for only 6.97% of total capital employed.

The only cause for concern is the reduction in net margin caused by the increase in expenses. We need to know which expenses have increased and whether anything can be done to control them in the future.

17 – Interpretation of Accounts and Ratio Analysis

17.4　Limitation of ratio analysis

Ratio analysis can be a very useful tool to aid our assessment of a company's performance over a period of time or to compare the performance of two companies. It does have its limitations which, however, we must not forget.

1. The balance sheet is only like a photograph of the business at a particular date. It may not be typical of the business.
2. The ratios are only averages.
3. Ratios are taken over the whole business, which may hide certain areas of business which are performing badly.
4. A ratio of 10 per cent can be good or bad. In isolation ratios mean nothing; we must compare either the *trend* or with other companies of a similar nature.
5. Companies may distort the true picture.
6. Reference should be made to the accounting policies adopted, e.g. different methods of valuing stock will produce different profit figures.
7. Inflation must also be considered. An increase in sales may not be an improvement in real terms.
8. Balance sheet values are based on historical cost which may be out of date and therefore unrealistic, e.g. stock may be unsaleable, debtors may include bad debts and the bank balance may have since been spent.
9. Examining the past is no indication of the future prosperity.
10. If we have only one set of accounts, i.e. for one year, we are not able to examine the direction in which the company is going.
11. Ratios often provide questions rather than answers you must consider *why* the trend is increasing or decreasing.

    We must critically consider other things as well as the ratios, e.g.

    - cashflow forecasts, considering whether forecast sales and expenses are realistic;
    - forecast trading profit and loss account;
    - cashflow statements;
    - trading outlook, consider the market and industry the company is operating in, what future opportunities and threats it is likely to face;
    - management capabilities; what are the company's strengths and weaknesses?

The Structure of Accounts

Summary

1 *Ratio analysis* is a method which can be used to assess a company's performance over a period of time

 or to compare the performance of two companies.

2 *You will need to be able to:*

- learn various accounting formulas
- extract the necessary information from the final accounts in order to calculate the ratios
- interpret the results of your calculations (the ratios).

3 *The major ratios you will need to learn are:*

 A. Profitability ratios

 1 Return on capital employed

 2 Gross margin

 3 Net margin

 4 Cost ratios

 B. Operating ratios

 5 Rate of stock turnover

 6 Debtors' settlement period

 7 Creditors' settlement period

 C. Liquidity ratios

 8 Working capital ratio

 9 Liquidity ratio

 D. Gearing ratios

 10 Gearing percentage

 11 Equity: Debt

Please refer to the table above for the formulas.

4 *When interpreting the ratios you should take each ratio in turn and comment briefly on:*

- What the ratio is designed to show
- The *trend*, i.e. the direction in which the company is going, by comparing the results of Year 1 with those of Year 2

17 – Interpretation of Accounts and Ratio Analysis

- Whether the *trend* shows an improvement or decline in performance
- Why performance has improved or declined

5 *Return on capital employed*
- This ratio measures the return on the long-term funds employed in the business and is an indication of whether the company has successfully utilized its assets during the period.

6 *Gross profit margin*
- This ratio measures gross profit as a percentage of sales
- It indicates how effectively a company has controlled its cost of goods sold (purchasing costs or manufacturing costs) and/or managed to increase its sales price, e.g. due to better marketing, without a corresponding increase in the cost of goods sold.

7 *Net profit margin*
- This measures net profit as a percentage of sales
- A declining net margin indicated that the company has been unable to control *all of its costs*.

8 *Cost ratios*
- These measure the particular expense (or total expenses) as a percentage of sales
- A declining ratio indicates that the company has been unable to control its expenses
- If we were give details of the expenses we could look to see which particular expenses have not been controlled and then ask why not. It may be for reasons beyond the company's control but it may also be due to poor management control

9 *Average rate of stock turnover*
- This measures how quickly a company is turning its stock.
- The quicker the turnover the better, because this would speed up the cashflow cycle and ensure that expensive stock is not sitting idle on the shelves.

10 *Average debtors' settlement period*
- This ratio measures how long (on average) it takes for debtors to settle their debts.
- If the debtors are taking considerably longer to pay companies may need to chase their debtors. An increased settlement period may be the reason for increased sales.
- The ratio indicates only the average settlement period.
- An aged analysis of debtors shows how much is outstanding between various periods

11 *Average creditors' settlement period*
- This ratio measures how long (on average) Poynton takes to pay its creditors

- If the period is getting longer it may be because management is taking full advantage of credit facilities, or it could be that it has a cashflow problem. We should therefore compare this result with our liquidity ratios.

12 *Working capital*
- This shows whether cash and items that can be converted into cash adequately cover amounts due for repayment within the next 12 months.

13 *Liquidity ratio*
- By deducting stock from the current assets we are able to compare the most liquid current assets with current liabilities to gain a more critical assessment of liquidity.

14 We need to consider *the operating ratios and the nature of the industry in order to determine whether the working capital and liquidity situation is good or bad.* Even cover of 3: 1 can be insufficient if stock includes unsaleable stock, debtors includes bad debts and creditors are pressing for payment.

15 *Gearing percentage*
- This examines the extent to which the company relies on borrowed funds.
- Where companies are highly geared (e.g. above, say, 55%) they are relying heavily on borrowed funds and will be faced with high interest charges and may find it difficult to raise further finance.

16 *Debt: Equity*
- This ratio also examines the extent to which the company relies on borrowed funds by comparing debt (funds borrowed long term) with equity (shareholders' funds).

17 *Limitations of ratio analysis*
- The balance sheet is only like a photograph of the business at a particular date. It may not be typical of the business. The ratios are therefore only an average.
- Ratios are taken over the whole business, which may hide certain areas of business which are performing badly.
- A ratio of 10 per cent can be good or bad. In isolation ratios mean nothing; we must compare either the *trend* or with other companies of a similar nature.
- Companies may distort the true picture.
- Reference should be made to the accounting policies adopted, e.g. different methods of valuing stock will produce different profit figures.
- Inflation must also be considered. An increase in sales may not be an improvement in real terms.

17 – Interpretation of Accounts and Ratio Analysis

- Balance sheet values are based on historical cost which may be out-of-date and therefore unrealistic, e.g. stock is unsaleable, debtors include bad debts.
- Examining the past is no indication of the future prosperity.
- If we have only one set of accounts, i.e. for one year, we are not able to examine the direction in which the company is going.
- Ratios often provide questions rather than answers you must consider *why* the trend is increasing or decreasing.

18 *We must critically consider other things as well as the ratios, e.g.*

- Cashflow forecasts, considering whether forecast sales and expenses are realistic;
- Forecast trading profit and loss account;
- Cashflow statements;
- Trading outlook, consider the market and industry the company is operating in; what future opportunities and threats it is likely to face;
- Management capabilities; what are the company's strengths and weaknesses.

INDEX

A

abstracts, UITF 227
account
    appropriation 108, 121
    bank 23
    capital 24
    creditor 26, 28
    current 110
    debtor 27
    discount received 30
    discounts allowed 30
    equipment 24
    manufacturing 136
    petty cash 24, 28
    profit and loss 66
    purchases 26
    ratios, interpretation 281
    rent 25
    returns out 28
    sales 26
    T 22, 23, 24, 26, 28, 30
    trading 65
    wages 25
Accounting
    concepts, key 232
    for depreciation 258
    policies, definition 231
    ratios 277, 278, 279, 281
        accounting 276
    Standards Board (ASB) 225, 226, 227, 228, 230, 262
        aim 228
        Statement of Principles 228
    Standards Committee (ASC) 224, 230
    Standards Steering Committee (ASSC) 224
accounts
    balancing off 31
    overdrawn 182
    preparation of limited company 118
    recording 33
    specimen layout of partnership 112
accruals 44, 45, 49, 232, 248, 269
    adjustments for 44, 45, 48
activities results from
    continuing 263
    discontinued 263
adequacy, capital 285
adjusting the trial balance 90
adjustments 53
    how to make 42
    needed 41
    prior year 269
    why needed 42
amortization 260
appropriation 248
    account 108, 121
ASB *see* Accounting Standards Board
asset 23, 67
    revaluation 262
    valuation 248
    values 248, 250
assets
    fixed 170
    current 167, 168
    net current 124
    tangible and intangible 124
assumptions, break-even analysis 160
auditors' remuneration 120
authorized share capital 125
AVCO – Average cost (Perpetual inventory basis) 253, 256
average
    creditors' settlement period 284
    debtors' settlement period 284
    rate of stock turnover 283

Index

B

bad
    and doubtful debts
        account, provision for 54
        provision for 57, 58
    debts 49, 50, 51, 55, 56, 178
balance
    sample trial 36, 43, 46, 47, 48
    sheet 15, 16, 77
        for manufacturing business 139
        forecast 215
        format 10
        partnership 109
        preparing 73
        speciment layout of limited company 121
    balance, trial 32
balances, different opening 185
balancing off the accounts 31, 31–32
Bank 23
    account 23
    of England 225
    reconciliation statements 179, 182, 183, 184, 185
board of directors 235
bonus issue 127
book
    loss 97, 99
    profit 192
        or loss 96
bookkeeping, double-entry 22
brands 260
break-even
    analysis 155
        and decision making 155
        as planning tool 155
        assumptions 160
        definition 148
        limitations 160
    break-even
        charts 151-153
        point 149, 150
            calculating 150, 151
    graph 151
budget 205
business entity 233

C

Cadbury Report 1992 234, 235, 237
capital 23, 125
    account 24
        fluctuating 111
    adequacy 285, 286
    and reserves 127, 128
    cost of maintaining working 175
    employed 79
    expenditure 65, 193, 196, 198, 199
    position, assessing working 168
    reserves 125
    working 79, 167, 173, 174, 175
carriage
    in 69
    out 69
cash
    book, updating 184
    cycle 171, 172, 173
cashflow
    and trading profit and loss forecast 213
    constructing 205
    forecast 213, 214
        and balance sheet 213
        constructing 204
        definition 204
        example 205, 207, 209, 212, 213
        forecasts, benefits 215
    statement 190, 194, 195, 197, 199, 200
        analysis of 201
        example 191
        preparing 193, 194
CCAB *see* Consultative Committee of Accounting Bodies
chairman 236
closing stock 66
    cost of 252
    summary, calculating 256
Code of Best Practice 237
Combined Code 1998 237
Companies Act
    1981 222
    1985 226, 227, 232
Companies Acts 223
comparability 231

concern, going 232
conservatism 232
consistency 232
Consultative Committee of Accounting
    Bodies Limited (CCAB Ltd) 225
continuing activities, results from 263
contracts, long-term 248
contribution/sales ratio, calculating 150
corporate governance 235
corporation tax 192
cost 251, 252
    behaviour 147
    definition 251
    historical 233
    of manufacture 134, 135, 137, 141
costs
    fixed 148
    of manufacture 132
    partly fixed and partly variable 148
    semi-variable 148
    variable 148
Council of the Institute of Chartered
    Accountants 224
credit 22, 212
    buying on 12–13
    selling on 16
creditor account 26, 28
creditors 124, 125, 192
cumulative preference shares 125
current
    account 110
    assets 167, 168, 250
    liabilities 167, 168

D

day book(s) 26–28
Dearing Committee 225
debenture interest 120
debentures 125
debit 22
debt: equity ratio 285
debtor account 27
debtors 169, 192
debts
    bad 49, 50, 55
        and doubtful 56

    doubtful 50, 51
decision making and break-even
    analysis 155
depletion 83
depreciation 93, 192, 207, 213, 258
    adjusting the trial balance 90, 92
    calculating 84
    causes of 83
    charge, calculating 83
    definition 83
    effects on accounts 86
    examination questions 89
    reducing balance method 85
    straight line method 84
direct
    debit 184
    expenses 132
    labour 132, 134, 148, 160
    material 132, 134, 148
directors 235, 236
    board of 235
    executive 235
    non-executive 235
    remuneration 120
discontinued activities, results from 263
discounts 28, 28–31, 29, 30
    allowed 31, 70
        account 30
    received 31, 70
        account 30
dividends 121, 193, 196
    proposed 124
double entry 16, 46
    bookkeeping 22, 90
doubtful debts 50, 51, 56
drawings 16

E

earnings per share 267, 269
Eighth Directive 223
entity, business 233
equipment account 24
equity dividends 193, 196
estimation techniques 231
EU 222
examination questions, depreciation 89

Index

exceptional items 268
executive directors 235
expenditure, capital 65
expense 53
expenses 25, 65, 248
extraordinary items 264, 267, 268

F

FIFO (First in first out) 253, 254, 257
    perpetual inventory basis 254
final accounts
    in a vertical format, presenting in 76
    of a partnership 106
finance servicing 196
Financial
    information, recording 4
    Reporting
        Council (FRC) 225, 235, 241
        Exposure Draft *see* FRED
        Review Panel (FRRP) 227
        Financial Reporting Standards (FRSs) 42, 224, 226, 227, 229
financing 196
finished goods 137, 139
fixed asset disposal 95, 97, 98, 264
fixed assets 10, 170, 193, 198, 199, 250
    purchase and sale 198
fixed
    capital 110
    cost element 148
    costs 148, 154
flow of funds 171, 172
fluctuating capital account 111
forecast
    balance sheet 213, 215
    cashflow 204, 213, 214
    example cashflow 205, 207, 209, 212, 213
    trading profit and loss account 213, 214
forecasts
    benefits of cashflow 215
    constructing cashflow 204
foreseeable losses 51

Fourth Directive 222
Framework for the Preparation and Presentation of Financial Statements (IASCs) 234
FRED (Financial Reporting Exposure Draft)17 229, 262
FRS *see also* Financial Reporting Standards
    1 239
    2 265
    3 239, 262, 263, 266, 267, 268, 269
    3, objective 263
    10 262
    11 262
    14 269
    15 – Tangible Fixed Assets 83, 245, 262
    18 42, 230, 231
FRSs 229, 230, 238, 239
    definition 224
    ones required for examination 238

G

gearing
    percentage 285
    ratios 278, 281
general reserves 126
going concern 232
goods, finished 137
goodwill 124, 250, 260, 261
    definition 259
    non-purchased 260
    purchased 260
    reasons for 259
    valuing 261
Greenbury Report 1995 236
gross
    loss 66
    profit 65
        margin 282, 286

H

Hampel Report 1998 235, 236
historic cost 233, 267

I

IASB 234
IASC 234
inadequacy 83
income 64
increasing output 154
    break-even implications 153
inflow 190, 193, 194
information, recording financial 4
insurance 44, 148
intangible assets 124
interest received 70
International Accounting Standards
    (IASs) 42, 233
    Board (IASB) 233
    Committee (IASC) 233
issue
    bonus 127
    rights 127
issued share capital 125

J

journals 26

K

key accounting concepts 232

L

legislation 222
liabilities, current 167, 168
    and deferred 14
LIFO (Last in first out) 253, 255, 257
    perpetual inventory basis 255
limitations making, break-even analysis 160
limited
    companies 117
        accounts, preparing 118
        liability partnership 118
limiting factor 156, 157
liquid resources 193, 196
liquidity 286
    ratios 277, 280, 284, 285
long-term
    contracts 248
    investments, financing 201
    liabilities 125

loss, gross 66
losses, foreseeable 51

M

maintaining records 22
make or buy decisions 159
manufacturing
    account 136
    business
        balance sheet 139
        trading profit and loss
            account 137
    calculating costs 132
    overheads 133, 134
margin 210
    of safety 151
marginal cost basis 251
mark-up 210, 211
    definition 210
matching concept 45, 51, 84, 248
materiality 233
measurement, profit 246, 248
money measurement 233
monopoly 260
movements in shareholders' funds 266

N

net
    current assets 124
    profit 124
        margin 283
    realizable value 251, 252
non-executive directors 235
non-mandatory recommendations 234
non-purchased goodwill 260
non-recurrent transactions 262
notes, balance 43

O

obsolescence 83
opening
    balances, dealing with different 185
    stock 67

Index

Operating
    activities 192
    and Financial Review 1993 235, 236
    performance 286
    ratio 277, 280, 283, 284
operation
    sale 264
    termination 264
ordinary shares 125
outflow 190, 193, 194
overdrawn accounts 182
overheads, manufacturing 133
overtrading 201

P

partly fixed and partly variable costs 148
Partnership 104, 105, 117
    accounts, speciment layouts 112
    Act 1890 104, 106
    agreement 105, 106, 107
    final accounts 106
    limited liability 118
patents 260
periodic valuations 254
perpetual inventory basis 254
petty cash account 24, 28
planning making and break-even
    analysis 155
preference shares 125
prepayments 44, 45, 49
    adjustments for 44, 45
primary statement, definition 266
prime cost of manufacture 134, 141
principal risks 236
Principles of Good Governance 237
prior year adjustments 269
production levels and profit 158
profit
    achieving maximum 155
    and loss account 66
        new format 263
        trading 64
    before taxation 195, 198
    gross 65
    measurement 246, 248

profitability 282, 286
    ratio 277, 280, 282, 283
profits and sales 159
prompt payment discount 28, 29
proposed dividends 124
provision for
    bad and doubtful debts 51, 56, 57, 58
        account 54
    bad debts 55, 248
provisions 248, 269
prudence 232
    concept 233, 248
purchase
    day book 27
    of fixed assets 198
purchased goodwill 260
purchases
    account 26
    of stock 209

R

ratio
    accounting 277, 278, 279, 281
    analysis 276
        definition 276
        limitation of 287
    calculating accounting 276
    debt: equity 285
    gearing 278, 281
    interpretation of account 281
    liquidity 277, 280, 284, 285
    operating 277, 280, 283, 284
    profitability 277, 280, 282, 283
raw material 156, 201
realization 233
reconciliation statement 178, 179, 182,
    183, 184, 185
    definition 178
reducing
    balance 89
        method 85, 92, 258
    output 154
        break-even implications 153
regulatory regime 222
relevance 231

reliability 231
rent 148
    account 25
    received 70
reorganization costs 264
reserves 125
    and capital 127, 128
restructuring costs 264
retained profits 121, 127
return
    on capital employed 282, 286
    outwards day book 27
returns
    in 28, 69
        and returns out 27, 68
    inwards day book 27, 28
    on investment 192, 196
    out 28, 69
        account 28
    outwards day book 28
revaluation, asset 262
    reserve 126, 262
revenue reserves 125
rights issue 127
risks, principal 236

S

sale of fixed assets 198
sales
    account 26
    and profits 159
    day book 26, 27
Secretary of State for Trade and Industry 225
semi-variable costs 148
separate valuation principle 232
servicing of finance 192
settlement period 174
share
    capital 125
    issues 193
    premium reserve 126
shares
    cumulative preference 125
    ordinary 125
    preference 125

sheet, balance 77
sole traders 104, 105
SSAP *see also* Statement of Standard Accounting Practice
    9 – Stock and work in progress 248, 251, 257
standard-setting
    process 224
    regime 227
Statement
    analysis of cashflow 201
    cashflow 190, 195, 197, 200
    definition of primary 266
    of Principles, ASB 228
    of recognized gains and losses 266
    of Standard Accounting Practice (SSAP) 42, 224, 225, 229, 237
        definition 224
        required for examination 238
    preparing cashflow 193, 194
Statements of
    Recommended Practice (SORPs) 225
    reconciliation 178
stepped fixed cost line 160
Stock 25, 44, 169, 178, 192, 201, 214, 248, 250, 251
    adjustments for 44
    closing 66
    Exchange 227, 235
        rules 234
    opening 67
    purchase 209
    turnover 173, 174
stocktaking 252
straight line method 84, 90, 95, 258

T

T account 22, 23, 24, 26, 28, 30, 31, 179, 181
tangible assets 124, 250
taxation 121, 124, 192, 196
    profit before 195
time factor 83
total cost basis 251

Index

trade
    discount 28, 29
    marks 260
trading
    account 65, 67
    profit and loss account
        64, 76, 88, 120
        example layout 71
        forecast 214
        limited company 119
        manufacturing business 137
        partnership 108
        preparing 72
        sample 66
transactions, non-recurrent 262
trends 282
trial balance 31–32, 32, 47, 48
    adjusting for stock 44
    adjustment for depreciation 101
    sample 36, 43, 46

U

understandability 231
unlimited liability 104

Urgent Issues Task Force (UITF)
    227, 231

V

valuation, asset 248
value, net realizable 251, 252
variable cost 148, 154, 161
    element 148
vertical format 77
    presenting final accounts in 76

W

wages account 25
wear and tear 83
work in progress (W.I.P.) 133, 139
working capital 79, 125, 167, 171, 173,
    175, 192, 196, 284
    calculations 170
    cost of maintaining 175
    importance 176
    position 173
    assessing 168
    ratio 171

Notes

Notes

Structure of Accounts

Notes

Structure of Accounts

Notes

Structure of Accounts

Notes

Structure of Accounts